ALIENATION IN PERVERSIONS

ALIENATION
IN PERVERSIONS

M. MASUD R. KHAN

INTERNATIONAL UNIVERSITIES PRESS, INC.
Madison   Connecticut

Library of Congress Cataloging in Publication Data

Khan, M Masud R
   Alienation in perversions.
   Bibliography: p. 229
   Includes index.
   1. Sexual deviation.   2. Alienation (Social
psychology)   3. Psychoanalysis.   1. Title   [DNLM:
1. Sexual deviation   2. Social alienation.   3. Social
behavior disorders. WM610.3 K45a]
RC556.K49   616.8′583   79-17210
ISBN 0-8236-0135-8

Second Printing, 1988

CONTENTS

7

PREFACE

In the nineteenth century two persons dictated the destiny of the twentieth century, Karl Marx and Sigmund Freud. Each of them diagnosed the sickness of the western Judaeo-Christian cultures: Marx in terms of the alienated person in society; Freud, the person alienated from himself.

The basic argument of this book is that the pervert puts an *impersonal object* between his desire and his accomplice: this *object* can be a stereotype fantasy, a gadget or a pornographic image. All three alienate the pervert from himself, as, alas, from the object of his desire. Hence the title of the book *Alienation in Perversions*.

If the reader has the patience to read my work, which has taken me twenty years and more to write, then my meaning will be explicit and become clear.

February 1979   M. MASUD R. KHAN

9

I

Reparation to
the Self as an Idolized Internal Object

THE human individual at the beginning is not a *subject* but an *object*. The human infant exists and experiences itself only through the mother's idolizing attention, hence he is the *object* of the maternal care. In recent years we have been so indoctrinated by a certain type of theorizing which argues that the infant's psyche is a cauldron of infinite and relentless anxieties and conflicts, that we tend to forget that at first the infant exists only as the object of the mother's care and love. Gradually as the maturational processes release the various ego and id apparatuses, the infant will begin to assemble self-representations that can then be described as the subjective self. As Winnicott has repeatedly pointed out, the biological givens and endowments in an infant are dependent on the actual maternal (environmental) care and facilitation for their articulation, differentiation and fruition, developmentally and maturationally, into what can later be identified as functions and properties of the ego and the id in the child. Winnicott especially stresses the necessity of a mother's capacity to meet imaginatively as well as affectively the first creative gestures of the infant-child and this forms the basis of the child's true confidence in his evolving and crystallizing sense of self.

The Concept of Reparation

One significant process involved in this complex interplay and confrontation between the infant and his environment (human and non-human) is that of reparation. Winnicott has described this variously as the environment meeting the infant's 'experience of omnipotence', allowing itself to be created by the infant as in the area of transitional object and phenomena, and allowing the infant to make his own contribution towards his caretaking environment. In Winnicott's frame of reference the reparative drive and process is an expression of the natural potential of the libidinal cum aggressive cum imaginative-affective forces operative in the infant-child's psyche-soma. Winnicott, unlike Klein, does not restrict the use of reparative drive to that of mitigating and neutralizing the damage done by the sadistic instincts in the earliest stages of infancy. In his theory, if for some personal or other reasons the mother fails to meet the reparative (creative) drive of the infant, then it leads to an imbalance in the whole articulation of the emergent ego-id differentiation and entails defensive use of the reparative drive (1948a). The reparative drive therefore uses all the available emergent ego-id processes to make a contribution towards the caretaking environment (human and non-human) and establishes the matrix of confidence in relating to and being creative towards this environment. And since this contribution (reparation) is reflected and mirrored back as achievement by the environment it leads to confidence in the growing sense of personal identity and in the authenticity of self-experiences in psyche and soma.

The Reparative Drive in Perversion-Formation

From the intensive analytic treatment of some dozen cases of perversion over the past twenty years a distinct pattern of early mother-child relationship leading to choice of perverse sexual practices (heterosexual as well as homosexual) has begun to crystallize in my thinking. All these cases were as infants and children much loved by their mothers. It is significant that though in every case the father was alive and around in the child's experience he was not registered as a significant presence or person. The mother lavished intense body-care on the infant-child but in a rather impersonal way. The child was treated by the mother as her 'thing-creation' rather than as an emergent growing person in his or her own right. It is this idolization of the infant-child that I am singling out for special emphasis and discussion. I am advisedly using the concept of idolization instead of idealization. To me the two processes seem distinct and different. Idealization is an intrapsychic process and is very much influenced by reverie. Idolization on the contrary is an explicit over-cathexis of an external actual object and is sustained by elaborate ego-attitudes and ego-functions which subsume id-investments and intensify these in the service of idolization. Idolization therefore entails a mental exploitation of instinctual components and primitive psychic processes in the relationship to an external actual object, in this case the infant-child. My clinical work here corresponds very closely to that reported by Greenacre (1960a).

To elaborate my argument a step further. In this climate of mother-child relationship, the child very early on begins to sense that what the mother cathects and invests in is at once something very special in him and yet not him as a whole person. The child learns to tolerate this dissociation in his experience of self and gradually turns the mother into his accomplice in maintaining this special created-object. The next step in this developmental schema is that the child internalizes this idolized self that was the mother's created-thing. This, in my clinical material, usually happens around the oedipal phase when these mothers suddenly become self-conscious about their intensive attachment to and investment in their child and withdraw abruptly. Hence these children seem to experience a belated separation-trauma at a stage where their ego can register it more acutely. They register this as panic and threat of annihilation and especially as abandonment (unconsciously). It is in this inner affective climate that they intensify the cathexis of their internalized idolized self and also hide it from their environment.

Two further features seem to be characteristic of this type of childhood: absence of playing and transitional objects. At first I missed these because the concept of transitional object was not as yet available to me. Only the genius finds what he is not looking for, the rest of us have to be content with re-discovering the discovered for ourselves. The lack of playing and transitional objects is further matched by a lack of initiative to contribute of these children. While they are astonishingly empathic to their mothers' moods they seem to resign prematurely from offering anything from their side. Instead they learn to augment the mothers' efforts and gestures towards them as the special created-thing. A child in such circumstances learns a specialized use of his reparative drive, i.e. towards the self as an idolized internal object.

I shall at this point jump a few stages and try to abstract the dilemma of this type of child at puberty and adolescence. All my cases seem to arrive at puberty and adolescence in a state of organized innocence. They had little capacity for sexual reverie and their first attempts at masturbation were pathetically unsatisfactory. They felt shut in, almost claustrophobic, rather depersonalized with a distinctly schizoid type of personality and yet seething with a latent urgency towards life and others, which they couldn't actualize in life-experience or contemporary object-relationships. Hence they felt eager and disregarded, intensely subjective and yet dull and depleted, full of themselves and with nothing to offer to others, and

13

above all else special. They had a distinct secret sense of waiting to be found and met. It is in such an inner climate of strangulated affectivity and instinctual tension that an opportunity or encounter with someone would provide them with an opening into life.

It is true of each of my patients that none of them ventured out from personal initiative at first. After the first few adventures the role of the ego-initiative changes – some remained passive *vis-à-vis* the object, others learnt to seek it militantly. For a long time I was deeply perplexed and confused by the character and style of their object-choice, object-finding and object-relating. With a little distortion I could always satisfy myself that it was narcissistic object-choice or regression to the part-object phase of early libido development, but none of this really fitted all the facts. Gradually I began to see that one of the unmistakable features of the chosen and found sexual object was its potentiality and talent to play the part of an as-if transitional object. But even that left a great deal of the richness of the patient's experience of self and object in the relationship unaccounted for. It was only when I was convinced that the gratification from sexual discharge is a screen-experience in these patients directed against anxiety states, and that the basic use of sexual apparatuses and instincts is of a reparative kind, that the clinical picture began to yield more clues.

The next question is towards whom is that reparative drive directed. One could not say the object as a person in himself nor the object as an idealized image of the patient's self. I felt there was some very important factor missing. Only an unprejudiced scrutiny of these patients' intensive and elaborate ego-interests and sexual rapport with their objects has helped me to realize that what was being enacted was a very special type of early relationship from childhood. This relationship, in spite of all the overt and ecstatic awareness of what they were doing, was hidden from the patient himself, and it in essence was a repetition of the mother's idolization of the infant-child as her created-object, which the child had internalized and hidden. The characteristics of this type of perverse sexual intimacy and relatedness between two persons (heterosexual or homosexual) are: (*a*) that both parties have a silent ritualistic acceptance of the play quality of the relationship. In spite of all their vociferous remonstrances to the contrary it is understood that the whole venture is transitional and uncommitting; (*b*) that the relationship in its true detail is private, secretive and something very special between the two persons concerned; (*c*) that each is in fact doing it as a reparative gesture towards the other. This is what makes it benign. The element of hostile and sadistic exploitation of the other is kept low to a minimum; (d) that each will grow larger and more whole as a person from the venture; (e) in spite of protestations of perpetual fidelity and devotion, each knows that separation and loss are inevitable and will not be too traumatic; (f) a basic shared sense of gratitude at the time at having been allowed a mute and unshareable experience.

The next and important question that needs to be answered at this point is: why does the reparative drive in these persons choose the sexual apparatuses and modalities as the basic vehicle of its expression. In my clinical experience perverts are not persons who impress one with being endowed with a biologically high or intense natural sexual appetite and drive. In my clinical experience I have yet to meet a pervert who was compelled from the authentic instinctual pressure of his body-impulses to reach out to an object for gratification. It is all engineered from the head and then instinctual apparatuses and functions are zealously exploited in the service of programmed sexuality. And how does it come about that the reparative drive expresses itself only in relation to the sexual object? Because outside such relationships these people were all very selfish, impatient, patently unempathic and un-generous as well as mean and coldly aloof towards others. The answer partially lies in the way they suffered the restriction and negation of their reparative drive in childhood at the hands of their mothers. A person has to have special attributes as a thing-person to trigger off their interest. They cannot offer any reparative gesture towards anyone who is to start with separate and defined as an entity in his or her own right. Also the potential object must share their bias for body-language communication. The soma of an infant-child is available to a mother's imprinting from a much earlier stage than his differentiated psyche (ego), and this com-pliance potential of an infant-child's soma is greater than the more developed and mature child's ego. Hence the bias is to regress to that phase and modality of interrelationship.

Furthermore I think the very subtle and discreet inhibitions of emergent aggressive potential in these children as infants play a role here too. Such mothers distract, diffuse and negate the aggressive gestures in the infant-child's reparative drive that draws upon his body-musculature. This leads to expressions of aggression in rage-reactions which are then dealt with by a precocious development of

15

defensive ego-mechanisms. When these patients sought out accomplices they had, as it were, a latent wisdom in choosing objects who would not involve their ego too directly and explicitly, otherwise their phobic and paranoid anxieties and defences would come precipitately into action and spoil the whole venture. This is a problem we get stuck with quite often in the treatment of schizoid characters with acute selective sexual inhibitions. The sexual intimacies anticipate a privacy and seclusion from public view and allow for private symbolism and rituals to be tried out, learnt and taught. They are relatively at one remove from the exigencies of ordinary reality and value-systems. Another factor is that in all perversions there is a definite lack of elaboration of body-experiences into psychic reverie. The overt fantasies of perverts are patently banal and repetitive.

There is one last point I want to state. All perversions entail a fundamental alienation from self in the person concerned and the attempt is to find personalization through the elaborate machinery of sexual experiences. The inconsolability of the pervert is matched only by his insatiability. The researches of Freud and his followers have gone a long way towards providing us with true clues to the predicament of the pervert, without all the mystifications of moral approbation or the envious adulation of the seemingly liberal social approach. But the predicament of the pervert is still far from clear. The experiential data is so cluttered with secondary elaborations and gains as well as distortions that even knowing as such constitutes a trap. What we need to establish more firmly is the positive trends that lie buried under the debris of the erotic expertise of the pervert. It is towards an understanding of this that I think a clearer definition of the role of the reparative drive towards the self as an idolized internal object may serve as a deeper understanding of this predicament.

So long as the pervert seeks to make the reparation to his own idolized self, either through masturbatory practices or through projective identification with another who represents his idolized internal self, there is no possibility of true relating or mutuality. It is important to distinguish three components in a pervert's relation to himself and to his object, namely idolization, idealization and narcissistic identification. In idolization the object is treated as a sacred fetish. In idealization only some aspect of the object is invested with an exaggerated intensity of virtue. In narcissistic identification the object is used to mirror the self in a defensive

16

attempt to hide feelings of inferiority and unworthiness in the self. In the transference of these patients one sees these processes very clearly. When the patient *needs* to be idolized any gesture of the analyst that indicates his separateness is felt to be traumatic and annihilating. The dependence on the analyst for total acceptance is maximal. The analyst has to make the reparation so that differentiated personalization can begin to operate. When the idealized self is presented by the patient often there is a subtle denigration of the analyst. In the case of narcissistic identification the demand is for an intimacy of effort and relating rather than working with the analyst.

2

Intimacy, Complicity
and Mutuality in Perversions

Aᴺᴰʀᴇ́ Gide quotes Oscar Wilde as saying:

There are two kinds of artists: some bring answers and the others bring questions. You must know whether you are one of those who answer or one of those who question; for the one who questions is never the one who answers. There are works that wait and are not understood for a long time, because they brought answers to questions that had not yet been asked; for the question often comes a frightfully long time after the answer. (Delay, 1963.)

Freud was one of those rare minds that gave us the answers in relation to which we are gradually learning to ask the right questions. When Freud characterized perversions as the negative of neuroses he had established a distinction the full meaning of which is beginning to be explored only now through the researches in ego-psychology and infant-mother relationship. The paradigmatic syndromes for the classical analytic theory and technique were the neurotic conditions of hysteria and obsessional neurosis. In both these cases the ego can be considered to have achieved intactness and coherence. The dysfunctions and disabilities that it experiences are due to its attempts to find a *modus vivendi* between the imperious and archaic demands of the instincts and the inexorable limits imposed by external reality. In its attempts to find a solution the ego uses defence mechanisms which either impair its effectiveness or lead to gross repressions of instinctual modalities. In cases of severe conflict the ego's relation to reality itself can suffer distortion. It is generally accepted that in these cases the ego does not lose its essential coherence or unity. Clinical syndromes where the very character of the ego has suffered pathological deformation were designated by Freud as 'narcissistic neuroses'; they were not thought to be readily accessible to analytic technique or therapy. In the transference neuroses, as against narcissistic neuroses, the capacity for object-cathexes remains intact, in spite of all the inhibitions and re-

18

pressions (Freud, 1916–17). In recent decades advances in analytic technique and a deeper understanding of the transference relationship and the analytic situation have made it possible to explore clinically the nature of ego-pathology in narcissistic neuroses (Balint, 1950; Stone, 1961; Winnicott, 1955). Here the treatment of perversions comes into the forefront of our clinical investigations.

In 1905, in *Three Essays on the Theory of Sexuality*, Freud established the role of infantile sexuality in perversions. He singled out for special emphasis two factors: the tenuous relation between the sexual instinct and the object in the practices of the perverts: 'in them [the perverts] the sexual instincts and the sexual object are merely soldered together'; and secondly, the role of a mental mechanism which leads to idealization of the instinct in the pervert.

In the five decades since the publication of Freud's monumental work a great deal of research has been done on the treatment of perversions (Arlow, 1954; Fenichel, 1945; Glover, 1940, 1959; Lorand and Balint, 1956; Rosen, 1964; Wiedeman, 1962). There is a consensus of opinion among psycho-analysts that in perversions it is not simply a question of ego-syntonic regression to pregenital modes of instinctual gratification. Ego-pathology is now considered to be inherent in perversion-formations. Gillespie states (1952):

> I have no doubt myself that splitting of the object and of the ego, denial and omnipotent manipulations of the relation to objects play a leading part in perversion formation and help us to understand its relationship to psychosis. Melanie Klein suggests that in this early phase such mechanisms play a role similar to that of repression at a later stage. Here we have an important clue, I think, to the striking phenomenological differences between neurosis and perversion, which led Freud to say that the one is the negative of the other. In other words, we are dealing not with a contrast between defence and no defence, but between repressive defence and more primitive defence of a schizoid or splitting character.

Glover has stressed the exploitation of sexuality in perversions to still mental pain associated with guilt, anxiety and depression; and to neutralize, suspend or sidetrack the impulses of hostility and aggression (*op. cit.*). In an earlier paper Glover (1932) had discussed the function of perversion-formations in preserving reality sense, when this is threatened by excessive quantities of infantile anxiety, hate and aggression (cf. Bychowski, 1954; Rosenfeld, 1949).

Greenacre (1953a, 1959, 1960b) and Sperling (1959) have discussed more specifically the genetic roots of perversions in a disturbed infant-mother relationship. Lichtenstein (1961) has perhaps offered the most stimulating discussion of both the role of non-procreative sexuality in the establishment of a sense of identity and its pathological deviations. Winnicott (1951), from his researches into the infant-mother relationship and in terms of his hypothesis of the transitional object, has sketched out the role of very early psychic functions in the aetiology of perversion-formations. His argument is that if the integration of the ego-functions is disturbed through inadequate holding (maternal) environment then what in normal childhood development are transitional objects turn into the perverse sexual relationships to objects, human and non-human, in adult life.

This chapter singles out for discussion the acting out of the perverse sexual fantasies and practices. The phenomenology of the technique of intimacy through which the pervert induces and coerces another person into becoming an accomplice is first elaborated. It is submitted that perversions are a social acting out of the infantile neurosis in the perverts. The technique of intimacy re-enacts the infantile neurosis. Through this technique another object is appealed to, involved, seduced and coerced to share in the enactment of the developmental arrest and cumulative trauma resulting in identity diffusion which constitutes this infantile neurosis (Khan, 1963a; and see Chapters 3 and 4, below). This technique of intimacy, of which acting out is the mechanism, combines in a subtle balance the defensive exploitation of regressive satisfactions of a pregenital instinctual nature as well as mobilization of archaic psychic processes in the hope of freeing and enlarging the ego into an independent and coherent organization and achieving a sense of identity (1964, 1969). My argument here is close to that of Schmideberg (1956) : 'With perversions the fixation is not on an object but generally on an activity. . . . Structurally perversions are similar to acting out in analysis.'

The Technique of Intimacy

The distinction between perversions from neuroses on the one hand and psychoses on the other is the specific modality of the object-relation involved. The concept of object is here used in its most comprehensive sense, that is, as an external not-self objective object, as the internal object and in the more primary sense of self-body as object, as in auto-erotic and masturbatory practices. In neuroses the object-relation, both internal and external, is well established. It is the instinctual and intrapsychic conflict in relation to it that constitutes the pathogenic problem. In psychoses the objective reality of the external object is in all essential dimensions negated by the omnipotence of the subjective intrapsychic processes and instinctual needs (Freud, 1916–17). In perversions the object occupies an intermediary position: it is not-self and yet subjective; registered and accepted as separate and yet treated as subjectively created; it is needed as an actual existent not-self being and yet coerced into complying with the exigent subjective need to *invent* it. Spatially it is suspended half-way between external reality and inner psychic reality. The narcissistic magical exploitation of the object is patently visible and has been discussed at length in analytic literature (Ferenczi, 1914; Freud, 1922*b*; Nunberg, 1938), and yet there is an intrinsic deficiency in the pervert's incapacity, as it were, emotionally to focus and relate to an object, externally and intrapsychically, that is not fully accounted for by the hypothesis of narcissistic identification and magical thinking. Anna Freud (1952) has emphasized this crucial lack in the pervert's object-relations in terms of the incapacity to love and the dread of emotional surrender. It is this basic incapacity in the ego to mobilize adequate sustained cathexis of an external object or its internal representatives (internal object) that I consider to be the motivating dynamism behind the technique of intimacy which the perverts employ.

My interest in this type of object-relationship, which I am designating the technique of intimacy, derives from the clinical coincidence of having concurrently in analysis heterosexual patients with a schizoid type of character disorder and overt homosexual cases. I was struck by the similarity of the technique of intimacy employed by both these types of patient in the area of their significant, private and personal instinctual relationship to self (body) and external object, in spite of the differences in the rest of their character problems. In both instances the technique of intimacy derived from the area of maturational failure in ego-integration in the developmental context of the infant-child anaclitic relation to the mother (cf. Khan, 1960*a*, 1964).

I am using the concept 'technique of intimacy' advisedly to designate the character and emotional climate of the object-relationship and endopsychic functions involved in perversions.

21

The noun *intimacy* is best understood in terms of its forms as adjective and verb. The Oxford English Dictionary defines the adjective *intimate* as: 'Pertaining to the inmost thought and feelings; pertaining to and connected with the inmost nature and character of a thing.' It defines the verb *intimate*: 'to put into, drive or press into, to make known, announce, etc.' It is my contention here that through the technique of intimacy the pervert tries to *make known* to himself and *announce and press into* another something pertaining to his inmost nature as well as to discharge its instinctual tension in a compulsive and exigent way. That this impulsion to announce and communicate himself in a bodily way relates to a pressing crisis of diffusion of self and identity has been sensitively discussed in recent years (Bychowski, 1954; A. Freud, 1952; Greenacre, 1959; Lichtenstein, 1961). Influenced by analytic researches a few very pertinent biographical essays and studies by literary critics of perverts among writers have also appeared (e.g. Gorer, 1962; de Beauvoir, 1953; Delay, 1963; Sartre, 1963).

The outstanding feature of the technique of intimacy is the attempt to establish a make-believe situation involving in most cases the willing seduced co-operation of an external object. In certain sadistic criminal instances the object is coerced against his or her will, as in the case of de Sade, but I have no clinical experience of such cases. Even in de Sade's case the unconscious co-operation of the victims must have played an important part. This is very clear in the naive, delusional negation and denial by his fictional characters as victims of what is in store for them. The capacity to create the emotional climate in which another person volunteers to participate is one of the few real talents of the perverts. This invitation to surrender to the pervert's logic of body-intimacies demands of the object a suspension of discrimination and resistance at all levels of guilt, shame and separateness. A make-believe situation is offered in which two individuals temporarily renounce their separate identities and boundaries and attempt to create a heightened maximal body-intimacy of orgastic nature. There is always, however, one proviso. The pervert himself cannot surrender to the experience and retains a split-off, dissociated manipulative ego-control of the situation. This is both his achievement and failure in the *intimate* situation. It is this failure that supplies the compulsion to repeat the process again and again. The nearest that the pervert can come to experiencing surrender is through visual, tactile and sensory identifications with the other object in the intimate situation in a state of surrender. Hence, though the pervert arranges and motivates that idealization of instinct which the technique of intimacy aims to fulfil, he himself remains outside the experiential climax. Hence, instead of instinctual gratification or object-cathexis, the pervert remains a deprived person whose only satisfaction has been of pleasurable discharge and intensified ego-interest. In his subjectivity the pervert is *un homme manqué*.

The pervert's talent at enlisting reality and external object as an ally in the service of his ego-needs and instinctual exigencies is what gives him a spurious and exaggerated sense of his own sensibility and its potentialities. The pervert's subjective experience of the technique of intimacy and its achievements can be categorized as sense of over-valuation of self and object, insatiability, a solitary game, and envy. The over-valuation and idealization are in lieu of true object-cathexis. The sense of insatiability derives from the fact that every venture is a failure for the pervert. The internal anxieties relating to the ego's dread of surrender never allow for a gratification of the impulses involved. At best there is more pleasurable discharge. This relates it to the experience of intimacy as a solitary game; even though two persons are involved in a heightened instinctual modality essentially it is all the invention of one person. There is no object-relatedness; hence no nourishment. It is dramatizing without affective or psychic internalization of the object. The envy derives from the actual perception and suspicion that the other person has got more out of it than the self. It is this element of envy which makes most perverts behave viciously and meanly to their objects and compels them to jilt and hurt.

Confession is another basic function of the technique of intimacy. It is a remarkable feature of the pervert's behaviour that he confesses with a singular unrestraint, lack of shame and guilt – both to the social object and in the clinical situation. Even in literature the extravagant sincerity of writers like Oscar Wilde, André Gide, Henry Miller and Jean Genet are outstanding for their intensity and absoluteness. My clinical material leads me to infer that this confession through body-intimacies and retrospective verbalizations is nearer to dreaming and a hallucinatory mode of psychic activity than an organized ego-activity (cf. Sartre, 1963). It is precisely this partial capacity to abandon ego-controls and regressively invoke and express modalities of sexual and psychic experience that make so many victims the envious collaborators of the pervert. But it is a confession doomed to failure because the accomplice can only help

23

to dramatize the theme, give it a concrete reality in behavioural experience and a body-compliance without being able to meet and make known the true ego-need and the latent distress in the pervert. Hence the inconsolability of the pervert, and his addiction to this charade of intimacy. The pervert tries to use the technique of intimacy as a therapeutic device and all he accomplishes is more expertise in the technique itself. This failure to achieve any form of ego-satisfaction is then compensated by idealization of instinctual discharge processes, which in turn lead to a sense of depletion, exhaustion and paranoid turning away from or against the object. This vicious circle gradually reduces the positive strivings and expectancies implicit in the technique of intimacy. Clinically we see perverts only when their auto-therapeutic attempts have totally failed. In the clinical situation they project their well-founded despair to small details of the analyst's inevitable lapses and failures of understanding at the beginning of the treatment. It is this testing of the analyst and the analytic process from the start which makes the pervert's transference so difficult to handle and stabilize.

Let us examine why intimacy is the pervert's preferential mode of object-relationship. At the beginning of analytic researches into human personality Freud had emphasized the role of auto-erotic experiences in infantile sexuality. But intimacy is not a simple regressive ego-syntonic repetition of infantile auto-erotism. It is auto-erotism à deux. It is an engineered re-enactment of masturbatory practices between two persons as a compensation for that insufficiency of maternal care which is the pre-requisite of infantile auto-erotism and narcissism (cf. Spitz, 1963). Researches into infant-mother relationship and direct child observation have enabled us to postulate that the child's capacity to enjoy auto-erotic body experiences is very dependent on the mother's nursing care. Winnicott (1948b, 1956; cf. Kris, 1951) has detailed how the mother's technique of nursing enables the infant to achieve reality contact, integration and sense of body. Lichtenstein's hypothesis (1961) is also pertinent here:

There is an innately determined readiness in the human infant to react to the maternal stimulations with a 'somatic obedience' experience. This 'obedience' represents, however, fulfilment of the child's own needs: in being the instrument, the organ for the satisfaction of the maternal Otherness, the full symbiotic interaction of the two partners is realized for both of them. It would, however, be a mistake to see this 'organ' or 'instrument' identity as too narrowly defined. The mother imprints upon the infant not *an* identity, but an '*identity theme*'. . . . Man thus makes use of nonprocreative sexuality in a unique way: he becomes an instrument for the fulfilment of another one's needs, needs which are conveyed and perceived as primitive modalities of sensory interaction within a symbiotically structural *Umwelt*. This link between sexuality and imprinted identity is supported by the observation of many psycho-analysts of a correlation between body image, sexuality, and identity problems (such as in fetishists).

It is this infantile unconscious knowledge of what the body can achieve by way of relatedness, and can reach out for through compliance and active expectancy, that provides the dynamics of search, appeal and hope in the technique of intimacy in perversions.

If the area of disturbance in the pervert belongs to that stage of infancy-childhood development where the self and (body) ego boundaries are in the process of being crystallized and established through maternal care and management, then it follows that the psychic processes that are phase-adequate at that stage and are the infant-child's mode of relating to and experiencing his human and non-human environment must also play a very important role in the pervert's involvement with and manipulation of his sexual object through the technique of intimacy. It is here that Winnicott's concept (1951) of the 'transitional object' supplies us with a creative instrument of research with which to examine perversions. Winnicott details the special qualities of the infant's relation to the transitional object as follows:

1. The infant assumes rights over the object, and we agree to this assumption. Nevertheless some abrogation of omnipotence is a feature from the start.

2. The object is affectionately cuddled as well as excitedly loved and mutilated.

3. It must never change, unless changed by the infant.

4. It must survive instinctual loving, and also hating, and, if it be a feature, pure aggression.

5. Yet it must seem to the infant to give warmth, or to move, or to have texture, or to do something that seems to show it has vitality or reality of its own.

6. It comes from without from our point of view, but not

so from the point of view of the baby. Neither does it come from within; it is not an hallucination.

7. Its fate is to be gradually allowed to be decathected, so that in the course of years it becomes not so much forgotten as relegated to limbo. By this I mean that in health the transitional object does not 'go inside' nor does the feeling about it necessarily undergo repression. It is not forgotten and it is not mourned. It loses meaning, and this is because the transitional phenomena have become diffused, have become spread out over the whole intermediate territory between 'inner psychic reality' and 'the external world as perceived by two persons in common', that is to say, over the whole cultural field.

I shall schematically state in terms of Winnicott's hypothesis that to the pervert his object has essentially the value of a 'transitional object'. Through its (his or her) readiness to comply it lends itself to be invented, manipulated, used and abused, ravaged and discarded, cherished and idealized, symbiotically identified with and deanimated all at once. What it cannot do for the pervert is to cure him of his developmental deviations in ego-integration resulting from the failures of maternal care and provision.

I have so far indicated some of the more positive strivings implicit in the technique of intimacy. But it will not be true either of the total clinical picture or the personal predicament of the pervert if I were to underestimate the organized, static and congealed patterns of defence mechanisms by which the pervert bolsters his ego-activity. It is precisely this effective and almost autonomous defensive ego-structure that presents us with some of the most adamant resistance against change and cure in the treatment of perversions.

I am inclined to place the flight from regression to ego-dependence as the most global defensive character trait typical of perverts. Through the technique of intimacy the pervert tries to compel and induce a regression to dependence and instinctual surrender in his accomplice. His own ego retains its defensive distance and dissociations. The elements of play, make-believe, omnipotence and manipulation of the object are all guarantees against regression to ego-dependence or investment in true object-cathexis or surrender to emotional experience. This self-protective vigilance and negativity in the ego also provides a screen for the basic mistrust and suspicion with which the pervert treats both his inner need to be related to an object and the object's emotional demands on him. Another over-all defensive function of the technique of intimacy can be defined as a sexual variant of manic defence. Winnicott (1935) has detailed the several different but interrelated functions of the manic defence as follows:

Denial of inner reality.
Flight to external reality from inner reality.
Holding the people of the inner reality in 'suspended animation'.
Denial of the *sensations* of depression – namely the heaviness, the sadness – by specifically opposite sensations, lightness, humorousness, etc. The employment of almost any opposites in the reassurance against death, chaos, mystery, etc., ideas that belong to the *fantasy content* of the depressive position.

If we examine the fantasy content and general defensive function of the technique of intimacy in terms of manic defence then we can see how it is exploited by the pervert to avert an intrapsychic trauma or crisis by eroticized flight to reality and an external object. In this way what would have been overwhelming for the ego in terms of passivity, guilt and anxiety is reversed into a predicament for the *external object*. This enables the ego to avoid abject helplessness and threat of dissolution and disintegration as well as depression. If the technique of intimacy is the basic vehicle of this defensive manoeuvre of the ego, the essential mechanism used for its actualization is acting out.

Role of Mechanism of Acting Out

Freud's concept of acting out to connote the patient's expression of resistance against the analytic process and as his alternative to remembering (1914g) has widened in its scope and application to cover a multitude of behavioural phenomena relating both to the clinical analytic situation and the personality structure as such (Bellak, 1963; Ekstein and Friedman, 1957; Greenacre, 1959, 1963; Kanzer, 1957a,b; Winnicott, 1954, 1956b; A. Freud, 1949; Sperling, 1959. The specific role of acting out in relation to perversions and impulse disorders is discussed in Bychowski, 1954). I shall confine my discussion of the mechanism of acting out to its functions in the service of the technique of intimacy in perversions. Some of these functions are:

1. It enables the pervert's ego to reverse an intrapsychic predicament. By displacing and projecting the need-tension to reality and another person the ego retains its executive capacity.

2. What threatens the ego with passive surrender is transformed into an active mastery of the impulse and the object. This has the added advantage that through exteriorization and sharing, the intrapsychic affects of guilt and shame are neutralized. The accomplice through participation replaces the super-ego's strictures. Furthermore the increment of pleasure through tactile experiences supplies a bulwark against depression and psychic pain.

3. The mechanism of acting out by introducing the elements of play, imaginatively shared activities and through mobilizing ego-interest mitigates the deadness in the internal world of the pervert. If over-excitement constitutes one source of internal threat another is inertia and apathy through excessive and archaic defences against unconscious sadism and aggression in the pervert.

4. Acting out also provides the ego with an opportunity for restitutive and reparative tendencies towards a *real* object. This is an important and positive aspect of the technique of intimacy. Because of the pathologically disturbed relations to internalized objects of infancy-childhood the pervert experiences in his inner world utter despair and hopelessness *vis-à-vis* his creative and reparative tendencies. The loss of narcissistic self-esteem through such gross and futile relations to internal parental figures can be partially remedied by the pervert through giving pleasure to a real external object and self.

5. Acting out is inherently a counter-phobic mechanism. It enables the pervert to escape from his congealed inner world of pathological parental relationships and archaic identifications. Anna Freud (1949) has described the role of acting out in the service of repressed fantasies of the phallic phase and their displacement to ego-activities through social maladjustment. Winnicott (1956*a,b*) has offered the concept of antisocial tendency to explain the acting out of developmental arrest which belongs to deficiency of maternal provisions in the sphere of child's ego-dependence on her. The pervert through acting out manages to avoid total ego collapse and an irreversible regression to psychotic states. It is this which links perversions so closely to psychoses rather than neuroses.

6. Acting out also enables the pervert to control some of the more primitive and archaic object-relations from his childhood and the identifications therefrom. The objectification through an actual

28

new object provides the chance to correct, no matter how minimally, the grossly pathological relationship to parents from early childhood which are always threatening to overpower the ego internally. This exteriorization also puts the pervert in touch with reality. Glover (1932*a*) has discussed very pertinently the role of perversion-formations in the service of retaining contact with reality and mastery of anxiety.

7. Through the libidinization of activity, acting out binds and partially neutralizes the archaic sadistic and aggressive impulses which the pervert's ego has no intrapsychic means of controlling.

8. Finally, acting out enables the pervert to establish at least a rudimentary mode of communication with an external object. In spite of the over-intimate early bond between a mother and child that is at the root of perversions there is little meaningful communication between the child as a separate person and self and the significant parent. Acting out through the technique of intimacy breaks down this primary sense of isolation and establishes contact with an object, and through an object with the self. Here the anti-social factor in perversions offers a vehicle for hope, appeal and help.

I have discussed some of the functions of acting out in perversions. I am not concerned with its aetiology here. I have stressed the important function of acting out in transforming passive traumatic intrapsychic states into active ego-directed experimental play-action object-relations. In spite of the gross pathology of these types of object-relationship in the pervert, there is little doubt that these relationships have a rescue value *vis-à-vis* the ego's internal anxiety-situations and archaic internal object-relations. The pervert's capacity to employ acting out in an ego-syntonic way is evidence of the fact that in his childhood ego-development he does achieve a minimal amount of maturational integration of ego-functions. It is relevant to state here that the ego of the pervert is more like a collage than an integrated coherent entity. It is this dovetailing of phase-adequate ego-capacities with unintegrated and unstable ego-functions that gives the pervert's ego its peculiar quality of resistive manipulative strength on the one hand and its panicky vulnerability on the other. The typical anxiety affect of the pervert is the dread of ego dissolution and disintegration. Through the mechanism of acting out and the technique of intimacy the pervert's ego concocts for itself a pleasurable negative identity. In no other character disorder do we meet such a consistent idealization of the reactive defensive self-image as in the pervert.

CONCLUSION

Perversions are more akin to dreaming than neurotic symptom-formation. The technique of intimacy is the vehicle of this type of dreaming and acting out is its preferential mechanism of psychic functioning. The ego of the pervert acts out his dream and involves another person in its actualization. It is possible to argue that if the pervert dramatizes and actually fulfils his body-dreams with a real person, he also cannot wake out of them. Here we meet with another formidable therapeutic task in the treatment of the pervert: how to wean and wake him from his specific mode of dramatizing his dreams. This confronts us with the pervert's inaccessibility to influence and change through his object-relations. No human being can do very much in ordinary life for a pervert because he can be as Lewis Carroll's Tweedledee would say 'only a sort of thing in his dream'.

3

The Role of Polymorph-Perverse Body-Experiences and Object-Relations in Ego-Integration

I. On a Specific Type of Emotionality met with in Schizoid Character-Disorders

IN 'Clinical aspects of the schizoid personality' (Khan, 1960a) I tried to give a general clinical picture of a schizoid type of character-disorder. Here I shall single out for discussion one aspect of these patients, namely a special latent emotionality and affectivity, which expresses itself through polymorph-perverse body-experiences and object-relations. My emphasis is on the role and pathology of these polymorph-perverse body-relations. I hope to show how they derive from specific disturbances in the infant-mother relationship, which result from pathogenic features in the mother's personality. I have been greatly helped in the formulation of my hypothesis by the researches of Deutsch (1942), Eissler (1953), A. Freud (1952, 1954a), Greenacre (1953a, 1959, 1960b,c), Hoffer (1952), James (1960), Lewin (1950), Milner (1952), Sterba (1957) and Winnicott (1949, 1951), all of whom have discussed this type of emotionality and body-ego disturbance from different angles.

The type of patient who is carrying this emotionality intra-psychically, at a first impression looks remarkably like a normal, effective, well-integrated human being who is successful socially and professionally and who claims to have fairly adequate, even though somewhat tenuous, heterosexual experiences. I have not seen any specific difference in the pathology of the male and female patients relating to this area of emotionality, apart from those one would expect. This, I think, is a significant detail, because it is my impression that bisexual strivings and confusion of body-image play a large part in this type of emotionality.

None of these patients had sought treatment because of subjective awareness of this type of latent affectivity, nor had they because of distress about the polymorph-perverse body-experiences. Characteristically they drift into treatment complaining of a general

31

lack of vitality, depressiveness and dissatisfaction with their mode of life. It is only through analytic work that both the analyst and the patient become aware of this special type of emotionality and the role this plays in their personality equilibrium. Each one of them had doubts both as to whether they were really ill and/or whether psycho-analysis could help them, but they offered to exercise a somewhat superior and good-humoured 'willing suspension of disbelief' and give the analysis a try. This aggressive defensive attitude is characteristic of their denial of their passive dependency needs.

In their overt behaviour they are characterized by amicable cleverness, tidy appearance, compliance and apathetic docility. Soon in the analytic situation their muted aggressiveness and hostility become apparent. Gradually what emerges clearly in the clinical situation is their excited emotionality and inflammable affectivity, which is controlled and regulated by depressive, phobic and paranoid defence mechanisms. This emotionality is a confused, formless, obsessive state of tension which they carry in their heads and nurture diligently, even though it is both painful and exhausting (cf. Greenacre, 1960b). They are rather secretive about it. Bouts of elation, hypochondriacal anxieties, conversion symptoms, at times even confusional states, extremes of restlessness and agitation are all exploited in a random defensive way to hide this emotionality and keep it dissociated. In their social behaviour they are genially feeble people with sensitive, alert minds. In analysis one finds them continuously fighting a propensity towards violence and affective-storms. Quite often their actual behaviour in the analytic situation is flat, listless, silent, self-pitying and morose. Detachedly they can present flagrant pregenital dream material and phantasies as well as body-states and sensations of eidetic and hypnogogic intensity and vividness.

If they nuture this emotionality secretively and with masochistic zeal, it also constitutes a threat to their ego-functions and their body-ego. Hence the marked 'resistivity' (Hartmann, 1952) of their egos, both towards the analytic process and towards their latent affectivity. They cling to their autonomous ego-functions and try to use them omnipotently. Their dread of resilence ('regression in the service of the ego' – Kris) is based on the fear that their ego-functions will be overridden either by this emotionality or by crude id-cathexis. This creates some very complex and bizarre confusions of intrapsychic functioning in them, e.g. massive libidinization of defences and/or erotic exploitation of body-organs in lieu of ego-relatedness. The relative failure of neutralization of id-cathexis and establishment of reliable ego-id boundaries leads also to a perpetual confusion between body-ego, ego-functions and id-cathexes. Their dreams exemplify this concretely and excitedly. They do not feel they are firmly and sentiently inhabiting their bodies. Their own bodies are in some ways external to them; they manage everything from the head, mentally. All the musculature is in their head and yet they use their bodies to *talk and communicate with*: which predisposes them towards these polymorph-perverse body-experiences (cf. Winnicott, 1949).

They have little capacity for real initiative; they rarely undertake any activity from personal initiative; they are mostly either intrigued, provoked or seduced into doing things. It is this exploitation of their ego-functions through seduction or provocation which makes them feel all their experiences and achievements as reactive, 'as-if' and false. They also rarely complete any experience with satisfaction: generally they exhaust themselves into uninterest. This peculiar technique of terminating every activity through losing interest and not through completion characterizes their object-relations as well.

They avidly search for contact and get passionately involved with people. While it lasts it consumes them with maniacal relentless intensity. What Lewin (1950) has established as the 'oral triad' in the psychology of elations is true of these patients in such moods. Their wish to devour and be devoured is ecstatic and ruthless, but equally vigilant and negativistic is the ego-defence against it. They just as readily fade out and lose interest. This ego-id involvement with people is not a true object-relationship. It might be fervent and ecstatic but it yields little satisfaction or pleasure. It is a defensive narcissistic alliance with another person, in which primitive identifications and exploitation of body-erotogeneity keep alive and sustain mutual ego-interest. Every such experience achieves a transient ecstatic quality and is grossly libidinized.

When one has watched their excessive ego-activity and sexual performances through the analytic material, what comes into sharp focus is their latent emotionality. It is an affective state which is most tangible clinically, though hard to define in words. It is this undifferentiated, confused emotionality and affectivity which they crave to materialize, actualize and share through sentient object-contact but never succeed in achieving. Their archaic anxieties and

33

random precipitate use of defence mechanisms continuously defeat every venture. What Alpert (1959) has called 'the point of *psychic satiety*' is never reached by them. Hence their own ego-functions, body and libidinal experiences, as well as experience of the external world and objects, constitute a persecutory threat to them and *flight* is a basic defence mechanism in these patients. I am using 'flight' in the sense Kaufman (1960) has postulated in his paper 'Some ethological studies of social relationships and conflict situations'. It is significant to establish the fact that search for 'comfort in contact and clinging' characterizes the dependence-need-attachment of these patients and also mobilizes to the maximum their negativity and ambivalence. They have to deny it as vehemently as they crave for it. Only in these patients the 'flight' is an intrapsychic process: it is flight into this emotionality which is then sustained in a dissociated satellite intrapsychic state (cf. Khan 1960*b*). This latent emotionality can be described as a pseudo psychic structure that is built out of the undifferentiated elements of the id and the ego, perception and hallucination, memory and apperception. It is the symptom of ego-distortion in these patients. The polymorph-perverse body-experiences and object-relations are both the vehicle of this emotionality and a self-engineered attempt to achieve, as it were, 'a corrective emotional experience' (Alpert, 1959) which will undo the split in the personality and the dissociations in the ego and lead to true ego-integration.

II. *The Nature and Function of Polymorph-Perverse Body-Experiences and Object-Relations*

It is important to distinguish these polymorph-perverse body-experiences from sexual perversions proper. All these patients had an adequate and intact genital capacity for sexual relationships. What I am characterizing as polymorph-perverse body-experiences can perhaps be best described in Winnicott's concept of 'transitional phenomena' (1951). They did not have a rigid defensive function or an organized repetitive pattern. They turned up spontaneously in certain regressive moods or tension states in these patients and before analysis were always as easily 'forgotten'. They were most often enacted with the person who was the habitual or normal object of heterosexual attention, e.g. the wife or husband. If they were acted out through masturbatory experiences, these never became organized into a static pattern of libido discharge. It is very

34

important about these body-experiences that in spite of their excited and ecstatic quality and value for the patient, they were at the same time felt to be traumatic, bewildering and shaming. In other words they were not ego-syntonic in the sense that true perverse sexual practices are. I should point out that none of the patients had sought treatment because of these polymorph-perverse body-experiences. They were not consciously aware of their significance or necessity for them. Once over they tended to regard them as ego-alien and dissociate or repress them from their self-image. Only through analytic work were these patients able to report truthfully and significantly about these body-intimacies of a primitive type. I am stressing this because though, I am sure, all of us have seen such material in our clinical practice, it has not been discussed as such. These experiences, because they are at once ego-alien, and acceptable to another person, escape attention. A mixture of instinctual impulsiveness, liberating ecstatic quality and ego-resistance, is rather typical of these experiences. In the phrase of one patient: 'I feel I get involved in a game to which I have lost most of the clues'.

In all the patients these body-intimacies had been experienced before they started their treatment and therefore these are not the result of the transference neurosis. However it was only through the transference and analytic work that it became possible to relate them to the infantile neurosis of these patients.

In content these polymorph-perverse body-experiences comprised libidinal regression to pregenital forms of foreplay and sexual intercourse. Apart from fellatio and cunnilingus, there was a craving for anal intercourse with a person of the opposite sex. These body-intimacies created a mild state of euphoria while they lasted. Touching, licking and 'devouring with eager eyes' played a large part in the foreplay. What was, quite often, frightening for the patients was a sudden realization during such an episode that they had lost sense of their own body-image. This fusion of body-images is significant. They felt confused and excited, traumatized and 'gorged' (to use the phrase of a patient). It often transpired that the men felt completely identified with the body of the female partner and experienced all her 'sensations'. Some of the oral and tongue-play was aimed at establishing this primary body-fusion with the partner. Even though they were able to perform genitally, they had no pleasurable body-sense of their own organ (Glauber, 1949).

These intimacies were precipitated by a mood of high tension,

35

apathy or restlessness. The enactment of the body-intimacies left them jaded, disoriented and they lost emotional contact with the partner. The same was true of their masturbatory experiences. If they masturbated anally they felt depleted and unreal afterwards, though the experience at the time of happening was felt to be lush, comforting and 'very filling'. In all my cases the masturbatory practices with the self-body followed experiences with a partner first.

The libidinal regression is also accompanied by affective regression to the object and is reflected in the choice of the object. They felt inseparably attached to the body and person of the partner in these moods. Contact by touch, penetration, sight and incorporation (taking some physical organ of the person into their mouth) was felt to be imperative. In one patient there was a distinct tangible sense that his hands were like his mouth: they could 'hold' and 'clutch' an object.

It was equally essential that the partner should wish, want and share with reciprocal avidity and zeal. Along with the compulsion to experience the *shared* sentience and physical reality of the partner, there was also a denial of their dependence on the object. The physical idiom of the body-intimacies and the permissive mutuality was idealized as an end in itself in these moods. The actual affective relation suffered from these body-mutualities. This element of body-involvement (as against phantasy elaboration) and activity (use of both skin and musculature) was felt by these patients to be very important. In the working through period one patient said: 'I feel it is more than an indulgence. I am trying to find out something. I know my body from outside only. I have no sense of being in it. Also I know other people exist, like my wife exists, but I have to *feel* it before I can be sure of her existence. I am sorting myself out into a separate person and getting to know and feel my own body-reality.' I think some sort of archaic body-reality-testing is involved in these intimacies. In the analysis they became a valuable source of information, both about the very early body-experiences and the relation to the mother in these patients. It is also surprising how accurately one could reconstruct the *actual* behaviour and relationship of the mother from these experiences.

If there was a search after passive, permissive, archaic and pregenital body-attachment to the partner, there was also an omnipotent control of her or him. Any resistance on the part of the object broke 'the magic spell' and wasted the whole venture, leading to rage and disgust both with the partner and self. This omnipotent control of the object in the service of idealized mutual body-love was the way these patients had of denying the primitive ruthless and aggressive elements in the instinctual cathexis of the object.

Only through analytic work and interpretation did it become possible to establish the link between these body-experiences and the latent emotionality in these patients. Once one established this link for them, it was not difficult to see how one way this emotionality could express itself for these patients was through this type of body-activity and intimacies. In analysis these activities were a form of acting out. The discussion of acting out by Greenacre (1950a), Bychowski (1945) and Ekstein & Friedman (1957) I have found most helpful towards an understanding of this type of behaviour. There is little doubt in my mind it is a 'special form of remembering' and what is being reproduced repetitively is 'a total experience'. What constituted this 'total experience' was the disturbed relation to the mother right from infancy, which has created ego-distortion and the dissociated emotionality. Just as the antisocial child makes *visible* through his behaviour the ego-distortions and archaic object-relations which he cannot psychically assimilate and communicate, similarly these patients use these body-intimacies to *make visible* and communicate the contents of their emotionality and ego-distortion (cf. Winnicott, 1956b; Shields, 1962).

III. *Mother's Pathogenic Role in the Disturbed Infant - Mother Relationship*

I shall now detail some of the salient features of the mother's pathology and character, which I could establish from my clinical material as being responsible for this disturbed relationship to the child and which created this emotionality and predisposition to enact it through body-intimacies.

In all my cases both the parents were alive and present during the early infancy of the patients. Therefore though their early background seemed to be stable, significant conflicts between the parents from this stage became obvious later, by which time mechanisms of denial and splitting had become firmly established as a way of dealing with any conflict. It is typical of these mothers that during the latency period they were compelled to involve the child in confidences relating to their husbands. This actual existence of parental conflict, and the young child's incapacity to sort its reality from personal phantasies, complicated and confused their Oedipus complex. Their mothers also had a way of making out their indispensability and exclusiveness for the child through precipitately dealing with every distress or stress situation. That they thus inhibited and interfered with the child's experimental and explorative activities did not seem to occur to them.

This type of mother does not denigrate or devalue the husband in her child's eyes. She makes the child precociously aware of her devotion to the husband and on this pattern demands devotion from the child. All these patients were deeply devoted to their mothers during childhood and latency. This intimate relation with the mother, with its 'peculiar union of the child's special need with the parent's special sensitivity', has been discussed by Greenacre in her paper 'On focal symbiosis' (1959). These children, through collusion of their body-ego processes and ego-functions, sponsor the mother in her self-deception that she is omnipotently good. What one rarely gathers from the anamnesis of these patients is any memory of both parents loving and looking after the child together and this is not due to repression of primal scene memories or phantasies. This failure of the parents, as a couple, distorts their capacity to enter into any affective bond which is not an intimate two-body relationship (Rickman, 1951).

All these mothers were adequate mothers of the infant. Their weaknesses, foibles and personal blindspots came into operation only when the infant reached toddler stage. This uncertainty of handling characterized 'the weaning period'. I am not referring to breast weaning here. I am discussing what Winnicott (1960) has described:

> In the ordinary case the mother's special orientation to the infant carries over beyond the birth process. The mother who is not distorted in these matters is ready to let go of her identification with the infant as the infant needs to become separate. It is possible to provide good initial care but to fail to complete the process through an inability to let it come to an end, so that the mother tends to remain merged with her infant and to delay the infant's separation from her. It is in any case a difficult thing for a mother to separate from her infant at the same speed at which the infant needs to become separate from her.

I want to emphasize this point, because it seems from the clinical anamnesis and transference recall of these patients that in each case

38

the mother certainly had a personal difficulty in handling this shift from primary identity to recognition of independence in the child. There was a random oscillation between continuing to treat the toddler 'as if' it were an infant or 'as if' it were more mature and integrated than its current development allowed for. I do not hold the early oral-sadistic phantasies as responsible for the ego-distortion in these patients. It is the mother's incapacity to administer 'doses of life experience' (Fries, 1946) that are phase-adequate for the child that causes this ego-distortion.

It is one of the consequences of this inconsistency that a precocious ego-development takes place, leading to a precocious identification with the mother on a mental level (cf. James, 1960). Contemporaneously a body-ego exploitation of a more auto-erotic primitive bond with the mother is sustained. I have advisedly used the term 'auto-erotic' because the emphasis remains on getting pleasurable satisfaction from the mother while she continues to be disregarded as an object. It is on this prototype that these patients seek erotic experiences and have singular dexterity in eliciting a maternal response from the sexual object who will voluntarily fit in with and sponsor their pregenital demands and impulses. In this context the relation never achieves true object-cathexis. The ideal is two people disregarding their identity and separateness to collude in the service of ecstatic auto-erotic intimacies. The historical inconsistency in the handling by the mother becomes apparent in the patient's ego as a split between a watching, supervising ego and a regressed primitive ego which is undifferentiated from id and operates essentially through the body-ego: its surface, organs and orifices. I think a lot of the bizarre contradictions apparent between the sophisticated ego of these patients and their extremely primitive body-intimacies can be traced to misidentifications with the mother. An example can make this clear. A male patient had felt compelled to induce his wife to masturbate and let him watch. After her orgasm he had made her masturbate him and watch him ejaculate. During the session next day he recalled how all through his childhood, right up to his adolescence, his mother had walked about naked in the flat, rationalizing that she had nurtured him as a baby and to her he was still a baby; and yet, when he was nine years of age, one night she had recounted to him how she had experienced orgasm as a girl of eighteen while sitting next to a man she had adored. And then had gone on to explain how men get erections and ejaculate. The patient had a clear memory of pretending to

39

understand it all so as not to shame himself in his mother's eyes through his incapacity to grasp fully what was being discussed. To him the link between what he had reported in the session and what he had acted out was quite clear. Another effect of the mother's body-exposures on this patient was that he had a compulsion to explore the genital of his wife in a variety of ways and could never discover its reality and nature. Keiser's (1958) intriguing hypotheses about the meaning of the invisibility of the vagina throw significant light on this material. This patient had not reacted with castration anxiety so much as an insatiable curiosity about a hidden organ. Quite a few of his compulsive anal masturbations during late latency were also attempts at discovering the vagina through exploring what felt to him an analogous organ in the self-body. This had completely 'estranged' him from his penis, even though he could use it for heterosexual intercourse. We have, I feel, not done justice as yet to the distortions in the male's crystallization of his body-ego through such confusion with the mother's body. This patient also had a compulsion sometimes after intercourse to make his wife digitally explore his anus.

The discrepancy between traumatizing and over-indulgent traits in the mother leads in these patients to an ego-dissociation where they as adults tend an undeveloped, infantile self; 'undeveloped' because it is in certain aspects a matter of arrested development. There is a form of developmental arrest in early childhood which is not so much a question of either the libidinal development or ego-development not progressing as such, but that there is a failure of significant interplay through integration between the two processes. It is one of the basic functions of mothering to sponsor this integration and facilitate its fruition and growth. It is precisely one of the 'progressive' functions of these polymorph-perverse body-experiences to find an object (a person) with and through whom this split can be undone. It is quite unmistakable that in all such pairs there is a subtle unconscious communication of basic needs: an appeal and a response. Where it always breaks down is that other conflictual elements enter the picture and distort the basic motivation. This is why, through the analytic process, the increment of insight makes it possible to transcend beyond the repetitive hankering after such experiences. Just as the analytic situation and transference relationship cannot supply physical satisfactions which these patients in such moods absolutely crave after, similarly a mere sharing of these experiences does not lead to psychical awareness of the unconscious processes involved. The libidinal regression entailed in the physical intimacies is bearable to the ego only if it keeps a dissociation throughout, otherwise the painful affects related to the historical experiences could break through the repressive barrier. The analytic process, through interpretations, administers to them in tolerable quantities the meaning of the 'staged experience' and thus makes it possible for them to resolve the dissociation. There is an unmistakable eagerness in these patients to explore their insides, both physically and psychically. The latter can be harnessed effectively in the service of the treatment if one can be tolerant of their acting out and search diligently for its meaning in their early childhood.

Typical of this disturbed infant-mother relation is a low toleration by the mother of distress and frustration in the young child. This again oscillates with a high expectancy from the toddler, in terms of ego-development, and avid affirmation of all their nascent ego-functions. These mothers barter with their children: for so much ego-development so much infantilism of libidinal body-experiences is allowed.

It is interesting to watch how during their latency period phantasies these patients translated this ambivalence in the mother into one of sado-masochistic teasing and traumatic deprivation. At the same time, through a complementary series, she becomes idealized into a magical person who was all-knowing and omnipotent. What they cannot find in their inner representations of the mother is psychic comfort and consolation. Comfort to them means seducing and being seduced into intimacies and this they re-enact in their adult body-intimacies.

Such a mother's low toleration of distress in the child is very closely related to depressive swings of mood in the mother. Because of her lack of personal stability of attentiveness towards the child at this stage, she is never sure of what is happening in the child so is always rushing to rescue and reassure. This interferes with what Hartmann (1952) has called 'intentionality' in these children. In spite of their precocious mental development they tend to remain 'fused' with the mother's mood. In childhood excessive daydreaming is one result of this.

A certain omnipotence of thought also characterizes these mothers. That is why they are good mothers to the infant. The toddler has a way of testing and teasing the mother's omnipotence. It is not yet independent enough, as it will be later, and yet it is not as pliable as the infant. This emergence of aggression, playful defiance and resistance in the toddler's behaviour is cause of great chagrin and fury to these mothers. The repression of their rage (hate) then leads to seductive manoeuvres on the part of the mother: a seduction which is both ego-seduction, i.e. sponsoring of precocious ego-maturity and id-seduction, i.e. through continuing to provide body-love. In three cases this peculiar technique of the mother led to a very marked split both in the ego and external objects. The relationship between mental-ego and non-sexual object was juxtaposed to libidinal id-ego and permissive sexual object.

One distressing aspect of this dissociation in the mother's orientation is that though she continues to comply with the child's body-needs in a primitive way, she no longer cathects her participation in these activities. In the adult patient's material this invariably turns up as their continuous anxiety and belief that their partner was not really enjoying it, was merely doing it for them for some social and personal gain which was nonsensual, or (in its more paranoid aspect) was merely doing it to laugh at them later. The extremes of psychic and emotional pain these patients experience through these doubts is very typical. In terms of the analytic process they feel one does not really care for them or credit their feelings. Every experience they receive loses its meaning because they cannot believe that the other person cathected the situation and experience with true feeling and libido and their last defence against this predicament is to turn against their own libidinal strivings and treat them as tools to play with. This way a severe form of self-denigration can take place, as well as devaluation of all libidinal relationships.

Another pathogenic effect of this type of maternal handling seems to me to be that though the mother fully boosts the young toddler's omnipotence of thought and action and indulges its auto-erotic activities, she fails to build a 'narcissistic capital' in the child's ego. I shall discuss the problem of the deficiency of primary narcissism in these patients under ego-distortions. Here it is sufficient to point out that exaggeration of erogeneity in fact leads to depletion of ego-libido in the child. Too great a discharge of pregenital instinct-tension devitalizes the building of cathexes into ego-libido (cf. Schur, 1953; Winnicott, 1956a).

Here the unconscious ambivalence of these mothers plays a striking role. Somehow their own instinctual problems lead them to put a very great deal of ego-interest in the child's activities, body-care and ego-development. But this ego-interest is patently lacking in warmth and affectivity. In their anamnesis all these patients recall their mothers as cold or wooden or impersonal and interfering.

In terms of the pregenital development of libido the maximum conflict between the child and mother takes place over body-excretions, i.e. over the anal and urethral phases. From my clinical experience it seems that though these mothers continue to sponsor auto-erotic experiences they have acute problems of shame and guilt *vis-à-vis* the cruder body-experiences. In certain cases I found that the mother's very permissiveness was because the mother had de-cathected her own involvement with the happenings. Seduction at this level is through sponsoring excessive displacements from pregenital libidinal processes to ego-processes, functions and defence mechanisms. This does lead at times to excessive neutralization of instinctual potential and leaves the ego out of touch with id-cathexes. There is a persistent dread in these cases, namely the fear of in-stinctual emptiness. And quite a lot of their craving after poly-morph-perverse body-experiences is motivated by this anxiety and dread. They have to find out that they actually do possess in-stinctual needs which can be made real and experienced within a shared mutuality with another person.

These unconscious but acutely shared and battled conflicts over anal and urethral experiences find a sudden relief at the phallic phase. At this stage this type of mother again comes into her own. She identifies with the child's phallic development (be it a boy or a girl) and over-invests it with ego-interest. The child becomes her phallus. It is a seduction which is very difficult for these children to fight off because it offers a magical solution to their interpsychic conflicts. On the one hand it leads to defensive narcissistic manoeu-vres and on the other it leads through bisexual identification to the regressive construct breast-phallus, i.e. a fusion of omnipotent breast and omnipotent phallus (Greenacre, 1960*b*).

This breast-phallus henceforth functions as a secret mental fetish (if I may coin a loose phrase) and is the source of a great deal of paranoid negativity and inability to surrender to true object-relationships (Greenacre, 1953*a*).

The mother's personality is neither excessively neurotic nor psychotic. She is a healthy mother whose sensibility and personal problems come into maximal pathogenic conflict with the child, just as it starts on its first experiences of differentiation from mother as a separate object and when intrapsychically the differentiation of ego-id boundaries begins to take shape. I have not done justice to the whole problem of aggression in this context. Briefly, I would say that these mothers deal with their aggression and hate through a curious type of manic emotionality. They are over-alert, over-eager, very vital and have bouts of depressive lethargy.

The fact that these patients have enjoyed a healthy infancy is very much the reason why they do not degenerate into perversions proper. Also a specific type of object-relation has been available to them right up to adolescence. This extended bond with the mother is aetiologically very significant, because it means that the relation, in its primitive and regressive affectivity, remains open and available to these patients through all stages of pregenital libido development and ego-maturation. This partially accounts for their over-sensitivity as adults. The significant aetiological point here is that these mothers do tolerate and sponsor certain types of discharge. This is protective even if it leads to ego-distortion.

This extended relation to the mother becomes the medium in which a great deal of primitive libidinal and psychic processes are kept alive. In these patients trauma is not so much a single event, or series of events in early infancy, as a long persistence of pathogenic interaction with the mother. It is this which has made it impossible to be more precise in delimiting the age-level at which all this takes place. These patients do not have an integrated ego so much as an ego that is built like a *collage*, i.e. the result of superimpositions at all levels and of types of libidinal stages, ego-capacities and object-relationships. To resolve this *ego-collage* into integration is the basic demand they have from their treatment. It is precisely this *collage* quality of their psychological and emotional make-up that they are trying to undo and correct (Gitelson, 1958).

Freud (1905*d*) stated very explicitly in *Three Essays on the Theory of Sexuality*: 'all through the period of latency children learn to feel for other people who help them in their helplessness, and satisfy their needs, a love which is on the model of, and a continuation of, their relation as sucklings to their nursing mother'. It is very typical of these mothers that they interfere with this process of displacement in the child. They remain the primary object. It is for this reason that at puberty and adolescence all these patients had to turn actively against the mother, and they did so invariably through *discovering* and idealizing the father. This is true of both the male and female cases, only in the female cases it led to very complex conflicts over heterosexuality.

It is not far-fetched to infer that the behaviour of these mothers is

44

both traumatizing and seductive. The role of actual infantile sexual seduction in the aetiology of hysteria was at first emphasized by Freud and later discarded. From the material of these patients it seems that the theory of actual seduction, as creating acute dissociation in the ego, is not so false after all. Only this seduction is not a single event but a mode of psycho-physical intimacy between the parent and child (Greenacre, 1953a). Freud (1905d) had postulated: 'it is an instinctive fact that under the influence of seduction children can become polymorphously perverse and can be led into all possible kinds of sexual irregularities'. This certainly is true of the polymorph-perverse body-intimacies of these patients, in so far as they are the result of their historical relation to the mother.

One further feature of these mothers' relation to their children stands out prominently. They had a compulsion, it seems, to leave the child for a certain period during the oedipal phase of its development. Suddenly they either went abroad on long holidays with their husbands or found some excuse for sending the child away. It represented their guilt *vis-à-vis* the husband and a final attempt to break free of the child. The child reacted to it in a confused, contradictory way: (i) as relief and freedom, i.e. experienced it as a positive experience, and (ii) as rejection and with rage and guilt. What defeated and undid the positiveness in the experience of being separated for the child was that the mother on return entered into competition with those with whom the child had established any bonds whatever and seduced the child back into the original relationship.

IV. *Nature and Function of Ego-Distortion*

Let us now define more specifically the nature and function of ego-distortion in these patients and its role in their perverse sexual practices. What I have aimed at so far is to give a picture of pathogenic maternal care-techniques in these cases. It is not my intention to put the blame on the mother and to present the infant-ego as a passive, helpless, innocent victim of these misdeeds of the mother. All our researches into ego-psychology leave us in little doubt about the extreme vulnerability of the nascent ego on the one hand and its innate potentiality for growth, structuralization and survival on the other. I am of the opinion that in so far as these mothers adequately sponsor the growth of all ego-functions, they

45

are setting the stage for the development of strong egos. This is why I have used the phrase ego-distortion and not ego-weakness. What characterizes the psychopathology of these patients is the relentless and wilful way in which they try to bring everything under the omnipotence of their ego (cf. Winnicott, 1960).

It is this feature of their psychical make-up we shall discuss first. In all these cases, as I have suggested, there has been a seduction into premature ego-development. But it is not a passive seduction. It is a shared seduction. The willing exploitation of every infancy experience towards ego-development is what creates a basic split in the ego. It is a shade fanciful to introduce the concept of will at this early stage of ego-development but I do not know how else to designate the strong innate tendency in the ego which Anna Freud (1959) has characterized as 'rooted in its biological reasonableness, towards assimilation, mastery and expansion'.

I think this early bias in the ego of these patients towards precipitate mastery of all conflict-producing experiences sets up a dual process: libidinally towards pregenital discharge processes and in ego terms to massive and random use of defence mechanisms. This prolix and precocious use of defence mechanisms leads also to their libidinization later on. Similarly, this heightening of ego-process in development, through premature identification with the mother's role, leads to severe disturbances of the development of pregenital sexuality. Because of low toleration of anxiety there is a continuous exploitation of erotic potentiality of the body-ego towards release of tension. This technique in turn devitalizes object-cathexes. Very early on true object-cathexes are replaced by ego-interest (cf. Anna Freud, 1954a).

One further consequence of precocious ego-development is that it leads to a decathexis of the person of the mother and of that part of the body which is related to her through primary identification and primary narcissism (cf. James, 1962). This is why in these patients' experience, in childhood and adult life, every object who colludes to yield 'body-need-satisfactions' becomes psychically obliterated through the very act of satisfaction. And though discharge-satisfactions become compulsive and idealized, there is little pleasure derived (cf. Glauber, 1949). These erotic and libidinal experiences do not lead to the capacity for 'object constancy' (Hartmann, 1952) or affective integration (cf. Winnicott, 1945, 1960). Anna Freud (1954a) has discussed the role this plays in the transference behaviour of these patients:

In analysis of such patients we find that there is no hidden fund of archaic love or hate on which the transference can draw. Relations to the analyst remain superficial and insecure, built on the only available pattern of relationships; since libido has never been concentrated fully on any one object, the concentration of material in a transference neurosis does not seem to come about.

(Also cf. Gillespie, 1952.) This, plus the denial of their archaic dependency on the analyst and the analytic situation, compels these patients to act out a great deal (cf. Bychowski, 1945).

I have already drawn attention to the excessive use of splitting mechanisms in these patients. Their identificatory mechanisms have some typical qualities too. The object is identified with and thereby replaced. It is an incorporative technique which leads to becoming the object rather than modelling and developing some ego-function through identification with an object. A very explicit example of this is how much these patients take over the caretaking function of the mother very early on and become their own nursing mothers (cf. Winnicott, 1949; Bychowski, 1945).

When this type of identificatory process is combined with splitting mechanisms, an interesting intrapsychic situation emerges. The patient is both the mother and the infant, but in any given situation of object-involvement he can play the role only of the one or the other. Therefore one part of the ego has to be projected on to another person. It is this which lends so many of the emotional and sexual relationships of these patients a characteristic aura of role-play and make-believe pantomime.

At this stage I would like to discuss the problem of deficiency of primary narcissism in the ego-structure of these patients.

The concept of primary narcissism has been brought to the forefront of our metapsychological researches in recent years through increased interest in and knowledge of infant-care techniques on the one hand and through more intensive analyses of cases of borderline and schizoid personality disorders on the other. What I offer here, by way of discussion, is extremely tentative.

In his paper on 'Narcissism' (1914c) Freud made the following two statements: 'not until there is object-cathexis is it possible to discriminate a sexual energy – the libido – from an energy of the ego-instincts' and 'there must be something added to auto-erotism – a new psychical action – in order to bring about narcissism'. What

47

has held up a clarification and assimilation of this most valuable paper of Freud's into our clinical work and theory is that Freud at that time was conceptualizing entirely in terms of the intrapsychic situation of the infant. Today, I think, given the researches of ego-psychology and infant-care techniques, we are better equipped to handle this issue. Let us first take the problem that Freud posed himself in this connexion: 'would not the postulation of a single kind of psychical energy save us all the difficulties of differentiating an energy of the ego-instincts from ego-libido and ego-libido from object-libido?' It is now feasible to postulate that at the start just as structurally there is undifferentiated ego-id, similarly, in terms of instinctual energies, there is also an undifferentiated capital of aggresive, libidinal and ego-energy. The question then arises: how does this undifferentiated energic capital get differentiated? To me the answer seems to be in a complementary threefold process: (i) the maturation of the body-ego which articulates the libidinal energy through pregenital stages; (ii) maturational muscular integration which binds and defines aggressive cathexes (Green-acre, 1960c); (iii) the growth of nascent potential ego-capacities into executive ego-functions. In all these three areas of articulation and differentiation the mother plays a central role. If she mobilizes the auto-erotism of the infant body through body-care, and helps to co-ordinate and canalize the infant's muscular development and its aggressive drive, she also lends herself as an ally, as an alter-ego, to the nascent infant-ego. It is only when she has enabled the un-differentiated id-ego to differentiate and build up libidinal cathexes and affects that the possibility of object-cathexes becomes feasible for the child ego. Therefore the 'psychical action' (Freud, 1914c) is composed of the activity of the mother, plus the ego's inherent developmental process. Discussing the early stages of infancy development, Anna Freud (1953) stated the basic problem of the infant-ego: 'whatever happens calls forth a response: what seems to be missing is a pulling together of experience'. It is the mother's basic function to enable 'this pulling together of experience'. By lending her own ego-function, affectivity and sensitivity the mother enables the following processes to materialize in infant-personality:

1. Differentiation of id-cathexes and affects.

2. Differentiation of libidinal from aggressive cathexes.

3. Assimilation by the ego of these aggressive and libidinal cathexes through body-satisfactions into primary narcissism.

4. Neutralization of a certain amount of instinct tensions and energy

through ego-structures that bind and serve discharge (cf. Schur, 1953).

5. Employment of the ego-libido, both in ego-functions and object-cathexes.

This naturally is an ideal diagram. In concrete experience certain deviations are bound to take place. In terms of the type of ego-development we are discussing, a dissociation between the mother's ego-functions and affectivity initiates a split in the child's ego. One consequence of this is that instead of interplay between ego-development and instinctual development a parallelism starts. The two develop independently of each other and each is continuously trying to bring the other under the dominance of its own aims and activity-patterns. This leads to exacerbation of both erotogeneity and ego-function. Consequently the transformation of pregenital erotogenicity into narcissism does not occur. Clinically one sees this both as an acute ego-depletion (apathy) and as instinctual impoverishment in these patients. Their ego-achievements are futile to them because they are devoid of libidinal cathexes and their normal instinctual experiences sap their ego-vitality. The wish to correct this imbalance motivates their search for an object who will enable them to unite and fuse these two parallel processes and polymorph-perverse body-experiences are one idiom of attachment to such an object. These patients, therefore, seek objects not only for discharge of instinctual needs but even more compulsively for satisfaction of primitive ego-needs. The aim is not to love and be loved but to find a special type of participation from an adult which will make what is ego-alien into what is ego-related. This ego-relatedness is a little different from the ego-syntonic. These patients have a way of making most experiences ego-syntonic in a pseudo 'as if' way through denial and splitting mechanisms. What their congealed and precipitate defence mechanisms never enable them to achieve is the ego-relatedness to both the instinctual processes and the external object (cf. Gitelson, 1958; Kaufman, 1960; Winnicott, 1958a).

I have mentioned intolerance of anxiety and frustration by these patients and yet in one particular way they show a craving for frustration. It is related to their dread of actual satisfactions. In the context of this type of ego-functioning and experience, any orgastic satisfaction is tantamount to annihilation. It is a trait of this type of ego-distortion that it builds up a craving for tension. It feeds on tension just as avidly as it is compulsively trying to discharge it. Schur (1953) has discussed this as 'reaction of primary anxiety with full resomatization'. Here the instinctual cathexes are subsumed in the defensive functions and mental hyper-activity. This emotionality of these patients has a manic quality. It leads them into extremely intense object-involvements and yet the dread of being swallowed up and/or annihilated through satisfaction is there. In terms of their adult psychopathology it all gets distorted into a game of emotional looking and being looked at: involving psychological processes as well as the body (cf. Lewin, 1950).

The vicissitudes of aggressive drives in these patients are equally complex and distorted. In childhood their mode of dealing with aggression was either affective storms or hyper-activity. In adult ego-activity it takes the form of compulsive and hectic 'love affairs' and excessive eroticism. This way of dealing with aggression through libidinization again dissociates it from the ego. One fateful and distressing vicissitude of it is that in unconscious phantasy repressed aggression becomes sadism and through ego-functions becomes a compulsion to control and dominate all objects. This is why a certain morbid apathetic passivity that one sees in their object-relations is a way of controlling sadistic phantasy and paranoid fears of retaliation. This unconscious conflict lies behind the seeming superficial docility and suggestibility of these patients and they have a great dexterity in exploiting this as a bait to appeal to and seduce others into collusive body-intimacies.

The underlying paranoid anxieties, castration fears and sense of acute split in the personality compels these patients into continuous acting out. What in analysis we regard as acting out in their previous life had been a proclivity to impulsive sexual relations and primitive body-experiences. This acting out is both a way of getting rid of conflictual tensions in the ego and a way of involving other egos (persons) into their service. In shared experiences they achieve control by playing master of ceremonies. It is *vis-à-vis* this compulsion to act out that they have to institute very subtle phobic practices and controlling mechanisms. Their sense of reality consists in selection of suitable but extremely limited areas of activity and willing objects. This naturally in turn makes their existence futile to them because they are fully aware of their ritualistic restrictions. Their omnipotence is impossible without their phobic defences. The polymorph-perverse body-experiences are both a way of making such existence pleasurable and carrying a hope that they might fortuitously reach beyond the rigid inner barriers of their personality. Their claustrophobic inner life is also made bearable through these sexual intimacies with people, though in turn every such relationship becomes claustrophobic and castrating and has to be dissociated from.

The failure in early development of neutralization of aggression compels their egos to deal with aggressiveness through displacement to pregenital body-experiences. The guilt and anxiety related to this is mitigated if an object can be found who will sponsor and share it. In this way these patients use the object as a permitting and sanctioning super-ego. One vicissitude of this is that the object who thus becomes the carrier of the projection of pregenital impulses is also judged adversely. The erotic activities shared with the object are split off as ego-alien and the super-ego is harmonized with the ego through adopting censorious attitudes towards the object. It is this that makes these patients give up their instinctual cathexis and ego-interest in an object suddenly, makes them bored and apathetic and to the other person they seem sadistically ungrateful (Bychowski, 1945; Winnicott, 1949).

V. *Quality and Role of Object-Relations*

I shall distinguish, for the purposes of this discussion, social relationships from affective and instinctual relationships in these patients. Their social relationships can be adequate and significant for those around them. In fact maintenance of good social relationships is necessary for the self-esteem of these patients. A weak super-ego also makes the personality dependent on social approval and support.

It is the personal and affective relationships which lead to these polymorph-perverse body-experiences. In our literature three papers describe succinctly the dynamics and pathology of these relationships. Winnicott's paper on 'Transitional objects and transitional phenomena' (1951) defines the area of primitive functioning to which these patients regress or at which they have remained ego-fixated and in the pattern of which they cast all their current experiences with instinctual objects. Anna Freud's paper on 'A connexion between states of negativism and of emotional surrender' (1952) describes how a predicament behind all their searching remains the inability to surrender emotionally and experience for themselves a true object-relationship and satisfaction. Marion Milner's paper 'Aspects of symbolism in comprehension of the not-self' (1952) details the vicissitudes of obliteration of body-boundaries and need for illusion of oneness as a precursor to differentiation of separate body and self identity.

What they are always trying to bring about is the achievement of a state of illusory oneness with another person, in which the other person will comprehend, sympathize with, articulate and fulfil all their ego-needs and instinctual strivings. But it is an unconscious condition of such a relationship that though the object promotes and fulfils these pregenital, auto-erotic and polymorph-perverse strivings, he or she should not need it for themselves. The fear that the other person might be a true pervert and thus seduce them into perpetual and abject collusion is a real dread in these patients. It is this inner untrust of the reliability of the object that degenerates the illusory state of oneness into a magical and omnipotent control of the object. Also the object, though making itself available for maximal dependency, should sponsor their denial of it. This extreme need to elicit and coerce total adaptation to polymorph-perverse body-intimacies, as an idiom of 'transitional object-relationship', is never successful in the adult person. Their own ego-pathology distorts the primitive simple state that they crave after. What starts as a search for an illusional primitive state of oneness pathologically degenerates into testing the object's credentials and potentiality. In this way the greater the 'resistivity' of the patient's ego the more excessive and ideal is the demand from the object for satisfaction and adaptation. Thus dependency becomes translated into compelling the object to adapt. Neither absorption in the relationship nor pleasurable satisfaction are possible. Intrapsychic and developmental conflicts are transmuted into ego-interests. It becomes the task of the object to heal and transform the patient's pathology into health through love and care. In the intrapsychic dynamics of these patients shame and concern play a more vital role than guilt and structural conflicts. Their reaction to frustration and disappointment is not so much depression as helpless inconsolability and confusion. Hence they teach the object how to become the ideal comforter. How compelling is the challenge and appeal of this offer of relationship for people in society is evidenced by the fact that these patients have a singular facility in finding accomplices. They hopefully tantalize others into collusion and then fail them. In their subjectivity it is, of course, others who always fail them. The irony of these relationships is that what is basically being sought is neither erotic nor libidinal satisfaction. These have been merely secondary gains from a technique of intimacy and a defensive mode of existence (cf. Winnicott, 1956a).

In so far as their ego-distortion has made an intrapsychic

52

experience of disillusionment, mourning and acknowledgement of object-love impossible, these patients are obsessed by a mental preoccupation with the search for an ideal object. Their primary need, as gradually becomes clear through the analytic process, is to find, or rather rediscover, an archaic dependency-stage relationship in which illusion, id-satisfactions and ego-relatedness can be achieved in order to experience psychically disillusion and separateness. What they are searching for is a relationship in which dissatisfaction, anxiety, sadness and loss can be experienced and psychically assimilated by the ego (cf. Winnicott, 1958*a*).

VI. CONCLUSION

My attention has been centred on a specific activity which involves the body-ego and expresses a particular type of emotionality that is a dissociated intrapsychic state in the patient. I am here following Kris's suggestion that 'study of specific activities represents an important subject for future psychoanalytic investigations' (Kris, 1955). I have tried to show how this specific activity, which consists of polymorph-perverse body-experiences, auto-erotically and/or with another object, is the result of ego-distortion which derives from a specific type of pathogenic mother-child relationship. This theme has been recently discussed by Greenacre (1959) in terms of 'focal symbiosis' and by Melitta Sperling (1959) as deviant sexual behaviour in children through intimate collusion with mother. I have tried to specify the pathogenic traits in the mother's character and handling of the child which lead to this type of behaviour.

Glover (1943) has postulated: 'however fragmented the early-ego, there is from the first a synthetic function of the psyche which operates with gradually increasing strength'. The specific pathology of the mother-child relationship in these patients disrupts and distorts this synthetic function of the psyche and leads to marked splits and dissociations in the ego. The elements of trauma, seduction and precocious ego-development that result from this lead to the intrapsychic formation of a dissociated affectivity which clinically becomes visible as tense emotionality. This emotionality is deviously and compulsively expressed through polymorph-perverse body-experiences and object-relations. The value, dynamics and meaning of these experiences become available to analytic examination and interpretation only very gradually, because the patients are very secretive about it. In four of my cases the patients had undergone long analysis before where this material had not come into focus at all. I have stressed the importance of this material towards an understanding of the psychopathology of these patients because regressive over-condensation from all phases of ego and libido development, as well as archaic object-relationships, results in an emotionality which is enacted through polymorph-perverse body-experiences.

I have postulated that along with a defensive-regressive discharge function these polymorph-perverse body-experiences are also the vehicle of a hope which can be perhaps equated with 'emotional corrective experience'. The mother's denial of the deprivation-value of her withdrawal of cathexis from the child's body makes it impossible for the child overtly to react with rage and aggression or to experience psychically mourning, loss and separateness. Instead the child institutes a dissociation which we can perceive clinically, in Szasz's (1957) description, as 'the ego treating the body (in contrast to the self) as the lost object'. The 'lost-object', which the body-ego becomes the representative of, is a composite constellation of (a) good memories of being nursed; (b) the lost good mother; (c) identification with the denial by the mother of her hate and rejection, and (d) repressed rage and aggression in the primitive ego. The polymorph-perverse body-experiences and object-relations are both a regressive attempt at the discharge of these affects and a mode of body-empathy in the service of new perception in order to sort out the confused images, memories and affects. If we succeed in clinically helping the patient to arrive at this psychic differentiation and discernment, then the dissociations and splits in the ego can be resolved (Greenson, 1960; Greenacre, 1956).

It has not been my intention to discuss the technical issues involved. I sincerely hope, however, that what I have said about the potentiality of these body-experiences to yield information about primitive and archaic levels of libidinal and ego-development will not be misconstrued as implying that I am recommending such experiences and acting out as essential and therapeutically necessary. That would be a gross error of clinical judgement. In fact the polymorph-perverse body-experiences and the emotionality in these patients constitute an adamant source of resistance. My clinical experience leads me to infer, however, that unless we can include this disturbed mother-child relation in the 'expectation' (Coleman,

Kris & Provence, 1953) with which we approach the task of reconstruction of the infantile neurosis in these patients, we cannot hope to evaluate judiciously the meaning of these activities (cf. Greenacre, 1956; Khan, 1962; Stone, 1961). It is my contention, however, that alongside a regressive defensive discharge function there is a latent rudimentary progressive potentiality in these polymorph-perverse body-experiences that can be therapeutically exploited towards resolving their ego-distortion and enabling them to achieve insight and ego-integration.

4

The Role of Infantile Sexuality and
Early Object-Relations in Female Homosexuality

THEORY

IN spite of the many and varied criticisms (Horney, 1939; Thompson, 1949; Robbins, 1950) of Freud's attempts at exploring and explaining the mysterious and complex processes of the female psychosexual development, there is little doubt that as yet we have no other set of hypotheses from any other source that help us clinically towards an understanding of this problem. Therefore, in this chapter I am going to restrict my range of hypotheses to the researches of Freud and his followers. I am not unmindful of the fact that valuable work has been done from other disciplines which throws a great deal of light on some aspects of female development and its role in culture, for example the work of Margaret Mead (1962) and Kinsey *et al.* (1953) to quote two examples from two very different angles. Similarly, there are some shrewd observations in the later work of Karen Horney and Clara Thompson on the cultural determinants that complicate and structuralize the role and function of femininity in Western cultures. But none of these help us with the therapeutic handling of intrapsychic conflicts or character distortion in our female patients. Since the exclusive aim of this chapter is to discuss a particular form of psychosexual pathology in the female, I shall first briefly and schematically state Freud's basic contributions to this theme.

It is typical of Freud's insight and integrity that he took a long time arriving at a discussion of the female sexuality and even then handled it with reserve and caution. No one was more aware of the tentativeness of his own hypotheses than Freud. In his final contributions to this problem he was very much helped and guided by the researches of Abraham (1920), Helena Deutsch (1930), Jeanne Lampl-de Groot (1928) and Ruth Mack Brunswick (1929).

Even though in his book *Three Essays on the Theory of Sexuality* (1905*d*) and through most of his papers up to 1925, Freud had

56

made little distinction between the sexual developmental process in the male and female child, he was, however, all the time aware that a distinction did exist. As early as 1897 in a letter to Wilhelm Fliess we find Freud (1950a) distinguishing between the course of sexual development in boys and girls: 'Disgust appears earlier in little girls than in boys', though here, as in his other works from this period, he still holds on to his point of view that the main distinction between the two sexes emerges at the period of puberty.

The three papers in which Freud revised, enlarged and explicitly stated his new hypothesis about the distinctive nature and course of psychosexual development in the female are:

'Some psychical consequences of the anatomical distinction between the sexes' (1925j);

'Female sexuality' (1931b);

'Psychology of women' (1933a).

Schematically one can detail the pertinent hypotheses as follows:

1. That there is an extended and complex phase of exclusive attachment to the mother in the girl, which precedes the Oedipus complex.

2. That this pre-oedipal phase which contains the pre-history of the girl's Oedipus complex and has fateful consequences for it, continues right into the fourth or fifth year of her life, thus involving most of the phallic phase of her libidinal development.

3. The girl's attachment to the mother is cathected with sexual aims that are first passive and then active and are influenced in turn by all the vicissitudes of libidinal development from oral, through anal sadistic to phallic phase. It follows that this relationship then bears all the stamp of the vicissitudes of aggressive and libidinal impulses that are faced at any given time through this period of psychosexual development.

4. The castration complex and relinquishment of this long attachment to the mother, that is the shift of her erotogenetic zone and in her object choice, are complementary. According to Freud, the Oedipus complex 'is not destroyed', but created by the influence of the castration, and the hostile attitude of the girl to her mother is not a consequence of rivalry implicit in the Oedipus complex, but originates from the preceding phase and has merely been reinforced and exploited in the Oedipus situation. Freud makes a very close link between the characteristic phallic activity of the little girl, that is masturbation of the clitoris, with all the vicissitudes of frustration and seduction that have been entailed in the long process of maternal

57

care of body-needs and the affective relation to mother as such. In this context then ambivalence towards the mother becomes very closely associated with both the attachment to the mother and the relinquishment of her at the discovery of castration.

5. The final transition from the mother to the father, that is the establishment of the Oedipus complex proper in the girl is, therefore, the result of two complementary processes: (i) the acceptance of castration with all its consequences, and (ii) the fulfilment of the biological drive by transforming the 'masculine' elements into feminine ones by drawing on her passivity and positive psychosexual trends. In this context the child-penis earlier on wished and fantasied from the mother is now transformed into an oedipal wish for a child from the father.

6. Freud saw in the particular difference between the male and female child in their way of arriving at the Oedipus complex very fateful consequences for the character formation and particularly for the development of the moral function, that is the super-ego, in the female. 'We should probably not be wrong in saying that it is this difference in the reciprocal relation between the Oedipus and the castration complex which gives its essential stamp to the characters of females as social beings.' When Freud made this statement he was fully aware that he would be accused of masculinity complex of the male and of an innate inclination to disparage and suppress women (Freud, 1925*j*, 1931*b*).

7. It is important to point out one particular postulate of Freud's about female sexuality, because it is pertinent to my discussion of the theme of female homosexuality. I shall quote the relevant paragraph from Freud, because it explicitly states his view on penis-envy in the girl which has been so emphatically questioned by some analysts of the culturist orientation, e.g. Horney (1939) and Thompson (1943).

There is yet another surprising effect of penis-envy, or of the discovery of the inferiority of the clitoris, which is undoubtedly the most important of all. In the past I had often formed an impression that in general women tolerate masturbation worse than men, that they more frequently fight against it and that they are unable to make use of it in circumstances in which a man would seize upon it as a way of escape without any hesitation. Experience would no doubt elicit innumerable exceptions to this statement, if we attempted to turn it into a rule. The reactions of human individuals of both sexes are of course made up of masculine and feminine traits. But it appeared to me nevertheless as though masturbation were further removed from the nature of women than of men, and the solution of the problem could be assisted by the reflection that masturbation, at all events of the clitoris, is a masculine activity and that the elimination of clitoridal sexuality is a necessary precondition for the development of femininity. Analyses of the remote phallic period have taught me that in girls, soon after the first signs of penis-envy, an intense current of feeling against masturbation makes its appearance, which cannot be attributed exclusively to the educational influence of those in charge of the child. This impulse is clearly a forerunner of the wave of repression which at puberty will do away with a large amount of the girl's masculine sexuality in order to make room for the development of her femininity. It may happen that this first opposition to auto-erotic activity fails to attain its end. And this was in fact the case in the instances which I analysed. The conflict continued, and both then and later the girl did everything she could to free herself from the compulsion to masturbate. Many of the later manifestations of sexual life in women remain unintelligible unless this powerful motive is recognized. (Freud, 1925*j*.)

8. The final shift from clitoral eroticism to orgastic vaginal capacity of the girl at puberty entails subtle and complex shifts not only in the dispensation of organ libido and redistribution of erotogeneity, but also a complementary rearrangement of active (phallic) strivings into passive receptive ones. This, Freud felt, entailed far more complex re-orientation and re-integration both libidinally and in terms of object-cathexis than we meet with in the evolution of the boy's sexuality from infancy to manhood.

Freud (1933*a*) summed up his general attitude towards the complexity of female psychosexual development in his statement: 'It is our impression that more violence is done to the libido when it is forced into the service of the female function; and that – to speak teleologically – Nature has paid less careful attention to the demands of the female function than to those of masculinity.'

Literature on Female Homosexuality

In the past four decades intensive researches into the psychosexual development of the female have been published in the analytic literature, e.g. Helene Deutsch (1944, 1945), Benedek (1952) and Bonaparte (1953), etc. I shall discuss the significant papers in the context of my clinical report. It is, however, worthwhile to single out for reference two exhaustive discussions, one by Zilboorg (1944) and the other by Lichtenstein (1961). Also Arlow (1954) and Socarides (1962) have reported two Panel discussions at the annual meetings of the American Psychoanalytic Association which are both comprehensive and stimulating in their contents.

There is, however, a paucity of clinical discussion in the literature, of actual female homosexuality or episodes of homosexual relationships. In a sense the situation in the analytic literature has not improved noticeably since Freud's complaint in 1920: 'Homosexuality in women, which is certainly no less common than in men, although much less glaring, has not only been ignored by the law, but has also been neglected by psycho-analytic research.'

Three cases discussed by Freud (1905e, 1915f, 1920a) of female homosexuality are all of an emotional homosexual attachment to another female; in two cases it was an unconscious and latent attachment and only in one case was it consciously acknowledged. There was no incidence of overt sexual intimacy in any of the cases. Jones (1927) had the most interesting coincidence of having five homosexual female patients concurrently in treatment but he did not report any clinical material, though his conclusions and inferences are profoundly helpful towards an understanding of female homosexuality. Fenichel (1929) reported an interesting dream-analysis of a homosexual female but did not detail any sexual experiences or their pathology.

It is to Helene Deutsch (1932) that we owe the most instructive and illuminating clinical discussion of female homosexuality. Her two contributions (1932, 1944) are the classics in this area of research. In my clinical and theoretical discussion I am deeply indebted to Deutsch's researches and shall discuss them in due course.

Brody (1943) presented some case material from the treatment of a female patient, tracing 'factors in the pyschosexual development of a girl which lead to homosexual maladjustment'. He singled out a rejective mother and poorly resolved Oedipus complex and an exaggeration of pregenital sadism as significant aetiological components.

Keiser and Schaffer (1949) have reported some very interesting case material from their observations of adolescent girls with broken home-life. Bergler (1951) reported four cases of lesbianism to illustrate his over-simplified thesis that lesbians are typically orally regressed people, with masochistic fixation on aggressive mothers. In a similar and superficial vein Caprio (1957) recounts brief life-histories of four female homosexuals in his book. Bacon (1956) and Wittenberg (1956) report a case each to show that homosexual relationships in the female can be an expression of developmental needs and therefore an attempt at growth and maturation.

Lichtenstein (1961) in his scholarly and profoundly interesting paper on the complex theme of psychosexual maturation and identity formation details material from the treatment of a girl with acute personality problems, gross heterosexual pathology and episodes of homosexual relationships. In some ways Lichtenstein's is the most stimulating and weighty contribution to this area of research in recent years.

Taking into consideration the relative scarcity of clinical discussion of female homosexuality, I have chosen to discuss this complex problem through the narrative of the treatment of a young girl, in whose analysis an intense and overt homosexual attachment played a very significant and dynamic part. It is important to bear in mind that my patient was diagnostically not a case of true homosexual perversion. In her life active homosexual intimacies with a female friend lasted for a short period of time and never became established as a permanent, exclusive and preferential mode of sexual gratification or object-choice. It can be argued that in so far as this was not a true and fixed homosexual perversion, what we can learn from this about the psychopathology and genetic development of female homosexuality is very limited. The clinical researches of Freud and his followers have again and again shown us the value of studying deeply the less extreme and bizarre instances and manifestations of human psychosexual pathology towards a truer understanding of the psychopathology of the gross disturbances and disorders: both sexual and mental, i.e. true perversions and psychoses.

In presenting the narrative of a long analysis it is unavoidable that one has to select and choose one's data. This, by definition, leaves out many aspects and thereby tends to distort others. My intention is to be able to convey the feel and rhythm of the clinical process and through it make visible the patterns of pathology, developmental arrest and psychosexual disturbance that can help us towards an understanding of the nature and function of female homosexuality. In one way to be able to delineate the emergence, working through and resolution of a transitory perversion has distinct advantages over discussion of organized and true perversion. The latter through the very fact of having achieved a rigid structure in habit and expectancy in the person concerned push under the more subtle and significant sources of distress and internal psychic conflicts. All true organized perversions present us with a false situation, where the secondary gains have become too rigidly integrated into the superstructure of personality and its modes of dealing with anxieties and instinctual conflicts. I have tried to give a detailed theoretical account of what I consider to be the significant patterns of psychosexual dynamics and early object-relationships in polymorph-perverse practices and intimacies in Chapter 3.

To avoid repetition, misrepresentation and to economize in the length of this chapter I have referred to the authors and their papers by indicating them in brackets where they are relevant to my discussion.

CLINICAL MATERIAL

From the material of a female patient I shall discuss some salient features of the psychopathology of female homosexuality in the light of psycho-analytic researches. What makes this material specifically pertinent is the way the patient acted out in transference neurosis her oedipal conflicts as well as her pre-oedipal conflictual attachment to the mother through a transitory active homosexual love affair with a woman a little older than herself. This homosexual acting out was intensively worked through and resolved in her treatment and the patient achieved a capacity for orgastic heterosexual experiences and has been happily married for many years now, without any recurrence of homosexual conflicts.

The patient, a college student in her twenties, had sought treatment because of difficulties in work. She enjoyed academic life and her relations with the other girls. Her difficulties in interpersonal relations arose always with the elderly female teachers, whom she was always trying to pacify and placate and of whose aggression she was always fearful. She had always avoided men and lived in close and tender attachment to girls.

The younger of two children, she had grown up in a stable middleclass family. She had throughout childhood a close and eager relation with her father, who was a sympathetic, affectionate and religious man and had encouraged the intellectual pursuits of his daughter. At puberty she had become rather belligerent with him and entered into lengthy intellectual discussions. He had died when she was in her early twenties (a few years before starting treatment) and she had been struck by her lack of grief and mourning at his death.

The patient had a conscious and good-humoured dislike of her mother. She described her mother as 'a very nice person addicted to doing good deeds for others'. Calm and steady of temperament generally she had been over-solicitous about the physical well-being of her children. The patient could not recall any intense emotional attachment to her mother, although she had always exploited her mother's infinite capacity for concern by running to her with little tales of woe or in attitudes of misery. Very early on she had learnt to exploit her mother through staging helplessness and bodily or mental discomfort. She had always used this as an effective weapon against the superior buoyance of spirit and strength which her elder brother possessed.

Her relation to her brother, who was four years older, had been a mixture of envy, jealousy, competitiveness and tender affection. Her memories of him from childhood were of always being teased to tears and helplessness by him.

The patient had lived a sheltered family life; smooth and uneventful. Her own behaviour during childhood, latency and puberty had been characterized by a delicate submissiveness towards her parents and teachers, diligence at studies and a lack of any boisterous exuberance of emotions or activity.

In physical appearance she was of short height, feminine and pleasant looking and tastefully dressed. She had always steered clear of any intense emotional involvement with men or women and had no sexual experiences whatever. She was very self-conscious of this lack of sexual experience and venturesomeness. She felt humiliated by it. Added to it was her awareness of her incapacity for any form of discharge through masturbation in spite of confused, excited, sensual reverie states. She felt prudish and inhibited. It had been becoming more obvious to her lately that her life was restricted by phobic and obsessional traits. She was also distressed by the general shallowness of her affectivity. All her experiences were entered on a make-believe as-if basis. Her personality integration and effectiveness was sustained through complicated defence mechanisms that reduced the verve and freedom of her inner psychic life as well as her social experiences. This type of benign ego-restriction, with phobic attitudes and passive depressiveness is readily compatible with personal and cultural expectancy from the females in her culture. In fact quite often it can be exploited as pseudo-femininity and becomes petrified into a character disorder that the person has no way of fighting free of. This patient had sought treatment from unconscious inner perceptions of her predicament and it is with the working through of this personality predicament in transference and through her homosexual acting out that we shall be most concerned in this discussion. Helene Deutsch (1932) gives a very clear picture of this type of character disorder:

> The economic advantage of this new turning to the mother lies in the release from a feeling of guilt. But it seems to me that the most important accomplishment lies in the protection from the threatened loss of object: 'If my father won't have me, and my self-respect is undermined, who will love me, if not my mother?' Analytic experience offers abundant evidence of this bisexual oscillation between father and mother, which may eventuate in neurosis, heterosexuality or inversion. We see the libido swinging between the poles of two magnets, attracted and repelled. Prospects of wish-fulfilment represent the *attraction* by one pole, frustration, fear, and mobilization of guilt feelings the *repulsion* from the other; and we see the same things happening in the case of other magnets; and as one of the most serious results of this oscillation, an obstinate narcissistic standstill appears somewhere in between. There are cases of blocking of affect, and especially clinical pictures of narcissistic disorders, which do not fit into any of the recognized forms of neurosis, but which do correspond to a standstill in the pendulum swing of libido as just described. If the oscillation is set in motion again in the analytic transference, the obsessional neurosis, whose oscillating ambivalence had been concealed by the emotional block, becomes apparent. There was in these cases of female homosexuality a longer or shorter phase of indecision, which offers proof that it was not a question of a simple fixation on the mother as the first love-object, but rather a complicated process of returning. The decision in favour of the mother as the attracting magnet lies naturally in the old powers of attraction, but also in the repelling forces from other magnets – denials, anxiety, and guilt reactions.

PHASE I

The Dread of Emotional Surrender

In the discussion of this phase which preceded the homosexual acting out and lasted for nearly a year or so, I shall single out first the social circumstances and relationships of the patient, then discuss the material collected in analysis through the analytic process and then detail the specific features of the transference.

When she started analysis the patient had come away from home. Her father had died a few years earlier. She was living with a family, consisting of a mother and daughter. The daughter was her friend. The patient had a very fond attachment for this girl who was a healthy, vigorous and athletic type and was very frightened of the girl's mother who she thought was jealous of the patient's relationship to her daughter. That she had taken flight into seeking treatment from the unconscious homosexual pressure of this relationship became obvious quite soon. It is significant to report that at this stage in her relationship with this girl-friend she played the passive, slightly masochistic and subservient role. She experienced a great deal of hostility towards all the older women and was reactively docile towards and co-operative with them. Invariably in her reveries she had excited hostile mental battles with them. That these teachers and older women were all mother surrogates was fairly easy to establish and for her it was not difficult to acknowledge this.

In her private experience she rarely allowed herself time to be alone and always carried an elated, anxious mood which very easily shifted to either depressiveness or obsessional rituals like tidying-up. For a long time she reported that she had been indulging in bits and pieces of fantasy but she could never allow them to develop. Consequently, she had evolved a technique of seeing hypnogogic images which were crudely related to the sexual organs of the body. She also from time to time was surprised by intense feelings in her genitals about which she did nothing. It is important to note here that she had developed quite an effective technique for splitting these images and body sensations off from herself and amusedly tolerating them and, as it were, looking at them from a safe distance. (Cf. Kanzer, 1958.)

Her very first remark in the treatment was to prove so complex and replete with her psychopathological state that it is worth reporting. On being informed of the fundamental rule, she had lain down and started by saying: 'I do not know what I am required to do'; in this she had epitomized her castration anxiety and her confusion about the functions of her body orifices, but this was to become clear only much later. How much this excited confusion and sense of castration plus helplessness were to play a dynamic role in the acting out into homosexual relationship we shall discuss in the second phase.

It is interesting also to report that she had started off by saying that she was not a lesbian. Her earlier material was, however, loaded with a mixture of anxiety about her femininity, a mocking attitude towards herself and a sense of humiliation lest she be stupid and I despise her. In the beginning she was rather insistent that I should take on a more verbally active role and talk. The castration anxiety was very obvious in her dreams and in her general anxiousness which compelled her continually to seek reassurance. (Cf. Abraham, 1920.)

Her transference was characterized by an excessive eagerness and by what I can only describe as excited pseudo-affect. It was typical of her at this stage that she arranged a neat role for me where she tried to win my sympathy and goodwill on the one hand and on the other was extremely suspicious and untrusting. In some moods she would take up a most ruthlessly nagging attitude towards herself and exploit it with masochistic fervour. She would weep copiously and self-pityingly. That she had cast me in the role of her older brother was quite obvious both to her and me. Her own memories of her brother were that he had been 'such an active nuisance' in her childhood and had always teased her. Her self-image from this period was of a meek, good girl, always easily upset who would run to mother to elicit support and sympathy which the mother had been only too ready to bestow. In the transference the analyst became in rapid succession the seductive teasing brother and the mother, who should console and be solicitous. It was very noticeable that subjective, instinctual states and impulses were being avoided. She was merely a passive victim. Isolation as a mechanism of defence played a very important role in her inner equilibrium, and in my clinical experience it is the combination of the defence mechanisms of isolation and splitting that compel the potentially homosexual person into actively seeking out shared instinctual relationships because the very success of their defence mechanisms leaves them stranded in an 'obstinate narcissistic standstill'. (Deutsch, 1932; Bychowski, 1956.) Consequently they feel their life becomes impoverished and depleted. Her tremendous attempt at

66

controlling the analyst's behaviour in the analytic situation on the one hand and eroticizing it into a 50-minute idyll were also characteristic of this stage of her treatment. She rarely remembered any dreams, though she dreamt profusely. Her dreams at this stage were full of exhibitionistic tendencies, movement and a phallic sort of vividness. They felt terribly unreal and unrelated to her. It is a significant trait of her psychic activity at this stage that so much of the repressed material was on the one hand so readily accessible in her dreams and diffused reverie states and yet she was so utterly unrelated to it in her wakefulness and treated it as both unreal and impersonal. The hostile negative feelings in her controlled ami-ability and co-operativeness too were easily distinguishable. A dream from this stage makes a clear statement of her intrapsychic situation and her transference relationship: 'she had been given the role of a maid in a play; had only three things to say; felt worried and con-fused because no one could hear her speak as she had not rehearsed enough'.

From the associations it was clear that she was protesting against the uneven balance in the relationship. She felt that the analyst had the dominant role: she was just allowed a passive function, even then she was not allowed to rehearse to her benefit. (Bacon, 1956.) She could identify the two roles as helping her friends and service to her analyst but what the third was she did not know. My remark that the third could perhaps be her self-employment in her own interests led to a spate of material about her brother: her hate of his strength and maturity in childhood. He could always do things better and in all her memories of playing with him she was reduced to helpless-ness and tears. She remembered one scene in particular. They had been sent out when she was three to sleep together and he had bumped about in bed and it had frightened her intensely and she had reported it to her mother.

Soon followed a memory of her sharing her parents' bedroom while on holiday at the seaside: she was about seven, and she heard her mother say to her father that if she had the strength she would throw herself down the cliff. The patient made loud noises to inform them of her wakefulness so that they would change the subject.

The working through of this dream led us into the complex and confused material of primal scene, penis-envy and castration anxiety. I have repeatedly used the word 'confused' in describing this patient's psychic and affective behaviour in this phase of treat-ment and I ascribe a significant role to this affective confusion in the psychogenesis of her homosexual experiences. In this confused state frightening perceptions, masturbatory reveries and a polymorph variety of excited body-states (with emphasis on orifices) were all mixed together and threatened her ego from within. This compelled her to take flight into sociability, but the guilt related to these inhibited her socially shared experiences and made her feel inferior, shallow and insipid. The homosexual relationship was a way of personalizing and sharing out this inner confused state and re-absorbing it into the ego in terms of its adult and differentiated capacities. It was also this latent confused affective state which her phobic and obsessional techniques were directed against.

That the episode recalled as sharing the bedroom and hearing her mother's remark was a screen memory there is little doubt. Its interesting denial was the zest and sensual pleasure of the mother. In fact as we were to discover much later this denial also carried a true perception of her mother's depression in it. At this stage she was full of contempt both for her mother's lack of sensuality and her own and felt the analyst would despise her for it and reject her. The oedipal implications of it and her bitter humiliation in not being able to 'do better' for the father were painfully obvious. This very explicit and precocious body-ego awareness in terms of the inadequateness of the child-body to meet the actual sexual demands, I think is also typical of this type of psychosexual disorder. It was this inadequateness which had made her turn to her brother in sadomasochistic excitedness to feel in turn equally overwhelmed and traumatized by him. This had then exaggerated her penis-envy and masculinity complex and she had reacted by trying to do better than her brother intellectually at school and she had partially succeeded. In this context her penis-envy was a defensive organization against a deeper sense of genital inadequacy. Horney (1926, 1933), Jones (1927) and Klein (1932) have very insightfully discussed this aspect of the feminine position of the young girl. (Also cf. Kestenberg, 1956a.)

In the transference working through of this material what characterized her current behaviour were quick oscillations of mood from depressive self-denigratory attitudes to hypomanic elated states of over-confidence in which she was condescending and contemptuous towards me. She extravagantly criticized the transference relationship and clung to it with vociferous demands for satisfaction. Her accusations that the analyst was both seducing and rejecting her were bitter and vehement. She felt ridiculed by the analyst's 'superior aloofness' and containment. She felt all men devalued women and yet in her social relations she treated the male students with contempt through an identification with the analyst.

The pregenital libidinal sadistic cathexes that fed her transference at this stage made her analysis an 'excited nightmare' for her. She was agitated and full of elation, with severe bouts of self-incriminations. Excessive transference-fantasying was her attempt to pull the analyst into an interpersonal relationship as a defence against the inner more primitive conflicts that were now pressing towards consciousness. She felt terrified that in one of these excited states she would burst into bits and pieces and this anxiety she would deal with by further intensifying her intellectual and narcissistic defences. She felt humiliated by her dependency needs in relation to the analyst. In her hypnogogic fantasies part-object images predominated. She reported 'seeing' a penis going into her mouth and being bitten, and this had filled her with horror. Splitting mechanisms alone enabled her to control this intrapsychic state of aggressive excitement and excessive emotionality. (Cf. Bychowski, 1954; Kanzer, 1958.)

Her anxiety states in this phase had a quality which I can best describe in Jones's (1927) term *aphanisis*: the threat of total extinction. She felt the fulfilment of her wishes and/or their frustrated fury would annihilate her. And yet such was the intensity of her splitting mechanisms and the efficacy of her phobic-obsessional techniques that one could not help sensing a staged quality about her affects. In her subjective experience it lent a sense of futility to all her relationships. She felt de-realized in a benign way, and exploited this state as a defensive ego-distance which shielded and protected her internally and socially. (Cf. Bouvet, 1958.) I interpreted her transference conflicts as the wish to be very dependent and fed like a child (cf. penis-image) and that then she was faced with her aggressiveness and need to castrate me. From here a lot of material full of persecutory anxiety emerged. And though at first it was all exclusively related to the analyst, it began to spread to her relation with women. She began to talk of her jealousy and the hypocritical nature of the goodness of her behaviour. She was amazed to discover that she got on so well – rather too well with the husbands of female friends, and felt anxious about her own impulses and their possessiveness and ruthlessness. She became frightened of her mean motives and the way she controlled her friends. She was panicky about the violence of her emotions as they surged up in her from time to time. Along with this her penis-envy and castration fears came to the forefront. She felt unwieldy and ineffectual. She felt that analysis had sabotaged the strength of her phobic distancing techniques and replaced them with nothing. She would feel desolate and her hectic and charming social life began to abate in its distracting intensity. (Cf. Nacht, Diatkine, and Favreau, 1956.)

When alone she began to feel miserable and under compulsion to fantasy about the analyst in a way that was clearly a substitute for masturbation. When this was pointed out to her she recounted how she had been surprised at the turn one of her fantasies took; she imagined herself sitting in bed, with the analyst's head in her lap and she was stroking it. Gradually it turned into a greyish sort of skull. She then thought she could keep it as a decoration.

From her associations it was clear that this was a very condensed statement of her inner feelings. She wanted sadistically to castrate the analyst on the one hand and on the other turn analysis into a substitute for masturbation. But its immediate relevance was her feeling of despair that she could not involve the analyst as an exciting object. She complained bitterly that I did not need her. The condensation of oral and phallic libido here was of great importance.

She had led in from this to an account of her parents' dismal and meagre sexual life. She was gifted with her polite sneers at them. But it was also now emerging that by freezing her own sexual impulses she was also controlling theirs. This gave us a good deal of insight into the way her social relations were a substitute for masturbatory activities.

Slowly the manic social fabric of her relationships began to break down and she began to be acutely distressed about what she sensed as the shallowness of her feelings and her lack of real emotion. How she found it very easy to ingratiate others by fitting into their need to be helped. She would blame the analyst for taking away all her surface relationships because there was nothing underneath.

Alongside this material her pregenital impulses were coming to the fore in her fantasies of exhibiting herself. She had started going to 'free dance' classes and felt in turns humiliated by her body and also an intense feeling of power from it. This phallic elation was usually followed by making herself miserable in bed with petty nagging anxieties.

At this time when she had felt particularly elated and been very satisfied with her dancing one evening she had the following dream:

'She was in a cathedral and it was full of half-dying bodies with tongues lolling out of their mouths'. She was highly amused by it. Nothing occurred to her in relation to the dream. Only one detail that her father used to preach sometimes in a nonconformist church, and she used to be very angry at having to attend and listen to him.

During the session her need to reduce the analyst's liveliness and youthfulness was very prominent. She wanted him to be much older, more sober and comforting. The interpretation that in the dream the exciting object (analyst) was represented in a corpse-like manner was scoffed at by her. The need to smother excitement was visible here. The ambivalence was firmly denied.

In her life situation she became more and more aware of the erotic and narcissistic value of her relation to women. In one dream she was with one of her close friends standing before a Gothic building and was urging her friend to explore it with her.

My pointing out that the building represented her body and her wish to explore it through the relation to a female she found very distressing and disturbing, and accused me of frustrating and aggravating her so much that soon she would have to throw herself into the arms of the first available male. She was very undecided which way to turn.

I want to stress the fact how the weakening of her manic defence and narcissistic character resistances led to an intensification of her predicament with her excited body. She gave the impression during this phase of being terrified by her impulsiveness, latent emotionality and aggressiveness.

We were now reaching the first long break in analysis. She was very melodramatic about it and about the analyst not caring for her. But the slightest scrutiny of her behaviour showed that she was not very deeply distressed on that count. As she was accustomed to doing with her mother, she had to make the analyst feel anxious and guilty about her. That this attempt to make the analyst feel guilty and concerned was her way of dealing with separation anxiety on the one hand and of repressing ambivalent sado-masochistic masturbatory fantasies relating to this separation anxiety now became apparent from her material. Recourse to magical thinking as a way of dealing with these anxieties was also prominent. A dream a few days before the summer break makes this clear:

'In the ground-floor room of her house, she is looking in to the garden where there are many relations and friends. She is lying on a couch seeing them come and go. Her mother calls her to come out, but she pretends that she has a headache. In the room also, her brother was lying on the couch reading Freud. They go out and she sees a big flower in the garden; it opens and closes in the middle. It frightened her intensely.'

She woke up to find that she had been sleeping with her hand tightly tucked into her legs near the genitals. This was her first approximation to a masturbatory experience.

The transference reference of this dream is obvious. What was important was that the dream portrayed the opposite of her behaviour in childhood, when she used to rush to mother, complaining and distressed, with some grudge against the brother. She was able to see how her need for the exploitation of the dependency relation to her mother was a defence against her own excitements. The brother was also used as a cover for her masturbation: he cloaked the distress from her genital sensations and their sadistic content. In her analysis, she wanted to involve her analyst in 'the circuit of her excitement'. (Cf. Deutsch, 1932.)

She linked this dream with the coming break. Her anxiety about deprivation in analysis and her no-longer 'potent' relationships with girls left her frightened with the prospect of masturbation. The fear of sexual excitement being combated through exaggeration of ego-syntonic dependency needs was a strong feature of this case.

After the holidays the analysis was full of resentment against her mother and her needs to be phallically independent. In her fantasies now I was employed more and more as a passive person in love with her. This eroticization of the analytic relationship was a defence against her fear of regressive dependency. Her efforts were to create a conflict in the analyst through imposing the dual roles of seducer and harsh conscience on him. Only later in her treatment did it become possible to work through the close parallel in this to her pre-oedipal relation to her mother, a relationship which the mother was sustaining currently through controlling the financial help she gave her daughter. She would suddenly feel very concerned about her daughter and bribe her with monetary gifts and then scrutinize her way of spending these. This conflictual and ambivalent relation to the mother had been exacerbated by their dealings over the holidays.

The castration anxieties inherent in excitement and sexual fantasies about the analyst (and in her childhood relation to her brother) were denied through dreams of urethral nature and dreams of exhibiting her naked body. (Cf. Abraham, 1920; Rado, 1933; Brody, 1943.)

The general picture was very confused. She oscillated rapidly from paranoid feelings to depressive ones, from exultation to misery. Even this confusion of emotional states one felt was a magical defence. The real castration anxiety was about being integrated in any specific way. She swung rapidly from the wish for a child from me to being as good as any man, to being helpless and needy of affection and solicitude.

She had an examination on hand and was worried. At times it looked as though she had decided to spite the analyst by failing. But she did very well. This was interesting because her capacity to be confused and bewail her insufficiency in herself in the analysis did not deeply interfere with the successful pursuit of her ego-activities. In analysis she strained every bit of herself to dish out her emotional confusions in order to leave the analyst (mother) 'hot and bothered about them' (her phrase). She was not without insight either. In the transference it was visible how as a mother-substitute she wanted me to partake actively in her sexually aggressive excitements. It would be wrong to say that it was all negative and that she wanted to victimize the analyst. Her distress was that there could be no free interplay between us: analytic 'aloofness' was traumatic and inhibiting for her. What she needed, she would say, was reciprocity and not this kindly inhibited insightfulness.

After the holiday break the patient's circumstances changed significantly. She had successfully completed her education and had taken on a job. She had exhausted the money left to her by her father and had thus become dependent on her mother for economic support. This caused her both acute pangs of guilt and humiliation. She was now also forced to face her jealousy of her mother's greater affection for her brother, whom the mother supported lavishly with money because it gave her access to the grandchildren. Also most of her friends had become pregnant which roused both rage and contempt in her. She felt lonely, unvalued and unloved: by her friends, analyst and mother. The oedipal resentment at not getting a child from the father played its full and bitter role in the transference and was a very weighty factor in her flight into the homosexual affair. This painfully bears out the statement by Deutsch (1944): 'Every individual act of homosexual in love expresses a nonfulfilled heterosexual hope. The more passionate a girl is in her narcissistic desire to be loved, the more ardent will be her active wooing of the *other*.' (Cf. also Abraham, 1920; Rado, 1933.)

Two further events played a fateful role in pushing her into the

73

homosexual relationship. During her holidays she had met a man who had taken her and her girl-friend out yachting. They had got stranded on return due to low tide and had had to wait in the dark. There the man had attempted to kiss her and make physical love to her. She had reacted with contemptuous permissiveness and only petting had taken place. That she had been frightened was obvious from her denial by ridicule while telling the story. But while re-counting the episode her mood had suddenly changed and she had burst into tears of remorse because she felt she had teased him into an erection and left him stranded. She felt frightened I would chastise her, that she had behaved delinquently. She consoled herself that she had done her best and added 'I really didn't know what else to do'. From here the guilt about having provoked the brother into 'sexual games' and then having betrayed him followed.

Now she began to put together the rudiments of a larval genital fantasy from her phallic and post-phallic stage of development. In this fantasy she actively instigated excitement, stayed in control of it, was active and the object yielded gradually in utter helplessness. At this stage of the fantasy she would get confused, awed and frightened. She could never quite distinguish whose body was supposed to be experiencing what. The helpless surrender was as frightening, in her imagination, for the object as for herself. She identified with both roles. Regressive measures were then taken to deal with the fantasy. Her dreams would be full of splashing streams of water. In one dream, in this phase, she was in a huge hall and there were lots of vomit on the floor and sheets of water pouring down to clean them. The vomit had looked like faeces and had resemblances of faces in them. Her associations led to a very recent birth of a child to one of her girl-friends. She now felt ashamed and enraged at her impotence, sterility and immaturity: both psychically and physically. The material in analysis essentially related to her body-ego fantasies. She felt her genitals were dirty, unlove-worthy, messy, faecal, too small, etc. She had distaste for her body: it was hairy and unformed. She felt desolate at night and had an agitated inner tension. She couldn't masturbate to relieve her tension: that would be the ultimate degradation she felt. And yet she remained curiously defiant and unrelated to all this chaotic emotionality.

The second fateful experience from the holidays was a visit to a Gothic church. While looking at a painting of Christ on the Cross she had felt a sense of warm yet chilling closeness to it and it had frightened her. She had related it to her lack of grief at her father's death. The experience had been as fleeting as it had been intense. After recounting it she had mentally put it aside. Only much later towards the end of her treatment were we to grasp its significance, and the contribution it had made in her *decision* for a homosexual love affair.

It was in this climate of emotionality that one day she had met the woman she fell in love with: passionately, blindly and wilfully. But before I describe that I would discuss some aspects of the analysis so far.

Early Psychosexual Development

I would like to discuss here what we can infer about her early psychosexual development. That she had developed through all the libidinal stages: oral, anal and phallic is quite obvious from her dreams and fantasies. It was characteristic of her libidinal development that each stage and zone seemed to have been hypercathected and intensely experienced. I consider this a pathogenic development of the body-ego. In her material there were unmistakable signs of precocious genital (vaginal) sensations in childhood which had left her excited and confused: the dream of the flower and the dream of the church gave explicit clues to this. What had created this precocious genital awakening was on the one hand the 'teasing' relation to the brother and on the other excess of anxiety in the ego. That her child-ego could do little towards either elaborating psychically or gratifying physically these tensions became obvious from the confused, hectic and masochistic way in which this was re-experienced in the transference and was epitomized in her 'clumsy affair' (her phrase) with the man. The ego's reaction throughout was defensive, now as in childhood, and led to excessive reaction-formation and phobic defences. In childhood it had also been expressed through mild hypochondriacal states which had been exploited to elicit mother's concern and also mitigate guilt about her pregenital impulses. That her phallic strivings in childhood had got exaggerated through identification with and envy of her brother was also quite clear from her material. The unsatisfactoriness of these competitive strivings led her to regress to anal-sadistic attempts at controlling her environment on the one hand and flight into post-phallic passive relation to father (and brother) on an oedipal level. The fact that too much masochistic cathexis of this position led to terror of being penetrated was very obvious in her

75

dreams. Quite a mass of her phobic attitudes aimed at establishing a relationship where contact with another object could be established and sustained without any danger of penetration. This is precisely what she aimed at in the transference relationship. This in turn led to over-stimulation and further threat of regression and inundation of the ego by uncontrollable id-impulses.

Helene Deutsch has succinctly described this specific predicament of the female homosexual's internal anxiety-situation:

> My experience substantiates my assumption that this change of object – the libidinal turning away from the mother to the father – is accomplished with more difficulty, the more aggressive and sadistic are the predominating dispositions in the little girl, not only because the change of object is hindered by the active strivings, but also because the change into passive attitude must, in cases of this type, assume a marked masochistic character and be repudiated by the ego as dangerous. (1932.)

Klein (1928, 1932) has made illuminating contributions towards our understanding of the 'feminine position' in the young girl and the role of urethral, anal-sadistic fantasies and their role in the object-relationships of that phase. She has most insightfully detailed the fear of being bodily intruded into and all the fantasies related to it in the 'feminine position' of the female child.

Horney (1926, 1933), Brierley (1932, 1936), Klein (1928, 1932), Jones (1927, 1933, 1935), Muller (1932) and Payne (1935) have emphasized the presence and importance of the 'vaginal infantile sexuality' in the evolution of the girl. They have postulated that the genital (i.e. vaginal) strivings are present there in a larval state right from the oral stage and that the confusion of oral, anal and vaginal orifices derives its maximal fantasy-content from this super-imposition. This is a point of view that Freud, Deutsch and Lampl-de Groot have not found acceptable. It is very difficult to establish the authentic presence of vaginal sensations and their psychic equivalents in the female infant. (Cf. Eissler, 1939.) The clinical picture of the girl-patient and adult female is so confused by a regressive confusion of genital, anal and oral cathexes that one cannot be certain what features were there from the start. It is, however, a misrepresentation of Freud's views to say that he considered the girl-child and females in general 'as *un homme manqué*' (as Jones phrased it in 1927). It is as erroneous to endow the female infant's earliest body experiences with an explicit awareness of the vagina and vaginal fantasies as it is to assert that early female development is basically masculine in character. What Freud stressed was the preponderance of active strivings at the phallic phase in the girl and their conflict with the passive processes in her libido and psyche (cf. Lampl-de Groot, 1928, 1933; Brunswick, 1940).

The barely cloaked elements of urethral and anal 'incontinence' in the dreams of this patient bear ample evidence to the intensity of intrapsychic conflicts in her about excessive ambivalence relating to the parents. (Cf. Brody, 1943.) The presence of this acute and over-excited ambivalence made her transference a very tortured and painful experience for her. In the homosexually predisposed female the existence of this acute ambivalence is a significant feature, since it vitiates any satisfaction from actual object-relationships and burdens the ego with guilt and creates a very real problem in terms of masturbation. This also forces them into relationships which will sanction such impulses and mitigate the guilt. Freud has stressed the difficulty the female experiences generally with masturbation and has emphasized the unsatisfactoriness of masturbation (clitoral) for the female child as compared with the male child (Freud, 1919e, 1925j, 1933a). The lack of penis not only exaggerates castration anxiety in the female, but also compels the libido, through unsatis-factoriness of the clitoral masturbation, towards a general and diffuse cathexis of the whole body as phallus. This displacement of libido can then involve the body-development of the young child in excessive guilt and inhibitions. One often meets with either exaggerated (manic) over-aliveness based on denial of castration anxiety, or intensification of dependency attachment to the mother in little girls. In both cases distortion of ego-functions takes place. In our patient the competitiveness and self-induced masochistic trauma-tization by teasing from the older brother had led to a flight into intellectual pursuits: which were then eroticized through father's encouragement and collusion. (Cf. Rado, 1933.)

One further complicating feature was the 'intrusion' of genital excitements, which again had to be displaced to phallic activities to be brought under ego-control. (Cf. Klein, 1932; Jones, 1933.) I think this precocious awakening of genitality is inherent in this patient's searching for a homosexual route towards discovering her true femininity later on. I am convinced from this patient's material (and this has been confirmed by three other cases since) that such

77

precocious vaginal sensations are a pathological phenomena in the development of a girl and beset her ego with very severe problems with which she deals through regressive techniques on the one hand and an intensification of her penis-envy and masculinity complex on the other. I have a feeling that such material must have led Jones (1927) into postulating that the 'phallic stage in normal girls is but a mild form of the father-penis identification of the female homosexuals, and, like it of an essentially secondary and defensive nature'. I think Jones's designation of the phallic stage in girls as 'of an essentially secondary and defensive nature' is a misrepresentation of the normal process from his being biased by the material of female homosexual patients. The phallic processes and attributes that we see in the regressive material of the adult patient are an over-condensation of the first experiences of her body-ego activity and 'masculine' strivings at the phallic stage as well as a distortion and defensive exploitation of these against the anxieties related to the post-phallic oedipal relation to the father with its masochistic dread and threat to the young ego. Jones's postulate that the anxiety here is of the nature of aphanasis (extinction) is very true. What we see clinically is a 'retreat' from an advanced position of libidinal development and new object-cathexis where the battle between passive and active strivings has not been successfully weathered and a regression has taken place. The regression here is not only libidinal. The object also changes from the male (father) back to the earlier mother (or mother-images). Complementary to this, in the instinctual process, libidinal and aggressive (sadistic) components are split off and dealt with separately. This leads to either attempts at projecting the aggressive drives on to the male object (in our patient to the brother, in puberty to the father, and later in treatment to the analyst) or directing them against the body through hypochondriacal states as in childhood, when she elicited and exploited the mother's concern and assuaged her guilt through her feigned illnesses and body-discomforts. In some instances this leads to intense craving for promiscuous and perverted heterosexual relationships in girls at puberty and adolescence. In our patient phobic devices and intellectual pursuits enabled the ego to survive puberty without sexual acting out. Instead a restriction and impoverishment of the ego-processes and phase-adequate libidinal satisfactions led to her loss of self-esteem, a crippling sense of inadequateness and inferiority feelings. She became very aware of the superficiality of her object-relationships and was distressed by her impotence as a person. (Cf. Greenacre, 1950*b*; Kestenberg, 1956*a*; Brierley, 1936.)

Freud has remarked repeatedly on the weak development of the female super-ego due to the belated crystallization of the Oedipus complex and the role of castration anxiety in the girl. In this patient what was most striking was the overwhelming preponderance of reaction-formations and 'sphinctral morality' (Ferenczi, 1925) in her behaviour. The greater the build-up of reaction-formations through toilet-training the weaker the healthy development of the super-ego. In this patient the reaction-formations were reinforced by obsessional defences in the ego. One of the major reasons why at this stage of the analysis I could not get at her pre-oedipal relation to the mother in any effective way was because this relation was embedded in her sphinctral morality, habits and reactions. A painful excess of loss of self-esteem plus her self-denigrating techniques added up to a very obdurate narcissistic-masochistic negative therapeutic reaction in the treatment. This sphinctral morality had deprived the ego of a full access to the instinctual processes and cramped it with defensive techniques and intellectual defences. In the analytic process it operated as a vigilant controlling observer that kept the affective processes dissociated and out of range. The specific nature of this patient's ego distortions we shall discuss in the next phase, because as Gillespie (1956) has stated, 'The ego's behaviour and defensive manœuvres are no less important for an understanding of perversion than are the vicissitudes of instinct', and I should add, the pre-oedipal object-relations.

The transference behaviour of this patient was characterized at this stage by an anxious and eroticized co-operativeness, in which militant demands for actual id-satisfactions on the one hand and clinging dependency attitudes on the other were very much in the forefront. Yet I had the persistent feeling that she was uninvolved in the analytic process. She engaged in a 'game' and traumatized herself with masochistic zeal which in turn justified and rationalized her aggressive and hostile resistances against the process of treatment. In spite of her real misery, helplessness and affective storms, she retained her psychic reserve and distance. Discussing the problem of affective inaccessibility of his female homosexual patient, Freud (1920*a*) had remarked, comparing her resistances to that of the obsessional neurotic, 'at last one perceives that everything that has been accomplished is subject to a mental reservation of doubt. . . .' I sensed this 'mental reservation' in this patient as a *staged* quality of affects and moods. The hysterical overlay of emotionality was also characteristic. It is not that these affects were insincere or hypocritically faked. They were both passionately intense and compulsive in quality. They 'happened' to her, as it were, without her experiencing them. The same dissociation and split operated in relation to her body-experiences. She reported genital excitement and sensations and it was painfully shaming for her to do so and yet it remained outside the range of her sentient ego-experience. As we shall soon see it was precisely this split and dissociation that compelled her into seeking an actual shared physical mutuality with another person of the same sex. I am inclined to believe, from my clinical experience, that one function of the homosexual intimacies and practices is precisely to *undo* this split, both in the male and female homosexuals. The body-ego pathology, ego-distortions and the disturbed primitive relation to the mother that lies behind this we shall discover in the acting-out episode in the next phase. (Cf. Bychowski, 1945, 1954; Greenacre, 1950*a*, 1953*a*.)

PHASE II

The Homosexual Episode

I have already stated that the homosexual relationship had materialized in a specific state of inner emotionality. This inner emotionality had been building up in her for many months after her return from the holidays. It was a very unstable mood of quick oscillations and general depressive agitatedness. No amount of interpretation of the content of her material and dreams afforded her any release from it. She felt elated and dejected, tense and apathetic, omnipotent and helpless in a rapid swing of moods. Her ambivalence in the transference relation was acute and dramatic. She also felt dissociated. She lived through her daily life in a dream-state: doing a lot of things but also sunk in an inner excited anxious reverie state. She brooded endlessly about her analyst. Her sleep was thin and restless and her dreams full of pregenital material. The 'impotence' (her word) with the man had deeply mortified her. In spite of her genital and clitoral sensations she could not masturbate. Too much inhibition and guilt was attached to it. She looked and felt as if she was barely controlling an explosive state of rage, excitement and fear: she was afraid she would go mad. I was rather afraid she would have a breakdown or break off treatment. I even considered advising her to change to an analyst of a different sex. But recalling the experiences of Freud (1920a) and Deutsch (1932), where such a measure had not been fruitful at all, I decided to continue and let her work her own way out. She was getting belligerently hostile and her relations with her girl-friends had deteriorated too. She felt too negative and aggressive towards them, though she maintained a polite submissive façade. I was fully aware that the analytic work done so far had loosened her character-resistances and manic defence and this had led to a serious threat to her ego from the resurgence of the repressed sexual and aggressive impulses. She couldn't be psychically receptive towards these any more than she could discharge them through masturbatory practices (though the urge to do so was nagging at her all the time) or express them through an object-relationship. She toyed with prostitution fantasies, accused the analyst endlessly of having provoked this emotionality in her and then sitting back and doing nothing about it. She was also terrified that her hostility might antagonize me and that she would then lose her only supportive object. I was idealized, berated, attacked and cajoled in turn. The transference relation and analytic work made her inner experiences only more confused and chaotic. What had gradually and inevitably coagulated mentally from all this period was an emotionality that she carried in her head and which was like an addiction to her. It had the function of a 'psychic fetish' that regulated her transference. It was also like a mental phallus which she had concocted from her repressed unconscious and the transference relationship: everything from the analysis had been fed into it. It had all the compulsiveness of an obsession and once when I had compared her mental emotionality to a 'pseudopregnancy in the head' she had assented saying it was not a bad description. But what was also evident was the negativity and omnipotence of this mood. It was threatening to wreck the analysis. She couldn't surrender to the analytic situation or to any social relationships or to her own body or her own reflective introspectiveness. (Khan, 1962.) Her dreams were crude and bizarre, her relationships shallow and passionate, her activities obsessional and hectic and all the time she was preoccupied with this *mental emotionality*. (Cf. Lichtenstein, 1961.) I could see it was a very narcissistic defence against surrender to a regression in the analytic situation. (Anna Freud, 1952.) Analysis and transference as vehicles of regression in the service of the ego were blocked out. Instead of a transference neurosis she had fabricated this mental emotionality and she was imprisoned in it. I deliberately abstained from an intellectual analysis of the psychic contents of this state, remembering Freud's remarks that one can collect a lot of material and analyse it and yet the patient remains securely embedded behind a 'mental reservation'. I tried, as well as I could, to show her her flight from her real feelings and anxieties; particularly her dissociation from her excited body-states. This mental emotionality was the transference-version of her infantile neurosis and an equivalent of her repressed phallic masturbatory activities: condensing into itself all the conflicts, cathexes and object-relations from the oedipal and pre-oedipal stages. It was this 'mental emotionality' that she now acted out in the homosexual episode. (Cf. Greenacre, 1954.)

Why I have so laboured this issue of the 'mental emotionality' in this patient is because I have clinically observed it in many cases of a schizoid type (see Chapter 3). Whether a patient will move towards regression in the analytic situation, or act out into heterosexual or homosexual perversions or have a severe breakdown first and arrive after it for treatment (as was the case with a patient, on whom I have reported, Khan, 1960*b*), or have antisocial episodes (which is more frequent in adolescence), depends on their ego-strength and capacity for instinct gratifications. Eissler (1953) has given a very vivid description of this type of emotionality in a schizophrenic patient and Sterba (1947) has described it in a female patient of his. One further observation about this 'mental emotionality' that I would like to venture here is that in spite of its flagrant exhibitionistic exposure in the analytic situation it was *hiding* something. It was a secretive state. For months I had an uncanny feeling with this patient that she had something up her sleeve, a secret ambition, which she was searching the right psychological climate to fulfil and enact in.

I would briefly detail the qualities of her friend that excited her most. Her friend was a little older than herself, and sexually a very experienced woman. She was handsome. It was her carved static face that attracted the patient most. She was having a hectic love affair with intense sexual activity with a much older man, which intrigued the patient. She was a very intelligent, sympathetic and sensitive person; according to the patient's phrase she was a 'breastful being'. Her partner had no previous homosexual experience either. Looking at the friend with fetishistic and idealized fascination was her chief mode of 'nourishment' in the relationship at this stage. (Cf. Greenacre, 1953*a*; Ferenczi, 1923; Arlow, 1954; Glover, 1938.)

The patient preluded the relation with acute feelings of misery, fear of inadequacy, of being rejected or being rebuked for improper insinuations. She was very guarded about telling anything about it, and considerably understated her passionate involvement to start with. In every way her partner was a superior being, who was heavily idealized. The patient had to boast a lot about her sexual experiences with men to get near her friend. She was too ashamed of her inexperience and innocence. She would get panic ridden at the prospect of her success in seduction and then not knowing what to do.

In transference she put the whole blame on me. I had aggravated her, excited her and frustrated her. After all these months she knew nothing about sexuality and now she was going to find out. The need to learn and know made the experience ego-syntonic. She also turned the analyst into a very harsh figure now who was threatening and demoralizing her, and against whom she had to protect her friend and the emergent relationship. In the sessions she was miserable, wept, felt guilty and ashamed, but nothing interfered with the zest of her relationship when away. She listened to interpretations sympathetically and neatly put them away. One had the feeling that she was possessed, impulse-ridden, wilful; and so events took as it were a predestined course.

It was one of the dominant demands of the patient that I should in no way disparage her relation with her friend in my remarks. On the contrary I should sanction it, as it was a great asset to her analysis. We could now deal with and understand feelings and impulses which she would never have attributed even to her unconscious. She could elaborate them, live them and not exist in a shadow world of goody goody friendships. This she would say was indeed education in the highest sense of the word.

At the beginning of this relationship, the patient was very afraid of becoming too violently involved and too possessive, too demanding. That she was sparing her analyst all this was obvious. But another important aspect was the acute need of someone who could share this with her, like her friend did: a sort of 'transitional object' (Winnicott, 1951) relationship (cf. Bacon, 1956).

In the beginning one night while she was absorbed in a reverie about her friend she got very excited and beating fantasies cropped up. She masturbated a little and slapped her behind. This was the first time she had reported actual masturbation. Feelings of shame and disgust had surged up in her and she had felt very abject and denigrated. (Cf. Freud, 1919e.) It was significant that masturbation should be experienced as a severe insult to the personality and lead to loss of self-esteem.

After this she plunged straight into physical intimacies. The relation between her masturbation and the new friendship could not be more obvious. It was essentially the fear of her surrendering to her masturbatory excitement that loomed large at this time.

The relationship started by her seducing her friend to let her lie in her lap: in a very marked dependency role. Gradually she began to reach out for the breasts, and when at last she was allowed to kiss them she was in absolute bliss. Ecstasy was a very marked feature in her accounts.

But she was also very concerned about what she could do for her friend. She knew her friend had a very eager sexual appetite, so she suggested masturbation. And her elation when she was able to produce an orgasm in her friend was limitless. Henceforth she always took great care to satisfy her friend before she took a 'feed' herself.

It would be a misrepresentation of the emotional experience of this patient to conclude in this context that she was behaving in a 'masculine way', was being a man or that the behaviour was unfeminine. That phallic identifications (with the analyst-father-brother) helped her to find her way to this 'infantile state of bliss' is true. But the aim was certainly feminine, tender and passive. Both Freud (1920) and Deutsch (1944) have emphasized the capacity of the female to play both roles in homosexual relationships and ascribed it to their greater bisexuality. 'A typical feature of overt female homosexuality is exchange of roles between the partners, even when one of them is more active and sadistic and the other more passive and masochistic. Because of their great facility in identifying themselves with love-objects of the same sex, women can play the two roles. This fact is one of the most powerful motives for female homosexuality.' (Deutsch, 1944.) Quoting from a case where a female patient had boasted to her female-partner 'No man in the world can give you what I can' Deutsch concluded: 'Her word "no man" unconsciously hinted at certain practices in which breasts play a prominent part. In this form of homosexuality the masculine gesture is only a means of wooing and a pretext, for the sexual goal that is desired completely excludes the masculine.' This

84

is very true of this patient's psychic state at this point. (Cf. Keiser and Schaffer, 1949; Caprio, 1957.)

The intensity and polymorph eroticism of the relationship, which consisted of kissing each other's breasts, masturbating each other: she could only enjoy clitoral masturbation while her friend was quite happy with having the genitals 'deeply penetrated', were coupled with a very keen sense of drama about the whole affair and acute sense of control. She did not want to fall in love; and it was obvious that she was manically attached to parts of her friend's body only, not the person who carried them. When a few months later her friend fell in love with her and broke off the sexual relation with her male friend, she was thrown into panic. And for a week she stopped physical intimacies. Their mutuality of surrender might become irrevocable, she feared. She would, during this period, have days of exaggerated buoyancy of spirits and elation. Their dialogue of bodies and erotic love gave her a unique sense of aliveness and well being, a freedom from fear and inner nagging. Her friend understood her needs instinctively, shared them and reciprocated them. Not like her analyst. Here she was holding a mirror up to him which ridiculed him, and gave her a superiority and independence of him. (Cf. Glover, 1932a; Lichtenstein, 1961.)

One particular body-organ and its use was rather significant: namely the tongue. Penetration by the tongue and licking of the genitals were mutually important. Freud had in his *Three Essays on the Theory of Sexuality* (1905d) commented: 'Among women, too, the sexual aims of inverts are various: there seems to be a special preference for contact with mucous membrane of the mouth.' Deutsch (1932), Bacon (1956), Jones (1927), and Caprio (1957) have confirmed this. Jones who stresses an 'unusual intensity of oral erotism and of sadism respectively' (1927) in the aetiology of female homosexuality reports that the identification of the tongue with the penis reaches 'a quite extraordinary degree of completeness'. In this patient's experience the tongue also played a very tender oral role of caressing. It was fantasied as healing the castrated genital. It had a restitutive role both in relation to the object and the self body-ego. In so far as it symbolized the penis it made good to her partner what she had been deprived of in being taken away from her male lover (father). Klein (1932) has stated: 'While her sadistic position, reinforced as it is by her anxiety, thus forms the basis of a masculinity complex in her, her sense of guilt also makes her want to have a penis. She wants a penis in order to make a restitution towards her mother.' (Cf. Riviere, 1929.) This was a prominent feature of this patient's oral-genital activity. But the tongue-penis equation also made restitution to her self body-image. It was a substitute for the clitoris and more effective and potent. She had once compared these tongue practices to the licking behaviour of dogs; it was affectionate and soothing. The ecstatic idealization of these practices was patently indicative of their denial function in relation to the sadistic impulses involved but I think the libidinization of the genitalia with the tongue served a very positive function in increasing the narcissistic capital of her body-ego. (Cf. Glover, 1938.) Another rather interesting function of the mouth-tongue-breast-hand activities was, that combined with hand-caressing, it was helping to differentiate the body-organs with their separate status and role. This extremely primitive function can perhaps be described as a sort of body reality-testing (cf. Spitz, 1955; Hoffer, 1949). Like many other body-intimacies involved in this relationship, this tongue-activity became the vehicle of a very primitive aspect of infant-mother relationship. Deutsch (1944) has remarked:

> The form that homosexual activity assumes . . . depends on the stage of development in which the relationship to the mother is determined. If the aim is to make good the genital trauma and to gratify penis-envy, a phallic activity will develop and the homosexual relation will have a masculine character. If, on the other hand, the renewal of the mother-child relationship is more infantile . . . the activity will be localized in those bodily zones that are connected with gratification of early childhood instinctual urges. The predilection for the oral zone in the sexual activities of homosexual women is connected with this mother relationship.

What Deutsch further describes as 'a typical identification with the nourishing mother' was also very true of the psychosexual meaning of these practices for my patient.

I want to interpolate here a discussion of a concept introduced by Greenacre (1959) which seems to me to throw a great deal of light, in retrospect, on one of the meanings of these mouth-tongue activities in our patient. Borrowing from Mahler's description and development of the concept of symbiosis Greenacre has coined the phrase 'focal symbiosis'. She defines it:

> I would conceive of a focal symbiosis as being an intensely

86

strong interdependence (usually between mother and child, but sometimes, as in my case, with people other than the mother) which is limited to a special and rather circumscribed relationship rather than a nearly total enveloping one. . . . Probably masturbation fears and their derivative phobias are the most frequent generators of the circumscribed anxious drives of the adult toward the child which result in limited or focal cords of attachment between adult and child.

I find this concept very illuminating in the understanding of intense perverse practices between homosexuals – male or female. The intense erotic cathexis of certain areas (the anus, or tongue and mouth, or vagina) is the vehicle of this focal symbiosis. We have seen how this patient did not want to be involved in a total love affair with her partner. They both met each other's needs at specific body organs with relish and abandon. It also became gradually clear that the patient's mother was a depressed obsessional person who had on the one hand toilet-trained her with impersonal vigour and on the other involved her daughter in her own hypochondriacal anxieties. She was perpetually watching the patient in her childhood for any symptoms of ill-health and then would coddle and nurse her. The patient's exploitation of these gestures of the mother to ward off her guilt and aggressiveness had restricted the full-bloodedness of her body-ego development at the phallic phase. At this stage her nascent active striving had been further discouraged and traumatized through the impact of her brother's superior phallic strength and aliveness and her resultant enforced acknowledgement of her own castrated body-image. She had vivid memories of how she used to get into 'obscene' postures, then would pretend to be asleep, and made sure she was seen either by the mother or the father. These strivings she had realized and fulfilled through her current relationship with her friend. They gloated in each other's nudity and through this mutuality of participation released and 'corrected' all the inhibitory influences of their original relations to their mothers. The clinging was *restricted* to body-intimacies and they retained their emotional independence of each other; in fact had always encouraged it. In this sense it could be said that this patient engineered a temporary 'focal symbiosis' in order to emancipate herself from the primary one which had seeped into her very character-structure and created a drastic inhibition of both her sexuality and ego-activities (cf. Lichtenstein, 1961).

I would like to stress one element of the situation. The importance of having a male in the background: her friend had her lover. She had her analyst. It controlled in their relationship the regressive potential of the situation: both in terms of instinctual and ego-processes. The analyst and the analytic situation were a security that she would not go beyond limits and thus get caught in an irreversible perversion.

It is hardly possible to exaggerate the threat of object-loss and separation anxiety in this patient. Behind her reduced and restricted affectivity she had all her life secretly cherished an ideal dream of shared body-love and emotional mutuality; that the two processes (the physical and affective one) had to be experienced simultaneously constituted an imperative demand and condition of this ideal dream of love. The danger lay in the fact that in any one relationship one of the two strands might get left out or become over-intensive. Hence her negativity and narcissistic defences. It was possible to interpret one cause of this patient's avoidance of heterosexual love so far in Jones's (1927) apt statement:

> . . . for obvious physiological reasons, the female is much more dependent on her partner for her gratification than is the male on his. Venus had much more trouble with Adonis, for example, than Pluto with Persephone. The last consideration provides the biological reason for the most important psychological differences in the behaviour and attitude of the sexes. It leads directly to a greater dependence (as distinct from desire) of the female on the willingness and moral approbation of the partner than we usually find in the male, where the corresponding sensitiveness occurs in respect of another, authoritative, male. Hence, among other things, the more familiar reproaches and need for reassurance on the woman's part . . . another consequence is that the mechanism of aphanisis tends to differ in the two sexes. Whereas in the male this is typically conceived of in the active form of castration, with the female the primary fear would appear to be that of separation.

It might well be asked here why this girl had waited so long to have a homosexual affair? The answer was her fear of true perversion. From her remarks and fantasies it was very clear that what had compelled her to avoid homosexual experiences was the dread of being trapped irrevocably in a perversion, should the other person turn out to be a true pervert. In this sense this patient was not a true homosexual pervert but passed through a phase of homosexual perversion *en route* to health and a true integration of her femininity. A development which her oedipal and pre-oedipal relationships had made impossible. It is my experience that such homosexual relations, unless they are a defensive organization against latent psychosis, enact a petrified developmental crisis. (Cf. Rosenfeld, 1949.) Quite often seeking a 'solution' the patient gets congealed in a false and static manœuvre through another person's influence or more ineradicable perversion. (Glover, 1932*a*.) Then secondary gains and further distortions of the libido and ego-processes make a release impossible. If treatment is started at the right moment it is not beyond our means to cure homosexuality which is of a psychogenic origin. (Cf. Nacht, Diatkine, and Favreau, 1956; Balint, 1952.)

This patient 'exploited' the analytic setting and its assets and limitations to act out her ideal dream. This ideal of love derived from the most primitive relations between infant and mother. (Glover, 1938.) The partner could provide all the shared body-love while her analyst and analysis kept a firm grip on her personal psychic processes and reality. The meaning of her homosexual experiences could be categorized as follows: (i) an infant-mother relation with her friend where all the primitive body-needs and wishes could be mutually shared and fulfilled, with equal enrichment of both parties concerned; (ii) the denial of the sadistic hate of the mother: 'I did not hate her because I love you'; (iii) 'I have not stolen the father's (analyst's) penis with sadistic greed but in love and I share it with you (mother)'; (iv) 'I am not castrated nor are you (the mother)'; (v) 'I am not incestuous because I love you (mother)'; (vi) 'You cannot swallow or hurt me because father (analyst) will protect me.'

The fight against dependency and fear of surrender to her excited impulses was a vital part of the whole 'staged set-up' of the homosexual episode. Anna Freud (1952) has elucidated succinctly this fight of the ego against regressive trends:

> . . . this fear of passivity is capable of a deeper, non-sexual explanation . . . the passive surrender to the love-object may signify a return from object love proper to its forerunner in the emotional development of the infant, i.e. a loss of personal

characteristics which are merged with the characteristics of the love-object. The individual fears this regression in terms of dissolution of the personality, loss of sanity, and defends himself against it by a complete rejection of all objects (negativism).

There was no mistaking the duality of the aims involved in the relation to her friend: she sought to surrender to complete love on the one hand, and on the other would strive hard to keep the boundaries of her personality defined and separate. Then she would feel cold within towards her friend and wonder 'what the whole palaver was about'. In no time this would change again to distress and guilt and she would strive after erotic love once again. All the time one could sense that she was bewildered and confused underneath. Interpretations in any direction evoked violent evasion and misery. The idealization of the erotic experiences covered her incapacity to give and yield herself totally to her own excited emotions or to her partner.

Helene Deutsch (1944) has given a beautiful description of this aspect of the homosexual love-life: 'The differences and similarity, non-identity and yet identity, the quasi-double experience of oneself, the simultaneous liberation from one part of one's ego and its preservation and security in the possession of the other, are among the attractions of the homosexual experience.'

Gradually we began to clarify another issue. Her partner was her own excited self in absolute surrender to her (the patient). She could thus reassure herself against the dangers of surrender. As the relation progressed the patient became the more active partner: it would not be true of her experience to say the more masculine one. By projecting to her partner her passive self (ego) and retaining the ruthless activity of the impulse in herself, she not only avoided the predicament but also brought these within the range of ego-activity. Thus she could elaborate it, master it. The continued physical presence and psychic intactness of her partner, and the evolution through excited hours to tranquil mutuality strengthened her ego-experience. Here perception was a check on apperception; through a two-body staging the fear of hallucination was neutralized. In auto-erotic or intrapsychic elaboration all this could easily become unmanageable and render her perverse or mad. These were her literal fears. This relationship brought her muted body-dreams and her mental-ego into a vital communication. No doubt it had its defensive role, but it also had a progressive one. The creation of an excitable and excited 'good mother' to whom she could come, to whom she could relate herself with emotional aliveness was of immense value to her. One day she humorously described it as her version of 'the nursing couple'. Now she could psychically tolerate her emerging awareness of her identification with the aggressive phallic mother, and how the role of this identification in her relation to her friend was a defence against the anxieties relating to the internal mother-imago. The primitive impulses to bite and castrate the phallic mother were neutralized in this case through the realization of the partner's needs to be excited and indulged. Thus she reduced the inner tension of the unconscious fantasy. Work on these lines enabled her to achieve a richer emotional rapport with her friend as against mere ecstatic discharge of pregenital id-tensions in a guilt-free way as in the earlier stages of the relationship. (Cf. Fain and Marty, 1960.)

A new feature now emerged. She felt very uneasy and in physical pain whenever her friend tried to penetrate her genitals with the finger. She would reflexively turn cold and aloof and shut up completely. Alongside, there was material which hinted at episodes of petty thieving in childhood. When I indicated to her that the excessive idealization of their play with the body-surface functioned as a denial of what was hidden inside, she was deeply perturbed and only gradually confessed to a shameful theft in her life. For years she had tortured herself about it. In her early college days she borrowed Marion Milner's book *A Life of One's Own* and she has never returned it. Its title had seduced her, and she was even more embarrassed by the fact that she had never succeeded in reading it through. Every attempt had to be given up because she would get too excited, hot and bothered. She could nibble at it endlessly. From here the theme of ruthless and excited love impulses began to take more shape. She now recounted how she adored licking the grooves around the neck of her friend, it always gave her a strange and uncanny feeling of her friend's wholeness and smoothness. The impulse to eat and bite was only thinly veiled here. The fight with the oral-sadistic and anal-sadistic impulses now came to the fore.

Gradually she had started to wean herself from her friend, the phrase is hers, and a true recall of her relationship to her mother in infancy developed. There is little doubt that this patient had a good mother; but to understand the total situation we must take into account the psychology of the mother. The mother's fear of her own impulsiveness and excited emotion had expressed itself in her relation to her daughter through the reaction-formation of over solicitude about the child's physical well-being and anxious protectiveness in general. In this relation to her mother, the patient developed her ego-functions well but to evoke a lively participation from the mother in moments of instinctual excitement was not possible. At her phallic phase this earlier rejection of her impulsive liveliness was repeated by the father's tender but exclusive interest in her intellectual development.

Hence the dissociated and undeveloped potential of the primitive ruthlessness of love impulses which the patient brought as her inner and unknown life to analysis. (Cf. Glover, 1943.) I consider this 'failure' of the real mother a very dynamic contributor to the homosexual episode (see Chapter 3). Even the manic erotic element in the homosexual relationship can be traced to the over-libidinization which the patient must in early childhood have experienced in her mother's intensive body-care. It would be difficult to ignore the patient's point of view that her relation to her friend had been a very vital way of correcting and elaborating this deficient relation to her mother. Why a real person, instead of elaboration through masturbation or transference neurosis, was indispensable for this patient can perhaps be answered on the lines suggested by Anna Freud. A hypercathexis of this internal situation in the self-boundaries could come too near to a psychotic state. Perhaps it would not be too gross a distortion of Anna Freud's remarks to postulate that in this patient the negativism and the fear of emotional surrender emerged in the relation of the patient to her own excited body as the object, and was rooted in her mother's depressive and anxious relation to her in early childhood. Hence the acting out into homosexual episode on the one hand to defend herself against these anxieties and on the other to find a milieu through which she could get at a life of her own with someone who was lively and equally desirous of such mutuality (cf. Fain and Marty, 1960).

Body-Ego Development

What I have tried to illustrate clinically here is, to my way of thinking, a vicissitude in the development of the body-ego. I am borrowing the concept of 'body-ego' from Hoffer (1952):

The developmental aspect of the drives expressed in their progress through the different stages of pregenitality to genitality has steered us to a new mental structure, the *body-ego*. According to Freud's description the body has to be conceived as the instinct's object and at the same time as a device for discharge closest to the source of the instinct. Instincts as such do not know or tolerate postponement of the discharge. They seek it in the object in or through which they can achieve their aim. They do not make their objects, they only make use of their availability. The 'making of the objects' of the instincts in addition to what is there from the start, the body, is the result of the functioning of the ego.

In an earlier paper, Hoffer (1950) detailed three sources of traumatization of the body-ego that contribute to its pathology in later life. Here I am concerned with the third, which he has termed 'Failure of the not-self': 'By this I mean the defect or excess displayed by the nursing mother, who is called upon to remove what interferes with the quiet growth of the self until it turns to the object as such. From the point of view of the infant's inner economy this failure results either in an increase of excitation or the self becoming inadequate for dealing with normal excitation.'

In the material presented we can see both aspects: the first in the excessively erotic love making (note the excessive use of mouth, tongue and hand in shared sensual experiences) and the second in the retreat to a dependency attitude. It is my contention that this failure of the mother at the oral level consistently operates through her reaction-formations and influences all the later stages, and though it may enable an adequate mental-ego development, it creates a trauma-prone disposition at the phallic level of the body-ego development and leads to acute inhibitions of auto-erotic play and psychic elaborations (fantasies) of the new excitements and experiences which are urgent and phase-adequate at this stage (cf. Greenacre, 1953a). Greenacre (1959) has suggested it can lead to 'focal symbiosis'. In latency this can be dealt with through continued attachment to the mother (through hypochondriacal anxieties in our patient) and a clinging attitude to the father. This displacement of the pre-oedipal bond with the mother onto the father can further both confuse and sap the oedipal strivings. At this oedipal stage then the penis is sought as a breast-object and dreaded in its own capacity and function. The splitting of the penis-image into a good idealized breast-object and a degraded and dreaded aggressive one, on to which repressed personal oral-analurinary sadistic impulses and fantasies are projected, leads to an impasse *vis-à-vis* the heterosexual object which can lead to both ego-distortion and pathological choice of love-objects who belong to the other sex (cf. Reich, 1940, 1953; Riviere, 1929). In our patient a dread of such misguided ventures with men, through confused and conflictual instinctuality, had been dealt with by phobic avoidances. As we shall briefly see in the third phase, once her internal conflicts and confusions with the mother had been worked through and her body-ego pathology and anxiety-situations resolved, she had little difficulty in finding a male love-object and enjoying orgastic satis-factions. What I am trying to clarify here is that an excessive pregenital eroticism can be exploited as a screen against this type of body-ego pathology. Also a vicarious exploitation by the mental-ego of the adult body in terms of its potential to yield pleasurable reassurances against inner anxieties can lead to pseudo-hetero-sexuality, promiscuity and addiction to perverse practices in homo-sexual intimacies. (Cf. Glover, 1932a, 1943; Lichtenstein, 1961.)

The Role of the Mother's Pathogenic Personality

We cannot over-stress the point that the mother plays a crucial role in the infant's discovery of its instincts, ego-capacities and its own body as object as well as the not-self objects. (Cf. Kris, 1951.) Consequently the quality of the mothering influence has a very fateful consequence as to how the inherent potentialities of the infant will differentiate into actual capacities and functions (cf. Greenacre, 1960c; Winnicott, 1960; Anna Freud, 1953). Mother's personality plays a decisive role and leaves a decisive imprint on 'the procedures by which the small body of the infant creates for itself the beginning of a mind' (Anna Freud, 1953). Here I will discuss one type of pathology in the mother that predisposes, in my clinical experience, the young child towards perversions, par-ticularly of the homosexual type (see Chapter 3). I have earlier discussed some aspects of it through using Greenacre's concept of 'focal symboisis'.

This type of pathology is related to latent depression or overt hypochondriacal anxious depressiveness and lack of true affectivity in the mother. Winnicott has provided us with a very succinct statement of this type of mothering-experience in his paper 'Reparation in respect of mother's organized defence against depression' (1948*a*). I shall briefly recount his argument:

> In the analyses that we do we can reach the guilt in its relation to aggressive and destructive impulses and ideas, and we can watch the urge to make reparation appear as the patient becomes able to account for, tolerate and hold the guilt feelings. There are other roots for creativeness, but reparation provides an important link between the creative impulse and the life the patient leads. The attainment of a capacity for making reparation in respect of personal guilt is one of the most important steps in the development of the healthy human being. . . . Clinically, however, we meet with a false reparation which is not specifically related to the patient's own guilt. . . . This false reparation appears through the patient's identification with the mother and the dominating factor is not the patient's own guilt but the mother's organized defence against depression and unconscious guilt.

Here I am suggesting that one of the ways that this 'identification with the mother' becomes visible is through the pathology of the body-ego development. A split takes place: the mental-ego development becomes dissociated from body-ego development. The body-ego carries in its development the closer and more intimate (unconscious) rapport with the mother's mood: because it has experienced it more tangibly through the mother's anxious and hypochondriacal concern and her lack of affectively vivid body-tone. Under these circumstances the mental-ego development, which invariably gets a precocious boost in these circumstances, tends to exploit the erotogeneity of the body-orifices and body-surface to make a restitution towards the mother, the deprived body-ego and against inner anxieties which have been provoked by exacerbation of muted rage and anger. I think the unmistakable sadistic strength of the oral and anal striving of these patients, on which Freud, Deutsch, Jones, etc., have all commented, partially derives its intensity from lack of fusion with the libidinal processes through early maternal failure. If maternal care does not fully materialize the libidinal potential of the infant-body then a reactive exploitation of body-surfaces, orifices and erogeneity can take place by the growing infant-child itself. This is not auto-erotism proper but a precocious form of masturbation as a self-consolatory technique. I am distinguishing masturbation at this early stage as an exploitation of auto-erotic potential through defensive ego-techniques. This inevitably involves the child with prohibitive and restrictive measures from the mother, which intensifies the conflict and 'guilt' on the one hand and yet turns these activities into an omnipotent means of *provoking* response from the mother. The sado-masochistic vicissitudes of these processes can lead to a very profound predisposition towards pathological object-relations and distortions of both the instinctual life and ego-functions later. (Cf. James, 1962; Lichtenstein, 1961.)

Because of the specially close rapport, affectively and physiologically, the disruption of the female child's psychosexual development by a depression in the mother is much more fateful than in the male child. From the material – remembered experiences with mother, transference behaviour and homosexual relationship – of this patient it is possible to define the pathogenic influence of her mother's depressive hypochondriacal mood as follows: (i) it led to a split between body-ego and mental-ego development; (ii) the mental-ego development had a precocious urgency and very early reached out towards the father (in a pseudo-oedipal relationship) for identifications, e.g. learning and interest in books; (iii) the body-ego suffered a dissociation within itself; in one part it was made over to the mother and kept in touch with her mood and gave her scope for her restitutive gestures, and another part, more deeply involved with instinctual needs and auto-erotic experiences was repressed and hidden from the mother and in time from the mental-ego too; (iv) the involvement with mother's depression and her reaction-formations compelled a severe and precipitate repression of all aggressive sadistic impulses, thus making the discovery of personal guilt feelings impossible; (v) the flight to an intimate seductive relation with the brother was little help. His superior strength and hyper-active phallic behaviour continuously traumatized the patient and made her acutely selfconscious of her weakness and castrated state and led to a severe loss of self-esteem; (vi) her solution to this had been a bifocal one, (*a*) regression back to the mother in anxious masochistic, and now also guilt-laden, hypochondriacal states; this constituted a severe threat to the developing ego's active phallic strivings, so further self-protective measures had to be instituted leading to submissiveness on the one hand and affective deadness on the other. Gradually as her relation with her friend evolved and a very profound depression had become apparent behind the vivid and vital façade of her friend's personality it was possible for the patient to recall and reconstruct her mother's depression and her own flat dullness as a child, her poverty at games and inventiveness, etc., (b) a further attempt at intellectual identification with the father. The vicissitudes of this we shall observe in the third phase.

In this context the homosexual practices served a twofold purpose. One was to enlarge and experience the fullness and intensity of the personal instinctual potential and through shared 'auto-erotic' activities build up the narcissism of the body-ego. I have used the phrase 'auto-erotic' to define their body-exploration of each other because it was essentially aimed at self-exploration: discovering what one's body can feel and do. Furthermore, I think there is a masturbatory type of homosexual sexuality which is a defensive organization against (psychotic?) inner anxieties relating to sadistic part-object internal imagos and cathexes. Here the masturbatory sexual technique is a way of omnipotently controlling and exploiting another object. It is this type of perverse defensive homosexual eroticism that breaks down into paranoid states and persecutory delusions. In my patient this was not so. (Cf. Rosenfeld, 1949.)

Winnicott (1948a) further makes the explicit statement in relation to children whose affectivity and psychosexual development has been intruded upon and distorted by the mother's pathology (Greenacre calls this focal symbiosis, I think): 'It will be seen that these children in extreme cases have a task which can never be accomplished. Their task is first to deal with the mother's mood. If they succeed in the immediate task, they do no more than succeed in creating an atmosphere in which they can *start on their own lives*.' In the displaced maternal relationship to her friend my patient had to deal with 'the mother's mood' extensively and only after it was successfully accomplished was she able to launch on her own separate and independent heterosexual life. I have already remarked on the depression in her friend. In fact the friend at one stage became dependent in a very primitive way on the patient and was threatening to smother her emotionally. Also she became acutely depressed and apathetic. The ambivalence and panic that this created in the patient were most striking and it is precisely here that she needed all the support and insight from her analytic relationship in order to cope and survive. Here the father's failure in not being able to come to the rescue of his daughter became very explicit. It also became clear that the mother's helplessness and inner panic, heavily defended against by her obsessional techniques, had not allowed the patient to react with aggression or hate. This denial and repression of all aggression and hate had led to the excess of free-floating sadistic impulses on the one hand and extreme dependence on the mother as a way of 'nourishing' her mood. In the relation to her friend she was able to maintain her distance, due to the transference relation to me, face her own sadism and hostility, and have a positive libidinal bond. Her friend's dream about her where her friend was kicking her head in a gutter had been most revealing and *releasing*. She felt at last she had got at her mother's unconscious hate and hostility and could cope with it. One reason this sort of child colludes so much with the mother's 'organized defence' is because of the absolute necessity of the relationship for the child. The child is totally dependent on the parent's livingness and, therefore, has to sponsor all the defences that enable the mother to live. The memory of mother's despairing remark to the father had a profoundly true perception in it. What had been repressed was the shame and guilt about her inability to be able to do anything positive towards the mother's mood and predicament. With her friend she could do and *did* much better. This released her from a guilty fixation on the mother. She was now gradually able to wean herself and enable her friend to tolerate this weaning. Here again one saw in very subtle detail how her mother had never 'weaned' the child. Ambivalence, love and hate, now became differentiated affects, that could be tolerated and sustained within the totality and wholeness of the relationship, where both she and her friend were separate persons. This separation into self and affective relationship to the not-self external object enabled her to surrender more to the transference relation and analytic process and get at her own instinctual needs, fantasies and a sense of guilt that was an intrapsychic experience within the ego (cf. Milner, 1952; Winnicott, 1958b; Lichtenstein, 1961).

It is noticeable from the account so far that though I have often mentioned this patient's use of splitting, projection, denial, phobic and obsessional mechanisms as a way of regulating internal tensions and social relationships, no clear picture of her defence mechanisms has emerged. This is rather symptomatic of this type of character disorder. The anxiety states are as diffuse as the defence mechanisms are confused with id-tensions. The defence mechanisms are not differentiated. What one sees is a general defensive personality structure. Winnicott has given us a very insightful account of this in his paper 'The manic defence' (1935): 'Its characteristics are omnipotent manipulation or control and contemptuous devaluation; it is organized in respect of the anxieties belonging to depression, which is the mood that results from the co-existence of love and greed and hate in the relations between the internal objects. The manic defence shows in several different but interrelated ways . . .' (see p. 27 above). I think it is true to say that this patient's behaviour and personality in the first phase was characterized by the manic defence. Analytic work by weakening the defences involved had created a threat to the ego which had been then dealt with through the creation of her internal satellite state of 'mental emotionality'. In the second phase the relation to her friend, supported by her transference, enabled her to experience and work through all the inner confusions and anxieties, and arrive at a personal identity where her own psychic reality could be tolerated and integrated. Marion Milner (1952) has discussed the problem of discovery of self-boundaries, separate identity and the problem of obliteration of boundaries. Discussing the meaning of her boy patient's play, she concludes: 'Thus a central idea began to emerge about what this boy was trying to tell me; it was the idea that the basic identifications which make it possible to find new objects, to find the familiar in the unfamiliar, require an ability to tolerate a temporary loss of sense of self, a temporary giving up of the discriminating ego which stands apart and tries to see things objectively and rationally and without emotional colouring.' The homosexual relationship and its working through in the transference enabled this patient to undo the defensive rigidity of the ego and arrive at a richer intrapsychic resilience and affective freedom (cf. Fain and Marty, 1960; Bouvet, 1958; Lichtenstein, 1961).

I have emphasized the role of homosexual relation to the friend in this phase. But the satisfaction, development and weaning from this relation would have been impossible without the transference relation and her analysis. If the homosexual relationship afforded her sentient body-experience and a shared most intense and primitive mutuality with her friend, it was her analysis that controlled its regressive threat, enabled her to relate it psychically to her past experiences with the mother as they conditioned the present, and gradually made it possible for her to achieve independence and identity through insight and understanding. The patient who, at the beginning of her treatment, had the muddled emotionality of a pubertal girl, mellowed and grew into a sensitive and alert womanhood. (Cf. Arlow, 1954; Socarides, 1962.)

ALIENATION IN PERVERSIONS

Problems of Technique

I shall now detail three aspects of the technical problems in the treatment of this case during the second phase: (i) the handling of acting out; (ii) the regulation and interpretation of the transference neurosis; (iii) the problem of counter-transference.

(i) Aspects of Acting Out

In any treatment situation the problem of acting out is met with at some stage or another. The intensity and extent of acting out is dependent on the nature of ego-distortions and the intensity of inner anxiety-situations. (Cf. Ekstein and Friedman, 1957; Greenacre, 1950*a*; Bychowski, 1954; Glover, 1955; Kanzer, 1957*a*.) In any type of perversion or perverse sexual practice acting out plays a very central role in the economy and dynamics of the patient's intrapsychic equilibrium (cf. Gillespie, 1952, 1956; Arlow, 1954). The impulsiveness of the pervert, his or her inability to tolerate anxiety, the pathology of the relations between the id, the ego and super-ego all compel towards a solution by dramatization and enactment. Fenichel (1945) has given us a useful statement on this aspect of the problem in what he calls 'the instinct ridden characters':

> There are various kinds of qualitative anomalies of the super-ego and its relation to the ego that figure significantly in the problem of impulsiveness . . . a more general mechanism which may or may not use 'bribing' was described by Reich as characteristic for instinct ridden characters: the 'isolation' of the super-ego. Whereas ordinarily the ego endeavours to meet the requirements of the super-ego and occasionally takes steps to ward them off, here the ego appears to keep the super-ego actively and consistently at a distance. . . . Closely allied to the 'isolation of the super-ego' is the formation of a kind of second, instinct-approving super-ego, of an idealization of instinctual activity, either by rationalizing one's own stubbornness as a 'fight for a good cause' or under the influence of instinct approving adults. . . . Related to the problem of impulsive behaviour is the problem of 'acting-out' in the psycho-analytic cure.

This plus the very primitive disturbances of child-mother relationship that every such case brings as an internal emotional constellation makes the analytic setting and procedure, with its emphasis on frustration and aim-inhibited verbalization, a 'traumatic' experience for them. They exploit it with masochistic wilfulness and heap on themselves acute privations that compel them to sanction acting out as relief and escape. I have tried to discuss this particular vicissitude elsewhere (Khan, 1960a, 1960b, and see Chapter 3). Recently, Stone has enlarged upon the inherently frustrating aspect of the analytic situation in his book *The Psycho-analytic Situation* (1961). I quote two relevant passages:

> The psychoanalytic situation is one in which two persons in the state of 'intimate separation', which we have already emphasized, express the whole gamut of tensions which arise between them almost exclusively through the medium of speech, sacrificing not only pedal locomotion, but that specifically human instrumentality which provides biologic relief of profound oral-aggressive tension, the use of the hands. To this extent, there is an obvious resemblance to certain of the normal conditions for dreaming. (Cf. Khan, 1962.)
>
> I have stressed the broad psychobiologic sweep of the psychoanalytic situation, a potentiality derived from the state of relative physical and emotional 'deprivation-in-intimacy' which it represents, and its mediation almost entirely through the complex psychosomatic activity of speech. In my view, it represents to the unconscious, in its primary and most farreaching impact, the super-imposed series of basic separation experiences in the child's relation to his mother. In this schema, the analyst would represent the mother-of-separation, as differentiated from the traditional physician who, by contrast, represents the mother associated with intimate bodily care. This latent unconscious continuum-polarity facilitates the oscillation from 'psychosomatic' reactions and proximal archaic impulses and fantasies, up to the integration of impulse and fantasy life within the scope of the ego's control and activities. The latter state is largely contingent on the development of true integrative insight and its ancillary phenomena, as autonomous ego functions. (Cf. Weigert, 1954.)

Since in the aetiology of this patient's anxiety about deprivations of impulse-aliveness and articulation, the mother's depressiveness played a vital role, the restriction of motility and contact aspects of behaviour in the analytic situation created a bias towards acting out.

It will be fatuous to conclude from this that any other type of therapeutic situation could have avoided this predicament for this patient. The great asset of the analytic situation is that it makes available for observation and interpretation what is being acted out and thus makes it possible for the patient to grasp its meaning and to integrate it gradually. Greenacre (1950*a*) has pointed out that in acting out we see: (i) 'a special form of remembering'; (ii) 'a compulsion to reproduce repetitively a total experience or episode rather than to select some small part of it as a token representation'. Supporting Fenichel's hypotheses she sees in the genesis of acting out strong elements of oral fixation, 'a special emphasis on visual sensitization producing a bent for dramatization and a largely unconscious belief in the magic of action', 'a distortion in the relation of action to speech and verbalized thought, arising most often from severe disturbances in the second year', 'inevitable increase in rapport by looking', 'activity seems to be increased by the effort to control the excreta', and traces it to a 'narcissistic weakness of the ego, with its accompanying over-dependence on dramatic activity rather than on work-directed activity as a means of expression' which is 'associated further with tendencies to exaggerated and somewhat detached fantasies which, in turn, impair the sense of reality or at the very least jade the perception of reality'. (Cf. Mittelman, 1955; Ekstein and Friedman, 1957.)

We have seen the presence of all these elements in our patient's relation to her friend. Specially worthy of attention are those aspects of acting out which are related to flight from surrender (Anna Freud, 1952) and denial of dependence in our case. Psychic passivity involved for this patient a very acute threat to her ego-functioning. The reversal of this passivity into magical action is inherent in her acting out. Furthermore her despairing and guilt-laden anxiety about her incapacity to make restitutive gestures, which led to almost melancholic bouts of loss of self-esteem and a sense of unworthiness plus the inner pressure of her sadistic impulses compulsively guided her into intimacies in which she could *see and sense* the pleasure she gave to the loved-object and also the pleasure she could experience in precisely those body-organs that in her internal body-image were too intensely cathected with aggressive and hostile impulses. This libidinization through sharing was her first attempt at fusing the aggressive and erotic components of her pregenital impulses; and it felt to her a necessary pre-condition for neutralization of the drive-potential and its availability for ego-functions (the narcissistic capital of the ego). It is my clinical experience that where a patient cannot tolerate such sexual activities through the presence of acute paranoid dread of the object and inner persecutory anxieties the analytic process creates a chronic state of psychic blockage, and through privation exaggerates the guilt and obsessional mental techniques of the patient. It often leads to a static emotional clinging to the transference. (Cf. Anna Freud, 1954*a*; Stone, 1954.)

I am not recommending acting out as a therapeutic device. What is important to realize is that if acting out can be regulated by the analytic process it can be a therapeutically advantageous process. (Orr, 1954.) But no acting out can be utilized in the transference if we are not aware of its aggression, flight from dependency and defiance aspects. It is the presence of these which makes the treatment of any type of perversion very much like the treatment of any antisocial behaviour. (Cf. Anna Freud, 1949; Schmideberg, 1956; Winnicott, 1956*b*.) Anna Freud has detailed the dynamics of acting out of the phallic masturbatory fantasy-content through antisocial behaviour very pertinently in her paper 'Certain types and stages of social maladjustment' (1949):

> In certain cases – this struggle against masturbation is abnormally successful. The ego then, and usually under the influence of castration anxiety, inhibits even the occasional, relieving masturbatory outbursts. As a result, the masturbation fantasy is deprived of all bodily outlet, the libidinal and aggressive energy attached to it is completely blocked and dammed up, and eventually displaced with full force from the realm of sex life into the realm of ego-activities. Masturbation fantasies are then acted out in dealings with the external world, which become, thereby sensualized, distorted and maladjusted. The acting out of fantasies (passive and active) sadistic or masochistic, exhibitionistic or scoptophilic, is therefore, a derivative of phallic masturbation, and in these cases, its substitute and representative.

Winnicott in his paper 'The antisocial tendency' (1956*b*) has emphasized that

> at the basis of the anti-social tendency is a good early experience that has been lost. Surely *it is an essential feature that the infant has reached to a capacity to perceive that the disaster lies in an environmental*

failure. Correct knowledge that the cause of the depression or disintegration is an external one, and not an internal one, is responsible for the personality distortion and for the urge to seek for a cure by new environmental provision. The state of ego maturity enabling perception of this kind determines the development of an antisocial tendency instead of psychotic illness.

Our patient sought the 'new environmental provision' through her homosexual love affair (cf. Milner, 1952; Bird, 1957).

(ii) *Transference Neurosis*

I have quoted Anna Freud and Winnicott because it is my contention that the dynamics of the perverse sexual practices derive from the fusion and confusion of two stages of early development: (*a*) the primitive relation to the mother and the distortion of both ego-integration and libidinal development from it, and (*b*) the failure of the attempts to deal with it at the phallic level of development, through magical activity and inhibited motility, restitutive masturbatory experiences and a submissive socialization process. (Anna Freud, 1954*b*; Greenacre, 1954; and see Chapter 3.) When the activity inherent to the phallic phase (both in boys and girls) fails to express and psychically articulate through phase-adequate behaviour the primitive conflicts and archaic affectivity then a regressive passive-masochistic solution is attempted. In our patient we see it clearly in her inhibited ingratiating behaviour and dissociated fantasy-symptoms riddled with chaotic pregenital impulses. Also striking was her cringing, ambivalent, peevish, dependency attachment to elderly women when she had started treatment. (Cf. Loewenstein, 1950; Mittelman, 1955; Katan, 1960.)

The transference neurosis of this patient materialized in a dissociated and bifocal manner: relation to the analyst and the relation to her female friend. The real task of the analytic work was to interrelate these two and gradually enable her to have an integrated personal ego and id. It is clumsy conceptually to talk of developing a 'personal id' and yet clinically it is true. The dissociations from earliest childhood of the id processes and impulses had put them out of range for the ego and made them ego-alien. Winnicott in his paper 'Primitive emotional development' (1945) has abstracted the processes of earliest development of the infant into (*a*) integration; (*b*) personalization, and (*c*) realization. About personalization he says, 'Equally important with integration is the development of the feeling that one's person is in one's body. Again it is instinctual experience and the repeated quiet experiences of body care that gradually build up what may be called satisfactory personalization.' This patient experienced the body-intimacies with her friend as an adult version of 'personalization' process. But the relationship would have degenerated merely into a perverse and magical defensive exploitation of pregenital instinctuality as flight from and denial of her inner hate, anxiety and ego weaknesses if the analytic relationship had not been available through the analytic work to make these sentient experiences available for psychic assimilation and integration in the ego.

It is precisely this antisocial element plus a very primitive level of body-ego pathology involving earliest areas of maternal pathology that put such a heavy burden on the counter-transference of the analyst. By counter-transference I mean the affective reactions of the analyst and *not* his unconscious conflicts. In every piece of acting out the patient is expressing hostility and defiance on the one hand and yet staking maximal claim on our understanding and support. The denial of dependency, the presence of very archaic ego-id processes, the phallic emphasis on action and activity, all directed against the transference, are bound to evoke hostility in the analyst. Perverse sexuality adds to this attack on the analytic process by being by its nature contrary to our normal social morality. It is easier to sympathize with a suffering inhibited human being trapped in his or her conflicts than to empathize with an antisocial person who has gone ecstatically berserk with his or her primitive sexuality, and is flaunting it in one's face. To keep in touch with the helplessness of the patient in spite of their omnipotence; to credit their suffering and confusion in the face of their manic denial and exaggerated eroticism; not to react to their activities with indirect and oblique interpretations which aim at causing guilt and are more based on our moral standards than on a true perception of the psychic situation of the patient, is a very heavy task. (Cf. Shields, 1962.)

(iii) *Considerations of Counter-Transference*
To weather such clinical crises and storms one has to be able to sense and deal with one's hate and distaste. These patients in such episodes have great and acute nuisance value and they taunt and challenge one with it. Masochistically they insist on being rejected

or reproached. It is their inherent need and demand that one should be able to *resist* them, show them one's 'hate' and the burden they are putting on one in a way that they can *realize* the meaning of their behaviour, and their own sadistic dependence. In so far as the patient is involved with *sorting out* the unconscious repressed hate of his or her mother it is imperative for him or her psychically and emotionally to be able to register the 'angry' elements in the analyst's experience of their acting out. If the analyst's 'angry reactions' are intruded into by his moral bias or envy or his incapacity to tolerate violation of his 'omnipotent control of the patient's emotions' then the clinical picture gets confused and the patient can only react with either panic and withdrawal or confusion and neurotic submissiveness. Winnicott has given us an extreme instance of this type of demand by the patient on the analyst's psychic and emotional capacity in his paper 'Hate in the counter-transference' (1947). When a patient splits and acts out the idealized good experiences with a sexual object then in the transference it is the aggressive, sadistic, dependency elements that need most urgent and consistent interpretation. It is the 'wholeness', strength and comprehension of the analyst which alone in the end can enable the patient to develop a personal and differentiated ego with which he or she can explore his or her psychic conflicts *vis-à-vis* instincts and not-self objects. (Cf. Bird, 1957; Shields, 1962.)

Gillespie (1952, 1956), to whose researches I am greatly indebted for the understanding of many vital aspects of my material, has particularly stressed the 'peculiar transference situation' met with in the treatment of perverts: 'the impersonal quality of the transference situation which the pervert attempts to maintain'. (1952.) I have discussed the defensive use of pregenital fantasizing and pseudo-hostility as defence against passivity, surrender, and dependency in my patient in the first and earlier part of the second phase. This dread of being penetrated, being compelled to yield and the masochistic erotization of these in the transference not only lead to splitting and controlling of the analytic situation but are specifically directed against the analyst's interpretations. The cravings for passionate erotic fusion with the analyst are another type of defence against his interpretative function in the analytic situation. Freud has drawn our attention to defence through 'a mental reservation'. This hostile (sadistic) attack on the analyst's role is then reacted to with fear and panic because it threatens object-loss and a most

FEMALE HOMOSEXUALITY

primitive type of separation anxiety. The patient thus finds himself or herself in a vicious defensive circle: his or her sadistic attacks on 'the penetrating interpretations' lead to fear of the loss of the analyst's support and also arouse acute guilt and anxiety. Attempts to deal with this lead to a very masochistic erotic craving to submit to the analytic process which is experienced by the patient's ego as total castration and annihilation. Their only way then of controlling and regulating the analytic situation is by acting out and splitting the total affectivity into two parallel relationships. The toleration of a certain amount of such behaviour and acting out is inevitable, from my clinical experience, if the patient's psychic congealed defensive states are to yield to the analytic process. What we have to keep in continuous and steady focus is the aim of the analytic work, which is to enable the patient to integrate in his or her psychosexual identity and gain insights into the unconscious conflicts and repressed oedipal and pre-oedipal object-relationships. Any experience in the patient that does not contribute towards this aim is injurious to the patient and any parameter of analytic technique that confuses or avoids this aim, through reassurance or sanctioning, is against the analytic process. Toleration of acting out in order to understand the patient's motivations and to enable him or her to gain enough ego strength to achieve insight and ego mastery is quite different from sponsoring and encouraging acting out as a therapeutic device. We can no more impose on our patients *corrective experiences* in their therapeutic interest than we can omnipotently dictate to them *how* their transference neurosis should work out.

PHASE III
Oedipal Relationships, Working Through and Integration

The homosexual relationship in terms of its physical intimacies had ended towards the end of the third year of this patient's analysis. The analysis lasted another two years and in this phase she achieved full genital orgastic heterosexual object-relationship and at the end got married. It is not my intention to discuss the complex and intricate material relating to her working through of the post-phallic phase, the anxieties related to genital (vaginal) sexuality and the intrapsychic shift from her unconscious identifications with the mother towards attainment of separate personal identity. This material does not fall within the scope of this chapter. I shall only select those aspects of it which throw light on the genesis and psychodynamics of the homosexual relationship. With this in view I shall discuss the material under three headings: (i) the relation to the brother at the phallic phase and its consequences, (ii) the belated oedipal relation to father and its collapse in frustration and despair, (iii) vicissitudes of body-ego development at the genital stage.

(i) *Relation to the Brother*

It was when she had weaned herself from her relation to her friend and the transference relation to the analyst had become recathected fully that we were able to see clearly the traumatic nature of her relation to her brother. He was in her early childhood highly idealized by her. She craved to have a close and intimate relationship with him but he treated her contemptuously. He teased her mercilessly and in every episode of playing with him that she could remember she had to be utterly passive and always ended up crying. From the dreams and the current transference behaviour, where crying was very frequent, it was evident that he had ridiculed her nascent and passive approach as much as her phallic strivings at identification. She had ended up with a very sado-masochistic relationship in which the flight was twofold: affectively to a regressive whining relation to mother and in ego development towards an intellectual identification with the father. It became also quite clear that she had seen the brother masturbate and urinate and there was one definite memory of being involved in all this. One dream from this period in analysis states the experiences clearly: 'A small boy is playing with her. He is playing with his penis. He puts it (the organ not clear in the dream) on her sleeve and it is wet.'

The associations were that she had woken up with excited wet genitals. She wasn't sure whether she had had an orgasm in her sleep. Other memories were of anxiety about bed-wetting (which had never actually happened) in her childhood, and recall of the game with her brother, where she had run to her mother crying and the brother had been caned by the father. She also related it to her own beating fantasies before sleep during the past year. One affect from the dream she had emphasized: she had looked with frightened fascination at the wet sleeve but couldn't quite focus the brother's organ (penis). In her own perception of the dream content she was aware of a sense of confusion between her body organs and her brother's. The 'wetness' also was related to mother's depressive tearfulness. The experience of her own body in the dream had been flat, wooden, inert, and full of fright.

The wish to share and be like the brother was present. That it was based on a flight from her relation to mother was also obvious. What had been prominent during this phase of working through was that once she had become confident about her own capacity to experience sensuous pleasure and give it to her homosexual partner it was possible for her to experience this masochistic fascination with the brother's sexuality and anatomy in childhood. This had further intensified her castration anxieties and sense of inadequateness, expressed in her acute selfconsciousness about her body clumsiness and general unattractiveness. Greenacre has given us the concept of penis awe in her paper 'Penis awe and its relation to penis envy' (1953*b*). I have found this an extremely valuable concept towards an understanding of this patient's phallic development. According to Greenacre penis awe develops when any or all of the four following conditions have been present in the girl's experience: (i) observation of the organ of the father; (ii) primal scene experiences; (iii) experiences of young children with exhibitionists; (iv) the chance observation of men or older boys urinating or masturbating. I shall single out two of the consequences that Greenacre relates to the 'extraordinary fascination and impressive awesomeness' that these experiences entail for the girl: (i) strong body-phallus identification; (ii) 'Penis envy of the more ordinary sort is never felt, but is turned into contempt, disappointment or an attitude of humour or ridicule towards the man who represents the brother or the contemporary.' The latter we have seen vividly in her transference attitudes towards the analyst. The first was a marked conscious experience of her body image throughout her puberty and later. What emerged very clearly was a specific anxiety associated with this body-phallus identification, which had militated against heterosexual intercourse and veered her towards homosexual intimacies. The anxiety was of getting torn apart and bursting into bits and pieces from intercourse; getting involved in a heterosexual relationship (like with the man) and feeling false and a phoney and not knowing what is expected of her. We have seen how she had reacted to analysis in this way in the first phase. The body-phallus, through regressive pregenital cathexes, also became a rectal penis, a secret omnipotent faecal object. But it had to be hidden and kept secret. From this derived most of her inhibitions about sports as a pubertal girl, her morbid shyness and her diffuse sense of disgust and shame about her body-image. Every heterosexual relation had threatened to expose her. The existence of this body-phallus as a secret possession had made the discovery of genitality at puberty difficult; because it meant tolerating castration anxieties in full strength. All her menstrual periods were accompanied by depression, disgust and distaste about herself. One defence against this was narcissistic investment of mental-ego functions. The body-phallus identification was also an omnipotent defence against the denial of the unresolved and regressive identifications with the mother. In this stage we were able to identify and analyse 'the mental emotionality' of the first phase as a specific affect related to this secret body-phallus image of the self. Hence its incommunicability and the avoidance of affective relationships. The sense of fear and awe had also been incorporated into the ego-attitudes and defences as phobic devices. Clitoral masturbation could not be taken recourse to as a means of discharging the excitement and tension built up internally because that led to the discovery of castration. Awe is a complex affect which consists of libidinal curiosity, anxiety, and aggression. Hence the fixation on the object or situation that creates awe. This inner image of the body-ego as a 'body-phallus' led to a distortion of the passive strivings of the post-phallic phase. She had obdurately rejected her father's tender and affectionate overtures all through childhood and latency. We know from direct observation and clinical experience that depressed children tend to over-invest looking as a means of feeling, perceiving and 'acting', i.e. expressing. In this patient experiences with the brother and the resultant penis awe had increased the use of looking as an ego-function and invested it with strong pregenital cathexes. It is also characteristic that 'masculine' phallic strivings in reaction to penis envy and castration anxiety were not expressed through exploitation of motility and body musculature, i.e. through an increase of body narcissism. The guilt about the secret body-phallus inhibited all exhibitionistic tendencies at the phallic stage and led to dissociated fantasying instead, i.e. a sort of intrapyschic exhibitionism. The psychic creation of the body-phallus also led to projection of all aggressive, sadistic fantasies to the male phallus. This predisposed her towards a homosexual solution where her body-phallus could be made available to a woman (mother) in a love relationship and hence be used for restitution. Only thus was it possible for her to rediscover her own female body, its attributes and its narcissism. And only in this third phase did an active receptive affective relation to the analyst become possible. In time she rediscovered her curiosity about and libidinal wishes for the male phallus and could reach out from a genuine female genital position.

(ii) *Relation to Father*

Freud (1931*b*, 1933*a*) and Deutsch (1932, 1944) have both strongly emphasized the existence and retreat from the oedipal relation to the father as a vital factor in the genesis of female homosexuality. Freud's (1933*a*) statement is explicit: 'female homosexuality is seldom or never a direct continuation of infantile masculinity. It seems to be characteristic of female homosexuals that they too take the father as love object for a while, and thus become implicated in the Oedipus situation. Then, however, they are driven by the inevitable disappointments which they experience from the father into a regression to their early masculinity complex.' Deutsch (1944) has strongly emphasized the fateful role of the father at puberty for homosexual object-choice in women: 'The father's favourable or unfavourable influence always affects the original mother tie during puberty.' Both these statements are true of my patient. Her relation to her father can best be discussed in terms of a dream during the last six months of her analysis: 'It is a seaside. Lovely blue sea. There is a very lovely building. It is a church. Outside it is a black chieftain who is looking curiously at her as she enters the church. She doesn't feel any anxiety.'

She had woken up feeling sad from this dream and had remarked that the emphasis on loveliness must have been a denial of the sadness. The black chieftain was easily identifiable as the analyst. Her next association was to her experience in the Gothic church three years or so ago, when seeing the image of Christ on the Cross had filled her with poignancy and chill. Now in the session she began to cry. It had reminded her of the gentle tender personality of her father; how in the latency period she had avoided him and clung to mother and brother. At puberty she had started trying to win his admiration and affection; her brother had left and there were only the parents and herself at home. But she failed because around that time her father had experienced a devout religious conversion, turned to church life and lost all zest at home. In analysis during the past months we had been dealing with this theme and it had become clear that gradually the father had despaired about the mother's depressive state. It was obvious beyond doubt to the patient, in her subjective recall, that the mother's depression had turned father to religion. All her attempts to revive his interest had failed. She had remembered her earlier dream of corpses in the church in relation to this dream. Now a strange memory came to her: quite often listening to her father preaching she would feel disgust and wish to vomit. She herself related it to masturbatory genital excitement. With distressing vividness she recalled many memories of seeing profound anguish and despair on her father's face and features at this time and she was deeply grieved at her impotence to do anything about it. Now she was able to mourn his death and the great loss from it, because he had been a very compassionate and gentle father to her.

At adolescence she had turned away from both her parents: in contempt and polite defiance. From this stage she traced her feeling affectively shallow and unreal on the one hand and carrying an anxious excitedness inside on the other.

(iii) *Vicissitudes of Body-Ego Development at the Genital stage*
The most important analytic work in the third phase related to the patient's discovery and experience of her vaginal sexuality and object-relationships. It is such a vast and involved phase of the treatment that I cannot do it justice here. However, I shall pick out one body organ, the vagina, and its rediscovery and assimilation into her total psychosexual integration and functioning. I have already said that this patient had experienced attempts at digital exploration of her genitals by her friend with pain. Her experiences had been restricted to the oral, visual, cutaneous and clitoral stimulations. She had explored her friend's genitals and experienced 'identificatory' satisfactions. It was this *lack* in their relationship which had been instrumental towards a successful 'weaning'. This particular aspect of the body-ego experience, i.e. a negative sense of the existence of an organ that could be felt as excited and which she had no means of psychically making real and psychically visible to herself played a significant role in her shift to heterosexual object choice. Sylvan Keiser (1956, 1958) has discussed the implications of the invisibility of the vagina for female psychosexual development in a most ingenious way. Keiser has tried to establish the *meaning* of the vagina as a recessive, invisible organ in terms of body-image awareness and its effect on ego development. Keiser's (1956) hypothesis is:

What is learned by deduction or derived from proprioceptive sensation is not equal to that which is acquired by the use of all sensory organs, particularly the visual. The female's body image should be considered as different from the male's; it is one which is not geometrically completed, since the figure is left with an unbounded area. But this is normal for the female. This could be a factor in the woman's feeling of incompleteness and her greater cathexis of the rest of the body. The wound, the castration, may also be a rent in her body ego which she is endlessly trying to repair. The penis envy may fuse with a wish to complete the body image, to do away with the opening in the body schema. The ego may struggle to deal with the id's instinctual demands without a clear representation of an executant organ. . . . The vagina is completely dependent on an external stimulus for sensation and entry into consciousness. Without the penis, there is no true definition of the vagina.

In a later paper Keiser (1958) has given some fascinating case material to show the contribution of denial of the image of the vagina towards inhibitions of ego functions.

When the need to deny the vagina is displaced to the other orifices, there is a regression to the earliest infantile state of no separation from the mother. . . . Acceptance of the existence of the vagina demands belief in knowledge by description and by deduction. To repress knowledge of the vagina not only leads to repression of abstract reasoning, but it becomes impossible for any knowledge to gain entrance into the body since no passage-ways are acknowledged.

With Keiser's hypothesis as a convenient and apposite frame of reference I shall now discuss some aspects of the emergence of genitality and their relation to the homosexual relationship. We have seen in the report on the second phase how the intimate body relationship to her friend had repeated significant archaic aspects of her disturbed relation to her mother. We have also discussed its defensive as well as releasing role *vis-à-vis* castration anxiety, penis-envy and restitution needs towards the mother and personal body-ego. It was when the patient had achieved a saturation point in her libidinal satisfactions and a confidence in the aliveness of her own body and the nourishing pleasure-giving (to the self and object) value of her instincts and body organs that she began to move towards a heterosexual object choice. She was thus able to gain insight into one specific defensive function of the passionate 'symbiotic' body rapport and body dialogue with her friend. It was aimed at denying the existence of affective confusion about her vaginal sensations. Now she was able to recall and comprehend what I had meant by my interpretations about her flight from her excited body. The 'excited body' was the excited genital and she *knew* nothing about it. She felt she should have known and yet all that turned up was the regressive confusion of other orifices and the fantasies relating to them. All her life she had felt that she had faked *knowing* things: in fact no idea ever 'penetrated into my head'. Hence her anxiety that she was pretending she understood and her certain feeling that she was totally blank and stupid. Or what was inside was faeces and useless stuff incorporated anally or orally. Now she wanted to find her vagina. At this stage, with painful embarrassment, she owned up to her primary wish from the transference relation and her analysis: the wish to be genitally masturbated. Though she could verbalize it only now and sense it, it must have been present at the very start, at which time she had only experienced confused excited tensions. She had described the tension as 'a dream one hasn't seen'. I think in this precipitate genital excitement in the transference situation we had confirmation of my inference that deprivations of body-cathexis from the mother had led to precocious and accidental genital sensations, perhaps from random manual explorations, in this patient (see Chapter 3). Greenacre (1950*b*) has discussed early vaginal awareness from stress and toilet-training (cf. also Kestenberg, 1956*a*; Eissler, 1939). It is my clinical impression that denial of the vagina becomes pathogenic when there has been a precocious *awareness* of vaginal sensations in the female child's body-ego development. And this leads to its confusion with other orifices and one defence against it is to seek body fusion with the mother, as Keiser suggests. In her relationship to her friend the ecstasy about oneness denied the separation of their body-egos. This denial of the vagina from body-image because of its precocious intrusion, which the young girl cannot psychically cope with, leads to a failure of neutralization of those larval genital impulses that belong to the post-phallic phase. Then instead of feminine receptiveness either greedy impulsiveness to incorporate objects and/or an obdurate negativity emerges in later character formation.

Once she had worked through the primitive anxieties of body destruction she could pleasurably anticipate discovering and using her genitals. (Cf. Klein, 1932.) She could also acknowledge the unsatisfactoriness of clitoral stimulations.

It is significant to report her experience of and reactions to her first genital intercourse. She had felt strangely full and satisfied. She had discovered that genital intercourse did not mean total passivity: she did not have to be a good child taking a feed (medicines) to please her mother, and she could be receptive and active. The vaginal spasms had neither the biting strength of the mouth nor the sadistic constrictive quality of the anus. In fact it was quite a unique organ with a unique function and capacity to yield pleasure and satisfaction. She was even more surprised about discovering the reality of the male penis. It was neither overwhelming nor terrifying; in her phrase: 'in fact it needs a lot of caring for and encouragement'. In short, she felt physically and emotionally confident that she could now experience genitality as a genuine function of her body-ego. (Cf. Zilboorg, 1944.)

In analysis her behaviour changed to quiet receptivity and capacity to converse. She could now understand the interpretations and elaborate them. She was a woman functioning as a whole person: physically, affectively, mentally and socially. (Cf. Payne, 1935; Brierley, 1932; 1936.)

(iv) *Aspects of Super-ego Development*
Super-ego and the unconscious sense of guilt is a very vital factor in the psychodynamics of any perversion and yet I have barely mentioned the role of the super-ego in the aetiology of this patient's homosexual episode and love relation. From my clinical experience of the first two phases of this patient's analysis I did not see any evidence of a true sense of guilt or a structured super-ego process. (Cf. Winnicott, 1958*b*.) This is not to say that she was amoral – very far from it: she was a fastidiously moral person. I am here discussing guilt in the sense that it is an affect of anxiety experienced by the ego in its internal relations with the super-ego. This patient's equivalent of guilt feelings in the first two phases was a complex and diffuse anxiety state, in which marked loss of self-esteem, a sense of humiliation and inferiority, dread of object-loss and separation anxiety, and an eroticized agitated anxiousness were the chief constituents. Similarly, I was very conscious of her lack of guilt about the abandoned and ecstatic way she submerged herself in the physical intimacies with her friend. Here again what was most noticeable was the acute anxiety about losing her friend, and an extreme form of brooding anxiousness that she would be sexually inadequate and therefore not be able to satisfy her. Concern about

the inability to give pleasure, make restitution, or failure to rescue the friend from the depressive moods she tended to get into, or incapacity to nourish her and make her happy played the dominant role. It is also significant to note that neither Freud, nor Deutsch, nor Fenichel, nor Bergler, nor Bacon discuss the role of super-ego or unconscious guilt in the psychogenesis of homosexuality in their female cases. The basic reason for this is that female homosexuality draws on a much more archaic level of libidinal relationship to the mother than male homosexuality, a point that has been stressed by Freud (1933a), Deutsch (1944), Fenichel (1945), Jones (1935) and Bacon (1956). In our patient the identifications with the father from the phallic phase derived from the 'active' elements and impulses in the phallic erotegeneity. They boosted intellectual development and also served a defensive function against castration anxiety *vis-à-vis* the brother and too great a regressive attachment to the mother. This I think further weakened the development of her Oedipus complex and consequently led to a more archaic sphincteral morality, with severe reaction-formations, derived from a very ambivalent pre-oedipal relation to the mother rather than a genital oedipal super-ego. In her affective states we see more separation anxiety, loss of self-esteem and dread of abandonment, with depletion of narcissistic supplies of the ego than inhibition and anxiety from guilt proper.

Freud (1925j) has stated explicitly his conviction that the super-ego in the female is less absolute and abstract than in the male and has related it to the anatomical difference between the two sexes and its psychological consequence in that the Oedipus complex in girls is 'a secondary formation. The operations of the castration complex precede it and prepare for it.' Freud's argument is:

> In girls the motive for the demolition of the Oedipus complex is lacking. Castration has already taken its effect, which was to force the child into the situation of the Oedipus complex. Thus the Oedipus complex escapes the fate which it meets with in boys: it may be slowly abandoned or dealt with by repression, or its effects may persist far into women's normal mental life. I cannot avoid the notion (though I hesitate to give it expression) that for women the level of what is ethically normal is different from what it is for men. Their super-ego is never so inexorable, so impersonal, so independent of its emotional origins as we require it to be in men. (Freud, 1925j.)

Recently, Keiser (1958) has given us another source for this lack of independence in the female from his study of a specific anxiety situation related to the female body-ego development, namely the invisibility of the vagina.

> The importance of the body image and the role visual factors play in early ego development is emphasized, with due consideration given to the penisless female genitals. What is not elaborated is the concealed nature of the vagina. It is not a direct sensory experience for the child and thus must have some effect on the body image. The existence of the vagina must always be deduced or accepted from authority. (Cf. Greenacre, 1948.)

I think that this dependence of the female on an external object for the *realization* of the chief organ of her adult instinctual strivings is another reason why female super-ego remains more diffuse, bribeable and permissive. (Cf. Brierley, 1936.)

One specific vicissitude of this patient's super-ego development is worth mentioning. From the analysis of her homosexual relationship it is possible to infer that her super-ego development consisted of two complementary processes: one was the flight from phallic traumata *vis-à-vis* the brother to an active series of identifications with the father on an intellectual mental plane and the other a regressive secret formation of an ego-ideal which consisted of the most archaic and positive aspects of body-love experienced from the mother in infancy and childhood. (Cf. Sandler, 1960; Milner, 1952.) The archaic wishes related to this ego-ideal entailed a passionate fusion and body oneness with a female object. Its defensive function had been to protect the patient in her childhood from too regressive an involvement with the mother's depressive moods. Through this ego-ideal of archaic body-love the patient had been able to postpone fulfilment into the future. (Cf. Schafer, 1960.) This ego-ideal sponsored the acting out of the homosexual solution. A true understanding of her acute loss of self-esteem became possible only when we were able to relate it to the absolute demands on the ego to fulfil the dictates of this ego-ideal. (Reich, 1960.) One further intrapsychic consequence of this secret creation of a body-love ego-ideal had been that it had usurped unto itself all the good and positive libidinal experiences of body-care and body-love of early infancy and childhood. Thus the patient's ego was left with only those identifications with the mother that were related to conflictual pregenital experiences (of toilet-training). The defences against conflicts relating to the mother took the form of either masochistic submissiveness or affective deadness and negativity. The homosexual relation was an attempt to break through these defences that were threatening to become rigidly established in her character-structure. In this context one could describe the homosexual relation as a regression in the service of the body-ego. (Cf. Ferenczi, 1923; Chapter 3.)

If the super-ego is composed of the introjected authority of the parents, and consists of identifications at the phallic phase which have replaced the incestuous object-cathexis of the current Oedipus complex with a corresponding and complementary desexualization and sublimation of the libidinal trends (Freud, 1924*d*), then it is possible to say that a more archaic and primitive psychic agency also exists in the human psyche, the ego-ideal, which subsumes into itself all the repressed or relinquished body-experiences belonging to infant-care and good-mothering and is more intimately connected with vicissitudes of the primitive body-ego development and is also the heir of the primary narcissism of infancy. The pathology of this ego-ideal depends on the pathology of the early relation to the mother. It is feasible to infer that because of her closer biological identity and prolonged pre-oedipal relation with the mother this ego-ideal plays a greater role in female psychosexual development than in the male. Perhaps the female's capacity to be receptive, empathetic and more tolerant of primitive body experiences, as one can see in any mother's care of her infant, is derived from the positive relation between the ego and the ego-ideal. The presence of this ego-ideal might also be the reason why female homosexuality is at once more archaic in its repetitions of mother-child relationship and why the presence of homosexual experience is less disruptive to the ego and is less ego-alien in the female than in the male. It is a fact that female homosexuals do not generally flaunt their psycho-sexual disorder as flagrantly in the face of society as the male homosexuals do. They also have not the male homosexual's compulsion to involve society and compel it to endorse their maladjustment with tolerance and adulation. Perhaps the fact that female homosexuality is more ego-syntonic and less destructive to the female personality has avoided its being noticed and censured too vehemently by society.

SUMMARY

From the clinical material of a young female patient evidence is offered to show:

1. The role of infantile sexuality in female homosexual relationships.

2. The specific importance of the disturbed and symbiotic mother-child relationship in female homosexuality.

3. The role of homosexuality as an attempt to repeat and elaborate the conflicts from such an archaic, collusive and disturbed relation to the mother.

4. The contribution of the mother's pathology towards predisposition of homosexual experience in the female.

5. The role of castration anxiety, penis-awe and modifications of the Oedipus complex.

6. The effect of conflictual early object-relations (mother, father, brother) on body-ego development, with special reference to difficulties about the discovery of the vagina and its psychic assimilation into identity formation.

7. The distortion of super-ego development through a regressive idealization of early body-care experience from the mother (ego-ideal).

8. The role of acting out in the treatment of homosexuality and the problem of transference neurosis.

5

Role of the 'Collated Internal Object' in Perversion-Formations

> It is impossible to deny that in their case, a piece of mental work has been performed which, in spite of its horrifying result, is the equivalent of an idealization of the instinct.—FREUD (1905*d*).

> It is true that the piece of blanket (or whatever it is) is symbolical of some part-object, such as the breast. Nevertheless, the point of it is not its symbolic value so much as its actuality.—WINNICOTT (1953).

FREUD had at the very beginning of his researches established the fact that it is 'a piece of mental work' that is at the root of perversion-formations. It was to take some half-century and more before psycho-analytic theory could account for the true character and role of this mental work in terms of precocious ego development (cf. James, 1960). Starting from a very different angle, Winnicott (1945, 1960) established the necessity and role of the *provided* object (maternal) if the psychic fruition of the innate maturational capacities of the infant-child are to actualize. In perversion-formations, the role of these two factors is perhaps more dynamically operative than in any other style of personality integration.

The hypothesis I wish to offer here is that during the infant-child stages of a pervert's development, there is a specific quality of maladaptation and/or excessive impingement by the primary (maternal) environment, which is compensated for by a precocious ego capacity of mental work that leads to the creation in the inner psychic reality of a 'collated internal object', which is the pervert's equivalent of what Winnicott (1953) describes as the transitional object in ordinary normal development. This 'collated internal object' the pervert can experience and actualize only through specific sexual events. For this argument it is necessary to establish three basic features of perversions: (i) The necessity of the presence and compliance of an external object. (ii) The nature and quality of an organized phantasy-system, unconscious and unknowable, in the subject (the pervert). (iii) The reality of an experiential situation in which the above-mentioned factors can be actualized. Space, motility, sight and touch are essential ingredients of this experiential situation.

A great deal of confusion in analytic theorizing on perversions derives from the fact that these three factors are not kept in focus. Pervert phantasies without practice do not constitute perversion. On the other hand, brutal, sadistic or masochistic sexual acts in mental defectives cannot be designated as perversions because they are lacking in that imaginative mental work which is, according to Freud and clinical experience, essential to perversion-formation. The pervert needs an object and his own phantasy-system to actualize that sexual event which alone gives verity and validity to his experience of himself in life.

Furthermore, it is necessary now to revise our preconceptions regarding the true character and nature of perversions. Perversions have a specific psychic structure all their own, which can on the one hand subsume neurotic and psychotic elements, and on the other can be compatible with normal living. The rigid bias of defining perversions as either the obverse of neuroses or a defence against psychotic states can and does hinder our true understanding of perversion-formation. Perversion-formations are much nearer to cultural artifacts than disease syndromes as such. This, of course, does not mean that perversion-formations are not pathological in their character; it only highlights the reality in the pervert's experience of his own perversion as something that is not necessarily sick and foreign to his sensibility and character (cf. Rosolato, 1967). Perversion-formations occupy a role in the total life of the practising pervert that is different from that of neuroses and psychoses in the lives of the psychiatrically ill persons.

The pervert is, to some extent, and significantly, distanced and dissociated from his pervert acts and devotes a mental care and effort to the fruition of his obsessions, which in many ways is comparable to an artist's pursuit of his vision and its actualization. It is this factor that *places* the pervert in a very special relation to his *sexual events*, and some of the inconsolability of the pervert and his sense of alienation from the very achievement of his wishes derives from this factor. To establish the personal equation between the private true self of the pervert and his *sexual events* is often as difficult as to identify how much of a writer's characters are him and how much generalized abstractions (cf. Smirnoff, 1968).

Concept of the 'Collated Internal Object' : A Case-History

Drawing on the researches of Freud and of Melanie Klein, Heimann (1952) has postulated: 'When the ego receives stimuli from outside, it absorbs them and makes them part of itself, it introjects them . . . we can define the beginning of the ego with the first introjections of another psychological entity.' It is not my intention to go into the whole complex theory of internal objects here. I shall restrict my discussion to a specific modality of this process in perversion-formation. In Chapter 1 I offered the hypothesis that in certain styles of mother-infant relationships what the infant-child internalizes is his mother's *idolized* image of him. This idolized self of the child is the mother's 'created-thing' and different from the child's total experience of himself. I then discussed some of the consequences of the child's relation to this idolized self as an internal object and how it distorts the person's future relation both to self and others (cf. Stoller, 1968). I stressed the fact that the relation to the idolized self as an internal object usurps most of the cathexis of the reparative drive towards others, especially in perversion-formations.

Here I wish to examine a specific use of the mechanism of introjection which leads to what I am calling here the 'collated internal object'. I shall illustrate my hypothesis with a case-history, because it strikes me as paradigmatic.

I shall recount the events in their chronological order in the clinical situation. A young woman of thirty years of age had sought treatment because of acute agoraphobic anxieties which were now paralysing her whole life. She was a very pretty and elegant woman, happily married with two sons. For her first consultation she had arrived with her *au pair* girl, who was barely eighteen years of age. The referring physician had warned me that she had great difficulty in travelling alone and being alone, and he had hoped I would not be too rigidly classical in my approach. So I was prepared to meet her companioned. What, however, I had not been prepared for was the fact that she would insist that the *au pair* girl sat with us during the consultation. I was a bit nonplussed, but accepted the situation. She gave a very good and lucid account of her life-history. She was an only child. Her father had been severely crippled by a car accident soon after her birth and had died when she was seven. She had very happy memories of him from her childhood because she had been his sole 'companion' while her mother went out to work.

The mother was an ambitious and rather intense person. After the father's death, her mother had brought her up very strictly, insisting she should work hard at her studies and get university education and go in for some profession. The mother re-married when she was thirteen. Her stepfather was younger than her mother and not very cultured.

At puberty she had suddenly blossomed out into a very pretty girl and was always being pestered by boys. So to avoid the nuisance of it all she suddenly married, at seventeen, a man some twenty years older than herself. He was a kind, gentle and wealthy professional person and her mother had made no objections, which had surprised her very much. She had her first son when she was eighteen and the second at twenty. She had enjoyed rearing them and they are both happy strapping young lads. Only the younger one has her difficulty about travelling alone to school. But once he is there he is all right.

While I listened to her narrative, I could not help noticing that the *au pair* girl had become noticeably dejected and apathetic and anxious. When she paused to ask me whether there was something else I would like to know, I merely enquired how long her *au pair* had been with her. She said for two years and they had brought her with them from their country of origin. Then she most genially and innocently asked me: 'Do you think you will be able to do anything? None of my doctor's pills have done much.' I asked her how long her symptom had been bothering her, and she said since they arrived in London, which was a year earlier. She now told me that in her home country she had led an active life of sport, with a great deal of sociability, though she had never been happy left on her own.

It was not possible, of course, to ask any personal questions in the presence of the *au pair* girl. I had deliberately allowed her full headway to arrange and organize the clinical situation as she pleased, because I felt she was enacting something very vividly and I should let it happen even if it made me look somewhat a fool. She asked me how the analytic treatment was *done*. I explained very briefly and added that in her case one difficulty would be how to enable her to use the couch *alone*. She thought that was a very funny way of putting it and added that of course the *au pair* girl would not be sitting with her in the future, only today she had to do it because the girl was studying psychology and was very interested to find out what an analyst does, and she had promised her that she would let her sit-in. This made me look even more of a fool, but I let it pass without comment. We arranged times and agreed to start her analysis the following week. As she was leaving, she remarked: 'Isn't it a great shame that I have been in London a whole year and have not been anywhere, seen anything, or done anything. But I really feel so terrified and helpless.'

She started the treatment and came regularly and chattered away pleasantly. It was one of those treatments where each session works all right: material is produced, interpretations given, and yet nothing happens. I shall now report her first dream after some six months of analysis.

She had managed to give her first dinner party, and it had been a success. Her husband had been very pleased and had given her a watch as a surprise gift. Socializing was very important for her husband's profession, and he also enjoyed having friends to dinner, and he was a person much liked by his friends and business associates.

Her dream was: 'She is expecting guests to arrive and is restless and on edge, fussing everywhere. No one turns up, and even her husband is not there. Suddenly, the door-bell rings and she wakes up in panic.'

In her association to the dream, she emphasized how very different the experience in the dream was from what had actually happened the evening before. She had in fact been at ease and had handled the whole evening both graciously and elegantly. The emphasis of my interpretation, however, was twofold. First, that through the dream she was trying to tell me that she was very much afraid that she would lose her symptoms without having been able to tell and share with me her true predicament. The bell which had woken her up in the dream I linked with the bell she always hears just before the end of her session, announcing the next patient. The second point I made was that it seemed to me that in this dream she was trying to show me an excitable and different aspect of herself, which so far she had not been able to include in her narrative of herself; and I felt very strongly that the dream was referring to actual experiences and memories.

We were only a few weeks from the summer break, and she reacted to the dream and the interpretations with a series of absences – some of them because of her having a cold, and others because of her children having some ailment. In fact, in the three weeks following the dream, I only saw her about four times. We were both aware that she was trying to postpone something until after the break, and I myself was not for pressing the point. It is my experience in the treatment of perversions that nothing is more damaging to the progress of the clinical process than curiosity, no matter how rationalized on the part of the analyst, to coerce a confession of phantasies and/or actual experiences from the patient, before the patient is ready to share them in a way that is meaningful to the patient. I had by now many clues which made me think that this patient had an extremely organized system of either perverse phantasies or practices. During the last session before the break she was very apologetic that she had not really succeeded in telling me anything about her 'other self', as she called it, but that it was all very acutely embarrassing, and she hoped that she would do better after the vacations. She also informed me that in her own country she had consulted a psychiatrist for some six months, and the whole thing had broken down because she could not speak in the face of what felt to her like accusations that she was deliberately hiding and holding back her material.

After the summer break, which in her case was rather long, extending over a period of some eight weeks, because she had to return to her own country with her children, she arrived in a distinctly different mood. She reported that her phobic states had definitely diminished, but instead, for the first time in her life, she had been overtly depressed and disinclined to do anything.

To summarize the work of the three months that followed, gradually what she was able to report was an event that had happened to her some five years earlier. Her husband had gone abroad for a week, and she had driven her sons to her in-laws for the weekend, which was some 200 miles away from their own residence. She was late on returning home, and something went wrong with the engine of her car. It was difficult to find a garage, but she did succeed in finding one – a rather shabby, old ramshackle place. The man agreed to look into the engine, and while he was trying to work she was very chirpy and excited, and teased him. He told her that he was going to gag her and tie her up so that he could get on with his work, and that he had no intention of staying there till midnight with all that interference from her. She provoked him further by saying, 'Well, you try.' Whereupon the situation evolved that he had tied her hands and feet, and tied her scarf around her face – all in play. And then, of course, as she put it, he 'raped' her.

While giving an account of this sexual event, she made the pertinent comment that though it had been totally unexpected, and

E   125

had both excited and terrified her very much in the beginning, at some point she had the same feeling as one does when reading a book and discovering half-way through that one has read it all before and the whole thing comes back to one. She assured me that she had been completely faithful in her marriage up to this point. In fact, she had experienced no heavy petting even in adolescence, which was very unusual for her culture. Another feature of this sexual event had been that it was the first time she had experienced orgasm – and yet in her description, she emphasized that basically she had been an onlooker, even though the whole thing had been experienced very intensely in her body by her. Furthermore, she told me that she had not felt guilty about it in retrospect, and had returned home and put it aside mentally. The man, however, had noted her address and came round a few weeks later, offering to look after her car. During the following two years, on one pretext or another, they met quite frequently and there was always intimacy. However, it never became a relationship – nor did it at any time threaten her relation to her husband.

I shall pick out from her long and complex account over the next three months only those elements which were instrumental in our putting together the history of her early childhood development.

The first thing that had struck me was that in all these sexual events, she was, to use her phrase, 'gagged' first, and then she looked on intensely with a terrorized fascination as he settled down to tie her in different postures before the actual consummation. I asked her about her father, and now she told me that he was a brilliant scientist, who was also an alcoholic. She did not know this, of course, when she was a child. He had had his car-crash when returning home in a drunken state. He was some ten years older than her mother, who was also a teacher and highly educated. As a child, during his lifetime, she was left to keep him company. The cost of the treatment and operations on him had impoverished the family very much, and therefore there was no help. He had suffered severe spinal injuries and both his legs were paralysed. Therefore he always sat in a chair, and 'to alleviate his pain', because that was the story told to her then, he would take huge gulps from a large bottle. He read to her endlessly from books, but she could notice that his eyes went intense and glassy towards the end of the afternoon, and his speech was slurred. It was only long after his death that her mother had told her that her father had been an alcoholic, and how tragic it had been, because it had not only ruined his career, but also killed him in the end. In her own actual postures in sexual intimacy, there were some very exact reduplications of what as a child she had seen and sensed in her father. For example, he was very adept at making little toys for her with bits and pieces which he would glue together, and had a very cunning way of using string to make them mobile so that she could pull them around. She had some of them still, and showed me a few. They were really very ingeniously made. Complementary to it was the fact that it was her mother's explicit instruction to her that she should not be rowdy and restless with her father, and she was therefore a very quiet, subdued, and compliant child.

The garage-man with whom she was having an affair was an uncouth young man, whom she described very vividly as always smelling of cheap liquor, sweat, and oil. From here, gradually another detail of her experience of her father very painfully came to the fore – namely, that after the car accident, her father had lost control of his bladder, and he was always, to use her phrase, 'dripping into a bottle'. She remembered very sadly how there was always a faint smell of urine about him. From these details, it was possible to collate part of the components of her internal image of her father – an image which had remained very hidden and unknown to her until this particular event. In fact, she had not been very much distressed by her father's death, and until puberty had been a very studious and withdrawn child. It was only at puberty that she had become a highly excitable, Lolita-type person, from which she had taken flight into the safety of marriage.

Another aspect of her latency was the lack of any cultural interests or games. She had lived in a somewhat somnambulistic state, and from puberty she could recall no phantasies or auto-erotic experiences. One of the gains to her from her affair with this garage-man had been that when he had left, she found herself masturbating in a ritualistic way, for the first time in her life. There was not very much phantasy to this masturbatory activity; only some of the features of her sexual intimacy with this man were repeated. She would lie in the bath and tie herself up, hand and foot, and somehow manage the tap-water to rush over her genitals in a way that would eventually lead to a sort of orgasm.

All this material occupied us for some three months. During this time she had become capable of travelling to analysis on her own, without a companion. During the last session before the Christmas break, she reported a dream. The dream was that she had come to a session and she was startled to find me dressed in a transparent skirt and blouse. Though she knew it was me, it did not look like me – I had long blonde hair and was smaller in height. She remarked how vividly she had seen the genitals through the transparent skirt. My only comment to her on this dream was that she had indicated to me that somewhere in the next phase of her treatment, she would need to use me in a feminine way, but with a masculine genital capacity.

She had responded to this by saying, 'You wait till you hear about it.'

She returned from the Christmas break in a very manic mood. She had managed to go abroad with the children, without the *au pair* girl, and had had a really gay time. But when she had gradually settled into the treatment, after having regaled me with all the gossip of her vacation, I reminded her about the dream that she had reported in the last session. It was here that she gradually narrated the second sexual pervert event in her life. About two years earlier from the time when she was talking, her husband informed her that most probably they would be coming to Europe for three years. This made her decide that she would like to learn a language – her children had grown up, and she had a lot of time. Somebody suggested that they knew a French teacher who was very good, and that she should take lessons with her. And she started the lessons. The teacher was a woman who was just a few years older than her, very intelligent and unmarried. She found it very difficult to start work and could not concentrate, and, to use her phrase, 'mucked about in the lessons'. One day the teacher remarked to her that she behaved like a fractious child of five, and that if she was not careful she would be spanked. This excited her enormously, and very soon she had tantalized and provoked the teacher into spanking her.

From here, the intimacy between her and the teacher really evolved very rapidly, and before she could realize where she was in the relationship, according to her, the teacher was having sexual intercourse with her with an artificial penis. She had told this teacher about her affair with the garage-man, and therefore the teacher had also tied her up. It was here that we were really able to collate a very great deal of significant material about her early memories of her mother, and it is these elements that I shall pick out from the total complexity of the material for discussion.

I shall summarize some six months of work here. She gave the whole account in great detail and with a manic exuberance at first.

She had *memorized* every detail. She went for her 'lessons' each day of the week, and they had become the ruling obsession in her life. She lived for them. They preoccupied her all day, and she was always preparing for the next 'lesson', she said, though this preparation was entirely a body-state with little conscious phantasy. She felt she was two distinct persons: the wife and mother who attended to the care of her family, and 'the other person' who was seething and frenzied within about what would happen in the next 'lesson'. It was a silently agreed part of the ritual that throughout the relationship, which lasted for some eight months, it was never verbally stated or acknowledged in any other way that they were having a sexual affair.

She went ostensibly for her French lessons and the teacher made her work really hard at them. Only during the lessons, some 'naughtiness' (her phrase) or other lapse on her part would start off the *game*. For example, the teacher would notice that she was wearing a torn stocking, or had a button missing on her blouse. At other times the patient would prearrange the 'naughtiness', like not wearing her bra or pants. Invariably, it would lead to chastisements, then caressing, and eventually intercourse with the artificial penis. Just as the use of the scarf to 'gag' her had yielded rich clues to the collated introjections of aspects of her father during her relation with the man, in this case it was the fetishistic use of the artificial penis that had been most symbolic and revealing. She described with what frightened fascination she would watch the teacher strap it on, and how bizarre, authoritative and awesome it looked. She was sort of hypnotized and intimidated by it. And it had an inexhaustible potency, unlike a male penis. One of her telling phrases here was how the sight and presence of the teacher with the artificial penis drove her out of herself. Here, her descriptions of the look and mood on the teacher's face were most instructive. She said that though the intercourse would always start very tenderly, gradually she could watch a violent tension and dismay creep over the teacher's face, and it would fill her with helpless terror and acute concern. She would feel as if the teacher would either explode or exhaust herself to death.

Another aspect of the same situation was sudden panicky feelings in her that the teacher would go mad trying to reach a climax, and in the process annihilate her. At some point, the teacher would stop and collapse into a dismayed exhaustion. It was this effect in the teacher's experience that preoccupied the patient most while away from her. She strove hard to see at least once a look of satisfaction on the teacher's face, but it never happened. She herself derived more satisfaction from watching what the teacher did to her and how she would do it, and did do it, than from the actual body-experiences. It was a complex ritualized game and they played it together with a fanatic seriousness and loyalty. She never once remarked that she loved the teacher or that the teacher loved her. From her account, it looked as if both of them applied the best of their individual talents to actualize a *sexual event*. Individually and privately they stayed impersonal and distanced from it. Here, one sees the essential paradox of most perverse sexual events and situations. Gorer (1962*a*), in his essay on Marquis de Sade, has offered the hypothesis 'that there is a close connection between theatricality and true sadism . . . the sadist is acting out a play with an audience of one'. From the patient's description, one was left in no doubt of an almost maniacal element in the teacher's role as the rapist with the artificial penis. And the patient, as the victim in this *game*, was always striving to assuage the violent inconsolability in the teacher's excitement and pent-upness. A task in which she never succeeded. In the end, she had got so run down in health from this manic frenzy in her and the sexual events, that her husband got worried and compelled her to see her doctor, who had sent her to the psychiatrist. It was during her visits to the psychiatrist that the agoraphobic symptoms started. She could not possibly have told him about the relation to her teacher, she said. Eventually, the treatment had stopped when they left for England. The relation with the teacher stopped at the same time, and she had experienced neither regret, nor sense of loss, nor nostalgia for it. Gradually, the phobic symptoms had taken over and paralysed her whole life before coming to her analysis with me.

Before I detail our reconstruction of her relation to her mother, I should state a bias in my handling of this patient's material. I knew she was leaving in six months' time to return finally to her country, and that was all the time I had to work in. So I decided to focus on the meaning of the fetishistic object – the artificial penis – and I exploited it to reconstruct her early relation to her mother. For my theory here, I was drawing almost exclusively on Winnicott's (1948*a*) paper. There he states: 'It will be seen that these children in extreme cases have a task which can never be accomplished. Their task is first to deal with mother's mood. If they succeed in the immediate task, they do no more than succeed in creating an atmosphere in which they can *start on their own lives.*' Just as in the case of her relation to the man I had not treated the affair as a heterosexual relationship between a man and a woman but focused on the enactment of aspects of the introjected aspects of the father, in this instance also I interpreted the sexual events as a way of *remembering*, and that my task was to help the patient cognize the introjections of her mother from her earliest childhood. Even at the risk of parodying Winnicott (1952), I would say that I considered these sexual events as dramatizing something that is before object-relationships – that is, a sexual enactment where 'the unit is not the individual, the unit is an environment–individual set-up'.

After I had collected sufficient details of these sexual events from the patient, I interpreted to her that the fetishistic artificial penis of the teacher represented the patient's mother's dissociated unconscious, which the patient had had to cope with throughout her childhood, and of which she could not possibly have a conscious and cognitive awareness. Now we began to get a most vivid and interesting recall of her mother's personality, from my interpretations of the teacher's mood and affectivity in the sexual events.

I have already mentioned how the patient in the very first session had talked of her mother as an ambitious and intense person. Now she gave a very vivid account of how her mother had to be active and busy all day. She could never rest for a minute. How well she remembered her collapsing into exhaustion every night when she could hardly move. That her mother was a frenzied and driven person, always preoccupied with some task or other – I linked this with the look on the teacher's face. Furthermore, she stated that though her mother could not have been more devoted to her father, or looked after him better, she had never heard her speak kindly to him or seen her kiss him tenderly; that she had always been afraid of her mother, though her mother had never punished her. From earliest childhood she had dreaded that her mother would one day blow up because she was so tense and pent-up. How her father's mood would change the moment her mother would return home: from a gay, playful, gentle person, he would shrivel up into a frightened, whimpering invalid. She even said that she could see now that her father would deliberately get drunk before her mother returned. In another context, she remarked that though no one could describe her mother as an unhappy person because she was always doing something, she had also never known her mother to be relaxed and happy. Similarly, though her mother paid great

131

attention to her clothes and body-care, she hardly ever gave her any toys or presents, or played with her. It was always something useful – like chalks, books, drawing-boards, etc. And until her stepfather arrived, they rarely had guests, and she had no friends of her own age to play with after her father's death.

Another meaning of this fetishistic artificial penis which her teacher had used came through very clearly in a dream that the patient had during the last month of her analysis. The dream was: 'She was standing, wearing this penis. Her mother was in the room looking at her, and the patient was crying.' In her associations, she had stressed how throughout her childhood her mother had dressed her in an indeterminate way – by which she meant that she was neither dressed particularly like a girl nor like a boy. Also she had always felt that her mother had very little understanding of girls. From this it was possible to say that the artificial penis also represented the mother's image of her whole self as 'a phallic thing'. It was following this dream that in this patient a very intense mood of disillusionment set in. It could not be described as depression. She felt very bitter at having been cheated of something throughout her life – to begin with by her parents; later on in a certain way by her husband, whom, because he was much older than her, she had always treated more as a father-figure than as a lover; and then from both her affairs, where she felt that though she had experienced a frenzied sort of passion and excitement in them, it had brought her nowhere near to feeling true emotions.

It was this mood of disillusionment in her that she found most unbearable to tolerate, and at times she would be very accusative that analysis had harmed her by spoiling her manic attitude towards life. And it is true to say of her that she had gone through life disregarding everything that was conflictual or psychically painful. Parallel to this disillusionment was a sense of alienation and distance from everything. She remarked often in this context that all her life she had felt that her way of experiencing was different from those of others. She could get very het-up, passionate and interested about people and things, but it was always transient. One day, she said with great sadness, 'If only I could at least hate someone' – because in fact she did not. Her whole life had been organized around libidinized ego-interests rather than proper affects and feelings or object-relationships. She had always been fair to everybody, but involved with no one.

From all this material it was possible to see very clearly how throughout her life she had been two persons. One who lived in reality, largely reactive to others, quite gay, and with a tendency to get run down every now and then, or to use her phrase, 'feel emptied out and drained'. And the other person who had stayed very latent and unknowable to her until these two affairs. One cannot really call this a person – it is what I am describing here as a 'collated internal object', which consisted of aspects of her father, aspects of her mother, and essentially the mother's dissociated unconscious, and an amalgam of self-experiences from very early childhood, as well as what her mother phantasied her to be. This 'collated internal object' inside herself she had no personal awareness of, and it is my contention here that one of the prime functions of such pervert sexual events and intimacies is precisely that they present the setting and the area for this type of intrapsychic structure to be acted out, actualized, and known.

Towards the end of her treatment and stay in England, some of the acute pain and bitterness of her disillusionment, and the sense that all her life she had been an alienated person, and hence a fake, abated. She began to talk of her wish to go back to university and get a proper degree. And that is precisely what she did, on returning to her country. In the four years since the end of this treatment, she has kept in touch with me by writing every Christmas, briefly and reticently, and giving me the news of her family and herself. She is about to obtain a degree in literature, and all seems to have fared very well with her – though she does persistently say that a certain glow has gone out of her life, and I can well believe it.

I have not said much about the transference of this patient, because I do not think the sort of use she made of me throughout her treatment could be accurately connoted by what we mean by transference. She was always genial, sometimes hostile and defensive in a self-protective way, and easily suspicious, but one felt that these were all oscillations of her own intrapsychic state. They really did not include me very much as a person in the transference. When she left she was sorry and sad, but again there was a sort of resigned acceptance of things. The absence of mourning, like the absence of real love in her life, is very characteristic not only of her but I think of perversions in general.

Glover (1933) has asked the basic question regarding perversions:

> It is worth enquiring whether a perversion is not in many cases
> a *symptom formation in obverse*, or the sequela or antecedent of a
> symptom as the case may be – a prophylactic or a curative
> device?

In my discussion now, I shall offer certain *ad hoc* propositions relating
to Glover's question and in the context of my clinical material:

1. At the root of the personality of the pervert is a *dissociation*. I am
borrowing the concept of dissociation from Glover (1943). He has
postulated:

> However fragmented the early ego, there is from the first a
> synthetic function of the psyche, which operates with gradually
> increasing strength. As development proceeds, the nuclei merge
> more or less . . . and a coherent and complicated ego structure
> appears . . . *the original state of nucleation of the ego is fateful for its
> later strength or weakness.*

Glover then goes on to say that the concept of dissociation is more
serviceable than that of nucleation. And elaborating his argument,
Glover added that, in addition to the dynamic, economic and
structural approaches,

> one ought to take into account the highly individual factors of
> *development*, and the *relation of the total ego to its immediate and
> potential environment*,

and advised that we should extend the concept of fixation 'to
include the fixation of the total ego to any one period of development'.

I shall extend Glover's concept further, in the light of Winnicott's
researches, to include a dissociation in the infant's 'immediate and
potential environment'. It is the central argument of this paper that
what the infant, who would become a pervert in time, introjects is
a dissociated primary object (maternal, paternal, or both). I have
tried to show from the material of my patient that what she had
introjected was not, according to Heimann's phrase, 'another
psychological entity', but disparate aspects of her father, her mother
(plus the mother's dissociated unconscious impinging on the child

through her reaction-formations and defences against it), and archaic elements of the primitive body-states which are indistinguishable from the object as a discreet not-self entity (cf. Milner, 1952; Mahler, 1969). The disparate introjections gradually amalgamate intrapsychically into a 'collated internal object'. This 'collated internal object' is the equivalent in the pervert's psychic inner reality to what Winnicott (1953) has christened as 'the transitional object' in ordinary development. According to Winnicott's theory (1953) the transitional object and transitional phenomena 'belong to the realm of illusion which is the basis of initiation of experience. This early stage in development is made possible by the mother's special capacity for making adaptation to the needs of her infant, thus allowing the infant the illusion that what the infant creates really exists.' In the experiential reality of a potential pervert, all these factors are reversed. He has to cope with maladaptive infant-care from the start, and what Freud has singled out as the role of 'mental work' I see as the capacity in the endowment of the pervert to compensate precociously by a dual process of idealization of those bits of environmental provision that *fit* his need and intensification by mental phantasy of partial and inadequate body-experiences of maternal care into a *collage*, which I am here designating as the 'collated internal object' (cf. Chapters 2 and 6). I am trying to differentiate the dissociation in the given object in the early experience of the pervert, from the later use of defence mechanisms and splitting of the object, which Payne (1939), Rosenfeld (1949) and Gillespie (1964) have extensively discussed in the psychopathology of perversions.

2. Winnicott's concept of the transitional object helps one to differentiate further the specific character of the 'collated internal object' in its role in the inner reality of the pervert. The transitional object is something external, and stays external as an entity in itself, even though brought under the imaginative and psychic omnipotence of the infant's experience. The 'collated internal object', per contrast, is something which is essentially intrapsychic – hence there is a continuous inner pressure to externalize it. This externalization is what constitutes the sexual event. It is inherent to this process that the pervert can never really achieve a complete embodiment of the 'collated internal object' in any external *found object*. In any given object which triggers off the *hope* in the pervert that this 'collated internal object' can be embodied and actualized, there is by

definition going to be a failure, because in the process of the 'game' of the sexual event and intimacy, gradually the external object's own needs and characteristics will begin to impinge – hence the inevitable result is disillusionment, and the primary affect in the pervert's inner reality is not so much depression as the pain of disillusionment.

3. Glover (1933) has exhaustively examined the various anxiety-situations against which all perversion-formation is both a defence and a curative technique. And he has emphasized the role of libidinization of anxiety as the basic self-saving technique in the pervert. I am here suggesting that the basic anxiety-situation in the pervert is twofold: (*a*) the threat of annihilation; (*b*) the threat of catastrophic disillusionment. One technique the pervert uses against disillusionment is to strive after *intensity* of erotic experience. This *intensity* is also the pervert's equivalent for object-relating. Hence, affective integration in the pervert rarely achieves the capacity of the depressive position.

4. It is here that Freud's emphasis on the role of the 'mental work' in the idealization of instinct in perversions can be seen most clearly. Intensity in the pervert's inner reality and enacted sexual events is his substitute for feelings and affects. In this context, and particularly in the case reported, one could very easily identify how there had always been a free-floating excited state in her.

This excited state has distinctly a manic quality, and displaces the pervert from his inner space to search for an external area of experience, where, through the instrumentality of another, this excitement can be processed and actualized.

5. The 'collated internal object' from another angle can be seen as the obverse of the process of personalization in the pervert. And one further consequence of the presence of the 'collated internal object' in the inner reality of the pervert is that it makes any further introjections of whole objects impossible. Therefore, from this angle, the pervert can be defined as a person who is his own invention and is perpetually seeking to substantiate himself through the personalizing participation of the other (cf. Bychowski, 1956). Bak (1968) has recently offered the hypothesis that the phantasy of the phallic woman is a ubiquitous phantasy in perversions, and that acting out

in perversions is an attempt at an 'orgastic affirmation of the truth of the primal phantasy . . . by actually engaging dramatis personae, the phantasy becomes indisputable reality'. It is important, particularly from the material of this patient, to reiterate that in fact the 'indisputable reality' of the fetishistic artificial penis was in itself an attempt to arrive at another reality, namely, that of the mother's unconscious. The function of the fetish, in this context, was both to create a new artifact, namely, the artificial penis, which is cognized and experienced as a separate thing in its own right, and at the same time which can subsume the unconscious signification of it representing the mother's dissociated self.

Stoller (1968) has given perhaps the most dramatic examples from his work with cases of transsexualism of how much the mother's mood, unconscious phantasy, and expectancies, can interfere with the gender identity of the child. One of the achievements of the 'collated internal object' in the psychic reality of the pervert is that it enables him or her to establish a paradox in inner reality which protects him from being completely overwhelmed in his person by the intrusive omnipresence of the mother's unconscious in his childhood experience (cf. Greenacre, 1968). But this technique of survival by dissociation alienates the pervert for ever from relating either to his own true self, or another person. At best, there can be intense episodes of intimacy. Hence, alienation from the self is the chief personal predicament in the pervert, as the patient I have reported stated so clearly.

6. The last point I want to pick out is that, though theoretically we know that sadism and hate are very basic to the potential affectivity of the pervert, in fact the whole machinery of the pervert's manipulation of self and object negates the experience of sadism and hate. What to the outsiders seems patently sadistic, in the pervert's personal experience is merely an attempt to reverse the threat of annihilation from within by gaining omnipotent mastery of the object. Sartre (1952), in his monumental study of Jean Genet, has shown very clearly how the incapacity in the pervert to arrive at personalization of the self continuously leads to what he calls 'being gives way to doing'. This emphasis on *doing* absorbs the pervert's sadism and lends itself maximally to the libidinized expertise of sexual intimacies, which are the pervert's substitute for object-relating on the one hand, and his way of denying the threat of annihilation of his being on the other.

7. I am grateful to Winnicott for pointing out a very significant implication of the type of work that I have reported with this patient. In so far as all perverse sexual events are an acting out of an intrapsychic situation in which the collated internal object plays a central role, it is important to keep in mind the inherent danger to life of this sort of actualization in lived experience. Here, a paradox is involved. If there are two people who are enacting this intrapsychic potential situation in the pervert, they can deal with it. But if through the analytic work somewhere, the pervert acts out his intrapsychic situation *in solo* through his masturbatory activities exclusively, then there can be a danger that the whole experience may take on a lethal maximalization, even leading to death, as a way of achieving orgasm. I think it is for this reason that very often, if the bias is against acting out in our clinical handling, the treatment of perversion in a potential pervert can get very stuck, because of the inherent threat that in a one-body situation the process will go beyond the means of the ego to control and regulate it. This may lead to an area where death or self-destruction is a by-product of this search for the completed sexual experience.

6
Fetish as Negation of the Self
Clinical Notes on Foreskin Fetishism in a Male Homosexual

THIS chapter gives an account in two parts of the treatment of a patient, relating to two phases of analytic work with him. Part I reports on the first five years of analysis. At the end of the first phase of treatment, the patient had gone abroad to take up an appointment. I saw him next ten years later, and the second part reports on a year's work since his return.

It is not my intention to superimpose an artificial unity on the two parts. Yet I hope that the inherent logic of the two phases will become clear in so far as such a logic can be conceptualized. One of the things that I learnt from the treatment of this patient is that some patients are enmeshed in a tradition of their own self-cure, which only gradually begins to manifest itself and follow its own relentless course. Inherent to any therapeutic effort that is true to the patient's need and character is one's capacity to allow for the full articulation of this process of self-cure. The title of this paper reflects largely the understanding of the fetishistic reveries and practices as we began to comprehend them in the second phase of his analysis.

PART I

In psycho-analytic literature the fetish has been discussed exclusively as an auxiliary object or device in the service of heterosexual gratification, and as a defence against perversions proper, particularly homosexuality. Freud (1927e) had derived the aetiology of fetishism from castration anxiety relating to the phallic phase. He had established the psychic contents of the fetish as denial of castration and had stated: 'The fetish is a substitute for the woman's (mother's) penis that the boy once believed in and does not want to give up.' By his emphasis on the singular importance of the mechanisms of denial (disavowal) and splitting in the ego's attempt to deal with the castration threat Freud (1927e, 1940e) had also established the beginnings of researches into ego-pathology and its relation to perversions which have since enlarged extensively the aetiology of fetishism to include: (a) primary pre-oedipal relation to the (breast) mother (Lorand, 1930; Wulff, 1946; Buxbaum, 1960); (b) internal objects and early ego development (Payne, 1939; Gillespie, 1940, 1964; Hunter, 1954); (c) transitional object phenomena and primitive mental functioning (Winnicott, 1953; Lacan and Granoff, 1956; Fraser, 1963); (d) separation anxiety and the dread of abandonment (Bak, 1953; Weissmann, 1957); (e) pathological body-ego development and threat of disintegration from disturbed mother-child relationship (Greenacre, 1953a, 1960a; Mittelmann, 1955); (f) bisexual primary identifications with the mother and the wish to bear a child (Kronengold and Sterba, 1936; Kestenberg, 1956b; van der Leeuw, 1958; Socarides, 1960); (g) flight from incest (Romm, 1949); and (h) a defence against archaic anxiety affects which threaten the relation to reality with the accompanying dread of breakdown into psychotic states (Glover, 1932b, 1933, 1949; Socarides, 1959; Katan, 1964).

In the literature, to my knowledge, there is only one case, reported by Bak (1953), where the patient indulged masturbatory practices with fetishistic homosexual fantasies relating to boys with buttocks of a certain shape and smoothness. I shall here present material from an overt male homosexual whose sexual interest and activities were exclusively centred round a fetishistic relation to the foreskins of uncircumcized youths. I shall try to detail the psycho-dynamics of this foreskin fetish and its defensive self-protective role in relation to the severe latent ego-pathology which derived from a grossly disturbed and intimate relation to his mother in his childhood.

Patient's Early History

The patient, a man of forty years of age, was one of four children. He had an elder brother and a sister two-and-a-half years younger. The parents had divorced when he was seven and the mother had married again soon afterwards; another boy followed within a year. Both marriages of the mother had been passionately, noisily and hysterically unhappy and she had intimately involved the patient in all her woes and emotional tantrums. She was a beautiful and ambitious girl who had miscalculated both times. According to her

FETISH, HOMOSEXUALITY AND EGO-PATHOLOGY

later insistent confessions to the patient, she had never loved her first husband whom she had reviled after divorce as a dirty man with nasty sexual habits. She had made out that the three sons (the youngest after the marriage) had all been her second husband's children, and to establish this fact she had their surname changed to his. The daughter she had conceived from another person. Her second husband was much older than she, and a rich and respectable citizen, who, however, lost all his wealth within a year of marrying her. This had exaggerated her terror of poverty and disease and the children were made witnesses of her eloquent complaints and grievances against fate and the husbands. Instead of improving her economic status she had, in fact, to do with a humble existence now. She was, however, very devoted to the patient who idealized her as a person throughout his childhood, and he had a profound attachment of love and affection to her right up to his adolescence.

The patient, who had been circumcized at birth, had a curiously vivid memory of isolated events as well as of fantasies from his childhood which he produced schematically in the first week of his treatment. They mostly belonged to the period between three years and six years of age. Briefly they were:

Memories from age about 3:

1. Sitting on a china egg and imagining he had laid it; feeling very disappointed on discovering it was not real.

2. Being very interested in the penis of the geldings and imagining himself united to them via the urethra. (This fantasy stayed with him till fourteen or fifteen years of age and had become absorbed into his masturbation fantasies.)

3. Tasting milk direct from a cow's teats during milking time and disliking it intensely.

4. He has been told, though personally had no direct memory of it, that one day his parents found that all the rhubarb plants had been nibbled and bitten at the root. First they had thought it was the work of rats and then discovered it was he who had done it.

5. He and his brother began going to the parents' bed in the morning and he started to entertain a compulsive wish to suck his father's penis and wished his mother were not in the way. Once he tried tentatively and was rebuffed. When he was seven, and both the mother and her new husband had started to revile the father as a man of nasty habits, he had confessed to his mother that he had actually sucked his father's penis and she had readily believed it.

6. His only other memory of his father was of the latter's once by mistake piercing the patient's foot with a prong while digging potatoes in the garden. Apart from this he had only the vaguest notion of his father and thought he had been a kindly person.

7. He remembers playing with his new-born sister by the fire and setting the blanket on fire. He burnt his hand and the nanny soaked it with the baby's wet nappy. He was very attached to this nanny. She had been sacked when the mother re-married because she had told the children that it was not their father who had been a nasty man but their mother who had loose morals.

8. His most vivid memory of his mother was of being tickled by her throughout his childhood, especially on the soles of his feet, and being reduced to ravished helplessness.

Memories from age 5 :

9. Of his mother's singing about fishermen lost at sea and his crying.

Memories from about 8 onwards :

10. Of his mother's bitter complaints against her first husband's sexual habits and her grievances against her second husband, with the patient always taking her side.

11. Of his mother's painfully congested breasts after her last child and his offering to suck them and being very relieved when refused.

12. Feeling terrified of his step-father on their first meeting and wishing he would go away and leave them alone. (He never got to know him well.)

13. Acute unhappiness when mother went on her honeymoon and starting sexual games with his brother and later threatening to tell on him.

14. It was also during this period (mother went away for six weeks) that he began noticing that his circumcized penis was different in shape from some boys'.

15. When he was eight, his parents moved to another country. From the period of his mother's divorce, remarriage, and move from home, started his obsession with foreskins. At first he had thought that the boys who had foreskins had an abnormality. At ten he wrote anonymously to the father of a boy in his class, advising him to have his son circumcized as his foreskin was abnormal. He was found out but not punished.

16. Of mother having an abortion done in the house, when he

was ten, and seeing the nurse and pans full of blood and other material.

17. His first masturbation activities started while he was listening to the hysterical rows between his mother and step-father, at the age of eleven.

18. When he was nineteen, his mother returned to the home country with her husband and left him at college. From this period his pruritis ani started and it persisted to the time of this analysis.

The patient presented these memories somewhat flamboyantly. Though he claimed to have a very good memory of his childhood, in fact there was very little else that he was able to produce during the first sixteen months of this analysis. Greenacre (1955) has pointed out the limited nature of the fantasies of the fetishist and this was true of this patient as well. He had almost no recall of any relationships to people other than his mother, brother, and father from his childhood and adolescence and all his masturbatory fantasying from puberty onwards had been almost adhesively centred on this foreskin fetish. Later in the discussion of his ego-pathology, it will be seen how much this blank affectless image of his own youth screened an extremely disturbed and crippled ego development as well as his incapacity for object-relationships (cf. Chapter 4).

Psychodynamics of the Foreskin Fetish

The patient had sought treatment because of what he had ironically phrased 'a theoretical dislike of homosexuality'. By this he had meant that he did not wish to become or be regarded as 'a queer', meaning a socialized overt homosexual. He had described in a euphoric way his current existence as dedicated to sexual love and the sexual seduction of young men with foreskins. The search for foreskins on beautiful youthful male bodies had become his chief private and personal preoccupation, although he had successfully integrated it with a sophisticated professional life. He was an educated person, well-groomed, slick and elegant of speech, and fastidiously polished in his manners. I have described the sexual cravings and pursuits of this patient and their relation to his identity diffusion during the first sixteen months of his analysis elsewhere (Khan, 1969). Here I shall detail the phenomenology of his specific sexual wish and activity: to find a youth with foreskin, perform fellatio on him, and then masturbate into the foreskin. The first phase of his analysis was filled up by euphoric and exhibitionistic accounts of his night-prowls in search of his accomplices. I have used the word 'accomplices' deliberately because he never once coerced a youth into sexual intimacy who had not been looking for a similar type of experience. There was also very little overtly nasty or sadistic or even unpleasant in his relation to his sexual object. The whole search for the suitable sexual object, the technique of seduction and the relation to the person of his sexual gratification were obsessionally ritualized. He had a compulsion to search for the foreskin object and if he failed, which was most infrequent, he was then reduced to masturbation. To this he always reacted with disgust, apathy, acute loss of self-esteem, and a sense of futility.

When the patient started the analysis his sexual activities had reached a crescendo of orgiastic excessiveness. He was fully aware of the dangers entailed (socially and legally) and early in his analysis had, as it were, reassured me by informing me that he had sufficient supply of poison should he find himself trapped, either through blackmail or police action. This type of splitting and denial was typical of him. Though he did his professional work efficiently and conscientiously he was concerned that he had lost all ambition and was living a day-to-day existence, without any real interest in his future.

The patient had had some sixteen months of analytic treatment in another country and it was during this previous analysis that he had acted out into real shared sexual experiences what had been till then merely obsessive private sexual ruminations with compulsive bouts of masturbation, which always left him disgusted with himself. Once he had started on his sexual adventures he had discovered his talent for such activities and when he came to me for treatment he could boast with some justice that there was not a youth he would wish to seduce who could resist him.

Though he had presented me with his stock of memories there was little material in the sessions during the first phase that one could relate to his childhood experiences with any clinical cogency. Of course his manic, perfervid, and impassioned sexual pursuit of the youths, his lyrical accounts of their beauty and his greedy consumption of their semen could be all too easily translated into patterns of childhood experiences with mother and father; but for me, at least, it was important not to be seduced into this type of intellectual analysis. I had also the fate of his first analysis as a good cautionary tale to guide my work. What had impressed me most from the start was that he had created for himself an ahistorical, as-if, screen identity in terms of his practices and pursuits relating to the foreskin fetishistic object. I have discussed theoretically this aspect of his behaviour in Chapter 2. During the first sixteen months analytic work had been concentrated on weakening his manic defence (Winnicott, 1935) as it operated through the sexual practices and on enabling him to bear minor anxiety states without taking recourse to automatic defensive manœuvres of the erotic or obsessional kind (Khan, 1964). It was when the patient began to relax his hectic and furious pursuit of sexual adventures that it became possible to examine in detail the psychic and affective contents of his foreskin fetishism. At this stage he became regressed in mood, apathetic and depressive in affect, and more dependent on his relation to me and the analytic situation.

Greenacre (1953a) in her definition of the fetish has stressed that 'in some instances it is not only the possession of the object but a ritualistic use of it which is essential'. The ritual in relation to the person carrying the foreskin fetish was most revealing in the behaviour of this patient. Equally important was the affective inner climate which would compel him into night prowling and searching for the foreskin fetish. This affective inner climate was an amorphous and confused state of excitement, anxiety bordering on psychically indecipherable terror, and a dread of collapse into total inertia and negativity (cf. Khan, 1964).

I am now condensing details which were laboriously culled together clinically over a very long period of time. The fetishistic reverie and pursuit organized this larval confused agitated affectivity into an alert and active state of elation. Hence the fetishistic search for an object both organized the patient's amorphous affectivity and, by transforming the latter into an active modality of behaviour, rescued him from apathy and inertia. The nourishing aspect of this type of acting out into reality as flight from an endopsychic crisis that the patient could not deal with had a definite self-protective role. How abjectly helpless and paralysed he could be would occasionally become visible in the early phases when he had to stay indoors due to weather conditions and was reduced to masturbatory discharge activities.

Relationship to the Fetishistic Object

I shall differentiate the total fetishistic practices of this patient into two component parts: (a) his ego-relation to the fetishistic object, i.e. the uncircumcized youths with foreskins; and (*b*) the intimate physical sexual relation to the fetish proper, i.e. the foreskin itself. The patient himself was fully aware of this duality in his experience of, and relation to, the youth and his foreskin. He had always idealized and boasted about the nature of his concern for, and appreciation of, these youths as persons, whereas he regarded his activities with the foreskin as in the nature of 'childish and absurd games'. It became quite clear to me very early on in his analysis that the type of affects and defence mechanisms involved in his relation to the fetishistic object were quite different from those expressed in his sexual play with the foreskin. The meaning and psychic content of the latter became possible only through analysis of the first and enabling the patient to see *himself* in the fetishistic object.

I have mentioned the amorphous mood of agitation and latent excitement mixed with anxiety and apathy from which the patient would launch himself on his night-adventures. This form of acting out of the endopsychic crisis enabled his ego to use objectifying and anticipating functions (Hartmann, 1956). Instead of a phobic negativistic state of apathy the search for the fetishistic object would mobilize a selective range of ego-functions. This patient had been crippled throughout his latency, adolescence, and earlier youth by an intense form of apathy and phobic-paranoid withdrawal into himself, in which state his only gratifications were the immediate discharge activities of masturbation with their stereotyped fetishistic fantasies about foreskins. The search after, and relationship to, the youths had enabled him to sense himself as a living, active, and effective human being. This had led gradually to an almost manic state of over-weening self-confidence and exaggerated self-regard. He now considered himself an omnipotent person, imperturbable and dedicated to the rescuing and nursing of beautiful abandoned youths. He felt not only in touch with reality but also omnipotently munificent towards it. His argument was that he helped these young men to become more conscious of their innate dignity and superiority and so enhanced their self-esteem.

He selected a very special type of youth for his fetishistic object: he had to be uncircumcized and, in physique, strong and beautiful. In mood he should be listless, depressed, at a loose end and searching for sympathetic contact. The fetishistic object should not be an avowedly practising homosexual, i.e. the youth should not have accepted homosexual relationships as an ego-syntonic mode of sexual gratification. On the contrary, he should profess an overt dislike of such practices. If the patient felt that the youth was in himself already excited and looking for homosexual gratification he would drop him immediately. This mixture of confused unease, apathy, and negativity in the mood of the youth was important for the patient because this alone established (unconsciously) the identity of the youth as one like himself. This type of projective identification as the vehicle of object-relationship I consider inherent in the ego-pathology of the pervert. Socarides (1959) has presented some very interesting clinical material exemplifying the role of projective identification in the pedophilic perversion in a male homosexual. Anticipating my discussion of this patient's ego-pathology I would like to comment here that to designate this type of relationship as projective identification is somewhat of a misnomer. This type of ego-interest and ego-cathexis of another person is more in the nature of a transitional state between relationship to the self and the relationship to the object, where neither the self nor the object are as yet fully differentiated as separate entities. I think we should use the concept of projective identification to designate an affective relationship where an internal object-representation is being displaced on to an external object and which further denies this object his own psychic and existential reality. For my patient the existential reality of the external object and its empathic perception were of vital importance.

Once he had established the significant and essential attributes in the object (the foreskin and the effective mood) he would then involve them in a verbal relationship. The youths he picked up were invariably 'lost souls' who felt abandoned, angry, suspicious, and ill-treated by life and worthy of a better deal. They were also as a rule grossly illiterate and quite often uncouth. The first task that he set himself in relation to the fetishistic object was to mellow the latter's mood and change it from negativity and suspiciousness into one of trust and co-operativeness. He always succeeded with remarkable ease and rapidity. That his successes were largely due to the simple fact that he had encountered the youths in an explicitly sexual situation and that sexual urgency goaded them into compliance he denied for a very long time. When eventually he had to accept this fact it drove him to bleak despair and he gradually gave up the adventures. He always tried to convince them of two things: (a) that they were uniquely valuable persons; and (b) that they should treat themselves with dignity, reserve, and reverence, and expect this of others in relation to themselves as well. I need hardly say that this is precisely what the patient wanted for himself. In order to promote this quality of narcissistic self-regard in them he would volunteer to teach them the proper use of language, good manners, and other cultural attributes. He would also feed them and show them the necessity of body-hygiene. The youths were generally unkempt, dirty, and undernourished. He would also give them a little money. All this in a matter of hours. This would invariably lead to physical intimacy, but before I discuss that I will make a few comments on the meaning of this type of relation to the fetishistic object.

That the fetishistic object represented the aspects of the patient himself as a forlorn, deprived, and abandoned, as well as idealized and special, person is obvious. What was significant for the patient was that the acted-out relationship enabled him to make a restitution towards his own ego as well as to the external object. This was in marked contrast to his inner hopeless relation to himself and his equally futile relation to his mother throughout his childhood. Furthermore, in his role as a provider of comfort and nourishment he was identified with the primary good mother; active, omnipotent, and full of nurture (cf. van der Leeuw, 1958). It is my contention that this type of relation to the fetishistic object enabled this patient to resurrect a good early relation to his mother which had got lost through the vicissitudes of his family life from about four years of age onwards. Winnicott (1956b) has postulated that behind the antisocial tendency there is a *memory* of a good (maternal) relationship that was present and got lost and the compulsion behind the antisocial tendency is to get back to this point and recover it. The patient in his relation to the fetishistic object was actively the good parent nursing the abandoned ideal child (youth).

The fetishistic object was also a whole person: intact and separate. The capacity to relate to him created the hope that not all was lost for ever. The illusional value of his type of relationship as a defence against a psychotic type of depression, apathy, and despair cannot be exaggerated. The relationship further established concretely the reality of the patient's identification with the good mother. He became and was the good parent (mother) in the transient expanse of such a relationship. It is possible to postulate here that in this type of patient the earliest relation to the mother has not been internalized. It is available only in terms of identifications and not as a stable internal representation of the good mother. Hence, when the patient was not operative in such an identificatory manner his sense of his self was one of bleak and morbid vacuity. The ego's incapacity to internalize the experience is also visible in the necessity to live through compulsive repetitions. The failure in his childhood development of a sustained good relation to the mother was dramatically repeated in the regressive breakdown in each encounter of the ego-cathexis in the fetishistic object as a person into the archaic and primitive sexual practices with the foreskin fetish.

Freud (1927e) has stressed the mixture of affection for and hostility to the fetish. Aggression towards the fetishistic object took a very peculiar form in this patient, namely that of exciting deviously and indirectly the youths to a pitch of sexual tension in which they would crave for discharge-relief. This was done so subtly that it is difficult to recount it. Through his verbal pattern and narcissistic boosting of these youths' self-regard he managed to get them 'sexually over-heated' (to use the patient's phrase). To deny the operation of this factor in the early phase of the activities was important. In fact verbally a psychic resistance was built up in the youths against sexual intimacy. The aggression expressed took the form of gaining a complete mastery over the excited state of the youth. This excitement was not allowed to be personalized. It was engineered furtively and obliquely. The youths had to experience it in a dissociated way: responding to his ego-solicitations their narcissistic self-regard was heightened and they had then to treat their excitement as a foreign body in their experience of self and treat it with casual cynicism. That they were used to sexual exploitation by their 'patrons' was adamantly denied, by him on purpose, and by them through collusion with his technique of relationship. So they invariably protested when he changed the direction of the episode from ego-support to sexual seduction. He knew precisely at what point their excitement had reached its peak. The role of sight and seeing was imperative here. He scanned every nuance of feeling and tension in their face and posture until he had worked up a 'colossal erection' in them. At this point his sense of achievement, triumph over, and mastery of the fetishistic object would be complete. He would now solicitously and compassionately offer to suck them and/or masturbate them. The excited helplessness of these uncouth, strong, aggressive youths had a specially pleasurable impact on the patient. Here a distinctly aggressive-sadistic element entered into his relation to them. He would secretly gloat over them: they were in his power. The more they got excited and frenzied with their sexual tension the more imperturbably quiet and gentle he became in his manner. He would often compel them to watch and see him masturbate them and make them ejaculate. He always swallowed the semen. The youth in the state of congested erection was both the mother and the excited self. At this point the inner status and psychic value of the object changed for him. He was the baby-person nourishing himself from the excited breast-penis of the youth (mother). He always had a guilty apprehension that this state of sexual excitement was not pleasurable for the youths. Here the identification of the youths with erection and the mother with painfully congested breast was complete. The youth with erection was also the phallic-breast mother. He had to hold tightly onto them while masturbating or sucking them. He could never cling hard enough and was for ever disappointed that this clinging grasping fervour in him meant so little to them. Here the disillusionment about the fetishistic object would already set in. He was also deeply aware of their humiliation and abject passive role in the masturbatory activity. Since he had first encouraged them to boast of their heterosexual inclinations and virility the situation of finding themselves homosexually seduced was negated by the youths through a rough and cynical attitude towards the whole activity. This would mortify the patient. Never could he get them to acknowledge it as a good experience and this caused him both sorrow and pain. On the other hand, whenever someone did become excitedly eager and involved in the masturbatory experience he would lose interest and become frightened and withdrawn. The dread of the excited and exciting object was intense in him. The excited state in the fetishistic object had to be an encapsulated and localized one and under his control (cf. A. Freud, 1952).

After the youth had ejaculated, the relation to the fetish itself would come into full operation, although this is not strictly accurate, because the relation to the foreskin was biphasic: as a property of the erect penis and as a sac into which he masturbated. The total fetishistic event can be differentiated into three stages: (i) ego-relation to the fetishistic object as a person; (ii) sexual passive oral and manual relation to the erect penis and the foreskin; and (iii) active intrusive ejaculatory relation to the foreskin as a receptacle.

Before examining the psychic contents of the foreskin fetish proper I would like to emphasize the importance for this patient of the relation to the fetishistic object. In heterosexual fetishism the fetish functions as a reassurance against the (castration) anxieties relating to the female sexual object and sexual organs. In my patient the ego-relation to the homosexual fetishistic object operated as a reassurance against the archaic and regressive nature of the relation to the fetish itself. Gradually it became quite clear to the patient and me that he had sought treatment because of the inner threat to his ego and personality from the chaotic and archaic feelings and excitements of the foreskin fetish practices. During the first year and more of his analysis, his idealized and ecstatic pursuit of the fetishistic objects screened his dread of what was happening in the sexual practices themselves. He tended breezily to slur over them and described his frenzied sexual activities as 'cure through exhaustion'. The elation and greed experienced in relation to the foreskin fetish was truly frightening for him. His dreams in the earlier stages of analysis were barely cloaked primitive wish-fulfilment of the wish to suck the penis with the foreskin and swallow the semen. That he never experienced any real gratification was hidden from himself and vigorously denied in the narratives of his sexual exploits.

Psychodynamics of the Foreskin Fetish

I shall first schematically detail the meaning of the foreskin-penis in the state of erection and the patient's relation to it. He attributed a very special magical significance to the foreskin-penis in such a state. To him it represented the ideal breast-penis from the first oral stage. It filled him with a sense of awe, fascination and excruciating excitement. By the time he had brought the foreskin-penis into this stage of congested aliveness he felt it to be his 'creation' and treated it as such. Sight, touch, and smell played a significant part in his relation to it. He could never fully digest the pleasurable possibilities of the situation. He wanted to fuse and merge with it. It was nearer to a hallucinatory imago than a perception of a separate organ on another person or as a symbolic vehicle of relationship. Lacan and Granoff (1956) in their discussion of the role of the symbolic, the imaginary, and the real in fetishism have discussed this point in an intriguing manner. This regressive mode of relationship to the foreskin-penis fetish involved the breakdown of symbolic and secondary process mental activity. The patient felt he had *created* this magical object and through visual and manual touch and oral incorporation *became* it. This meant to him refinding and recreating concretely the original unity with the omnipotent nourishing breast-mother. Nunberg (1947) in his study 'Circumcision and problems of bisexuality' has established the fact that circumcision can mean loss of mother and has further detailed the meaning of the foreskin as symbolic of vagina, rectum, and femininity. The wish to suck father's penis had arisen in this patient following his younger sister's birth. He had always felt his own circumcized state a deficient, inadequate, and maimed gender identity (cf. Greenson, 1964; Stoller, 1964). The fusion with the foreskin-penis re-established the lost omnipotent unity between the infantile pleasure-ego and the breast-penis-mother. It also served the function of denying the later traumatic separation from the mother through her marriage as well as negating his discovery that she was a castrated penis-less object. Nunberg (1947) has discussed his patient's fantasy that the female labia are a sort of foreskin that hide and protect the female penis. In my patient's fantasy and image this was true of the foreskin-penis. It was the ideal bisexual organ composed of the glans penis and foreskin-vagina united in inseparable (non-castrative) oneness. Hence his extreme delight and pleasure in it. The glans penis protected by the foreskin, which he could manipulate without injuring, meant also the primitive infant-self of the patient in the ideal protective nurturing ambience of the mother (foreskin), safely and pleasurably held by it.

The oral craving to fuse with the foreskin-penis and his idealization of a trance-like state of bliss that he experienced bear out the hypotheses offered by Greenacre (1953a), Bak (1953) and Socarides (1960) that separation anxiety and the fear of abandonment are the primary anxiety affects in the fetishist. In this patient the repetitive recreation of this illusional oneness with the mother through the concrete and physical idiom of his oral and manual relation to the foreskin denied the separation from her and at the same time established a new transient *event* that was its own reality and negated the affects related to the (internal) maternal imago. This capacity to carry contradictory affects and motivations seems to make the fetishistic practices particularly effective in the ego's defensive manœuvre against primitive and archaic emotional needs. The temporal element plays an important part here. The foreknowledge that the whole engineered event would last a short while and would be terminated by discharge (ejaculation) lessened the threat from the eruption of the very primitive body-needs and experiences with their traumatic genetic associations. The element of pleasure through gratification, the transience in time and the as-if make-believe of the whole fetishistic sexual game enabled the ego to split:

thus if one part was involved another looked on with bemused objectivity. This dissociation defeated, however, the regressive motivation to fuse with breast-mother and in retrospect the patient had no internalized satisfactory image of the whole experience available.

Just as the attempts to boost the narcissistic self-regard of the fetishistic object (the youths) ended in compelling them to submit to the sexual orgy and thus experience humiliation, the oral-manual relation to the foreskin-penis with its exaggerated and idealized excitement and fervour also ended in a collapse (detumescence) of the omnipotent organ through ejaculation. The patient always felt sorry and apologetic towards the youths and had a sense of them as having suffered a pain and an injury. The unconscious intention cannibalistically to murder the loved object in an excited frenzy was clear here (cf. Payne, 1939).

Before I detail the third phase of the total fetishistic activity, i.e. the intrusive (aggressive) relation with the foreskin, I would like to single out the importance for this patient of swallowing the semen. He had a distinct notion of it as a very powerful substance with magical attributes and constituting the very essence of the vigour and beauty of the youths. It was both comic and pathetic the way he always tried to make them promise not to let their girl-friends perform fellatio on them. The rationalization he offered was (and this neatly betrayed the sadistic greedy and hostile intent in his behaviour) that the girls would not respect them afterwards. The patient had at one time talked of his greedy compulsion to swallow semen as an addiction. An addiction it was too. It had the unconscious significance of incorporating a good substance which would neutralize his bad inner substances. We shall see later its magical curative value as a defence against hypochondriacal states. Glover (1932b) has pointed out how transitory fetishistic phenomena appear when an alcoholic gives up his compulsive drinking. Here we see an addiction introduced into the very structure of a fetishistic practice. The infinite complexity of archaic body-processes, pregenital impulses, archaic primary process mentation and affect which the fetishist can tolerate in an unorganized state is a remarkable phenomenon that still needs proper explanation.

It was only after the youths had ejaculated and detumescence had set in that the third phase started and the patient moved from a passive-oral relation to an active intrusive phallic one. His wish was always to penetrate the sac of the foreskin with his penis. This was another variant of symbiotic fusion, but at a phallic level. And here he experienced his most painful mortifications because the youths never reciprocated his feelings. He wanted to be held tight and to be loved, and they were generally bored and aloof by this time. So his penis was never appraised as a good object and it ended in a mere discharge gratification for him, which left him sad and disconsolate. One important fantasy involved was the wish to enter the womb of the mother, to be engulfed and enveloped. The submergence of his penis into the foreskin was both a wish-fulfilment and a defence against it. There was a profound dread in him of his passive masochistic desire to submit to the phallic-omnipotent mother, as represented by the foreskin. This was borne out by his dreams in which claustrophobic anxiety played a prominent part and he felt trapped or asphyxiated.

His ejaculation brought the fetishistic activities to an end in a dismal bleak way because he never experienced pleasure in his orgasm and had a sense of disgust about his own semen. The termination of the excited events in this meagre way was counteracted by a ritualistic nursing of the fetishistic object. He would wash and clean the youths, reassure them that nothing deleterious had happened, and through speech and conversation create a sort of benign amnesia about the whole episode. He rarely repeated these experiences with the same person. The person who became his first stable, social, and affectionate love-object was a circumcized youth, and by then his fetishistic manic pursuits had given way to a depressive hypochondriacal withdrawn state where the true nature and extent of his ego-pathology became fully visible. Before I discuss this I shall summarize the three main motifs that were enacted in myriad, amorphous, and fragmented ways in the relation to the fetishistic object and the foreskin fetish: (i) the wish to have a baby, i.e. give birth; (ii) the erotization and control of rage and murderous impulses regarding the mother, father, and siblings; (iii) the craving for, and dread of, a passive masochistic sexual surrender, which was the most potent unconscious wish and also a threat to the unity and existence of the ego.

The wish for a baby in the male child and its specific importance for fetishism has been discussed by Kestenberg (1956b), van der Leeuw (1958), and Socarides (1960). They have further related it to Winnicott's (1953) concept of the transitional object. Van der Leeuw has postulated that 'the transitional object is not only breast and phallus, but also the child made by the mother'. In my patient's ego-relation to the fetishistic objects there was the expression of the wish for a baby in terms of endowing the youths with a new identity and sense of self, and facilitating 'a psychological birth' in them. They were for him, in the context of the excited interchange, his *creations*, his babies: his own ideal self born through his psychological actions and activities in their shape and contour. The identification with the procreative, active and omnipotent mother was obvious here. But also present was the knowledge of its impossibility, hence rage and sadistic attack. This expressed itself through the compulsion to break down the identity of the whole fetishistic object into the regressive part-object, the foreskin fetish. The psychologically enhanced self-esteem of the 'created' youth was 'murdered' through sexual attack on it. The same theme expressed itself in the relation to the foreskin fetish: the mouth-manual-cannibalistic relation to the glans penis was the vehicle of the wish for oral impregnation. The unconscious fantasies behind making the glans penis emerge and submerge in the foreskin and making the youth look at it, as well as making the glans penis enter and retract from his own mouth (vagina), were all variations on the theme of giving birth to the self and the youth, symbolized by the penis. It also served the function of reassurance against being devoured. One element of castration anxiety in this patient was the dread of being eaten up (overwhelmed) by the mother.

This also ended in a fiasco through ejaculation, and here the sadistic delight in their helplessness at the point of orgasm and the consequent detumescence of the penis were in his unconscious fantasy an attack on the pregnant mother and her baby-phallus. The swallowing of the semen now endowed him with the magical power to impregnate and the use of the foreskin as (vaginal-mouth) sac for his 'intercourse' was a wish both to impregnate and to be born from this foreskin-uterus. This also ended in discharge-futility, and was followed by psychological nursing of the fetishistic objects and the need to reassure them as well as to re-establish psychic mental distance between the self and the object. The third element, that of the masochistic passive wish for total surrender and the dread of it, we see in his coercive stimulating the youths to a pitch of intolerable sexual excitement. Their egos, and not his, experienced the abandon to excitement. This way of splitting off the masochistic passive wish, projecting it onto the youth and then making them *live* it through his kindly sexual ministrations was one of the self-protective functions of the fetishistic practices (cf. Chapters 2 and 3).

Klein (1932) has detailed the complexity of the boy's fantasies in the 'feminine phase' of development. She has designated it as 'the period of maximal sadism'. She postulated: 'In this phase the boy has oral-sucking fixation on his father's penis, just as the girl has. This fixation is, I consider, the basis of true homosexuality in him.' In the fetishistic fantasies and practices of my patient the regression from the phallic phase to this feminine phase is explicitly clear, with all its omnipotent sadistic wishes to enter and possess the father's penis, as well as to attack the body-contents of the mother's inside. One consequence of this regressive intensification of the 'feminine phase' fantasies and part-object relations was the dissolution of his emergent phallic identity. Payne (1939) stated in her discussion of fetishism: 'The weakness of ego development is one aspect of the weakness of genitality and denotes interference with the libidinization, formation, and integration of the body ego, especially of the *penis imago*. This brings about an exaggeration of the first mechanisms and an exaggerated dependence on the introjected objects, but no sustained identification with any.'

The regression from phallic strivings in my patient led to a basic diffusion of the *penis imago* as a narcissistic model of self and the collusive sexual relationship with youths was an attempt to seek reassurance against the disintegration of the *penis imago*. In this aspect relation to the fetishistic whole-object was a defence against the persecutory anxieties inherent in the fantasies belonging to the foreskin fetishism. Sight of the whole-object as a sexualized phallic object also reassured against anxieties relating to sensations of the changing size of the phallus in sexual behaviour (cf. Greenacre, 1953*a*).

Ego-Pathology and the Disturbed Mother-Child Relationship

The analytic work of the first sixteen months had gradually enabled the patient to tolerate his inner panicky anxiety states without immediate flight into the idealized and erotic reassurance of the sexual practices with the foreskin fetish. Correspondingly he began to be disillusioned about his relation to the fetishistic objects. They were not such ideal and lovable human beings after all. He could now see that his programme to provide love for the 'outcasts for whom life had made no provision' had not succeeded, for three reasons: (i) his inability to love; (ii) their inability to receive love; and (iii) his choice of youths who had psychopathic, delinquent personalities, verging on the criminal. It was very humiliating for him to acknowledge that they had never cared for him, had stolen his money and goods, and treated him with scorn and derision.

He could now say that he did not want anyone to be dependent on him. He wanted to be dependent himself and be loved and taken care of. In this mood he began to search for a more human and what he had described as a 'personable' relationship. He met a youth and started a relationship which was neither fetishistic nor compulsively sexual (Khan, 1969). The youth was circumcized and quite a decent person. It was this relationship that revealed the true nature of his ego-pathology and the extent of his identifications with his mother. Soon after starting this relationship he found himself delusionally jealous and hysterically emotional all the time about the activities of the youth. He lived in a nightmare state of anguish when the youth was away, compulsively imagining the latter being seduced by someone else. His state of imperturbability gave way to fits of raging jealousy and a crazy sort of possessiveness. He would question the youth, endlessly row with him, search his underwear for signs of sexual activity, etc. Meantime he himself was furtively faithless to the youth with others – as his mother had been.

He now began to realize this was exactly how he had seen his mother behave to her second husband. She felt wronged, betrayed, jealous, and inconsolable. The patient had been her chief confidant and had shared all her moods and sympathized with her grievances. His stepfather had often remarked to him that he should not take every statement of his mother's as if it were God's written word.

The relation to this youth had led to the recurrence of his two old symptoms: anal itching and nightmares. He scratched himself furiously at night and could not sleep because of ghastly nightmares which frightened him so much that he could never remember them. They had mostly to do with a physical sense of body-dismemberment and/or fantastic enlargement of certain limbs. These latter he could experience in fleeting sensations during wakefulness as well (Greenacre, 1954a).

Here we were able to identify another motif in fetishistic practices with the foreskin: the sadistic wish to dig into another's body and discover the truth – to rob it of its precious contents which were his right and were being withheld from him. His anal itching also led to a general state of hypochondria. Gillespie (1940) and Greenacre (1953a) have stressed the importance of hypochondriacal states in fetishistic perversion. In this patient the hypochondriacal states could be divided into two distinct moods: (*a*) those relating to acute sense of personal unworthiness and loss of self-esteem; and (*b*) those relating to a disgust with the personal body and its secretions. They were intrinsically related to his jealous fits of rage about his new friend and his dread of being abandoned. This dread of abandonment was also a recurrent theme of his mother's emotionality. She had two terrors that ruled her life: (*a*) of being deserted by her husbands; and (*b*) of poverty, of being left destitute.

The history of his relation to his mother as we reconstructed it now from his memories, his acting out, and his transference relation can be presented schematically as follows.

His mother, a beautiful young woman, had started on her adult life rather traumatically. Her father had committed suicide and the ambitious girl had decided to make a rich and secure marriage. She had married an affluent farmer but had been unfaithful to him throughout (by her own confession). When the patient was two-and-a-half years old she had conceived extra-maritally and this had led to overt discord between her husband and herself. She had dealt with the guilt and anxieties about her pregnancy by turning passionately to her youngest child (my patient) and had taken over from the nanny who had looked after him till then. The nanny had stayed on till the divorce four years later when she had been sacked for telling the children that it was not their father who was a nasty man but their mother who had been a fickle wife with loose morals.

It was in this context that the three memories of the wish to suck his father's penis, the wish for union with the urethra of the geldings, and his sitting on eggs imagining he had laid them began to be integrated into a more meaningful pattern. We could see how the young child had reached the beginnings of the phallic phase. The parental discord and mother's pregnancy had a traumatic effect on him. He had reacted to it (*a*) with the wish to be like his mother and have a baby from father; (*b*) the dread of father's penis and rage at it (and the baby as father's penis) expressed in his biting the rhubarb plants; (*c*) the response to the sudden influx of insecurity in the mother and her involving him with it by flight to a magical fantasy of being united to the urethra of the geldings. Here the urethra meant the father's penis as a hollow womb-like secure place as well as the safe inside of the mother.

The patient as a child had made repeated observations of his mother's body and his younger sister's genitals. His mother had kept up a curious myth of the innocence of childhood and had exposed herself frequently, though inadvertently, right up to his eleventh year. She had stopped when one day she suspected he had started to masturbate and had then volunteered to tell him how if boys rub their penis a white fluid comes out. The relation of all these elements of his childhood experiences with the mother to his fetishistic practices was clearly established in his treatment.

His current relation to the youth settled down to a relatively stable and affectionate bond between them. He also had to accept that the youth helped him more than he helped the youth. Here the futility of his childhood efforts to help the mother, soothe her impassioned hysterical states, reassure her against her dread of abandonment and poverty all came to the fore. We could now see how the restitutive element of providing sexual pleasure to the fetishistic object was a great asset to him. He had grown up feeling and seeing that people only traumatize and hurt each other and are inconsolable.

In the treatment he now started to sink gradually into total apathy, inertia, and a helpless state of bleak withdrawal. All his phobias returned as well. He felt he could not face people and had an excruciating sense of his inadequacy and poverty of being. He could not go to work and took two years' unpaid leave, which was granted him. He now contacted his father whom he had not seen for over thirty years and who agreed to pay his living expenses.

The patient's state became one of a deep regressive dependence, in which the only thing that kept him going was his treatment. This phase lasted for nearly a year. It repeated in all essential elements the way he had lived his youth before his sexual acting out had started. Once he had left home and gone to boarding school he had become a shy, timid, withdrawn boy. He had made no friends; lived by his fetishistic reveries and masturbation. Even though he had done well at the university and got a good degree he had not felt up to the rigours of a competitive professional life. After his college life he had felt so frightened of going mad that he had decided to become a labourer and worked in a coal mine till the war started. Soon afterwards he had been called up and was taken a prisoner of war. He had survived the frightfully arduous and dismal existence in a Japanese camp without much sense of the dangers involved – at one time he had said how to him it had felt like being in a lunatic asylum and no more. The grim reality of the Japanese prisoner-of-war camp rationalized his worst terrors. His apathetic mood and mechanical obedience saved him from being victimized by the

Japanese soldiers. After the war, when he returned home, he had been given a good job and advised to have psychiatric treatment. This had led him to his first analysis and the acting out of his fetishistic masturbatory fantasies into actual relationships.

In his regressive illness in analysis the patient again decided to become a labourer because he could not bear the emptiness of his life, and it was indeed most painful to watch him live it. This alone, however, enabled us to work through the traumata of his relation to his mother.

We could now see how his mother's seduction of him as a child, which he had passionately reciprocated, had made no allowance for his emotional and developmental needs. He had felt unloved, abandoned, and terribly frightened. Added to this was the weight of the mother's hysterical emotionality. He had dealt with it by surrender to her moods and seduction on the one hand and a secret splitting off of his personal self into the masturbatory fetishistic reveries on the other. This had constituted the only private life his mother had no access to or control over. I cannot detail here the complexity of the material and analytic work involved in this phase. At the depth of his depressive apathy, phobic withdrawal, and feeling of total collapse the patient had the following dream which tells the whole story very vividly:

'On a table is a rectangular bowl three to four inches high, generally used for fruit or flowers. It is full of turds that look like sausages and bananas. He feels an acute sense of apprehension that at any time the pretence will break and they will be visible for what they are. There is a bit leaning over the edge of the bowl and from its soggy consistency he fears it will break off and fall. He takes it with a silver spoon to save it from falling on the tablecloth. Pretending it is a sausage, he puts it into his mouth, discovers it is shit and spits it out.'

This dream succinctly portrays the patient's inner emotional perception of his relation to his mother (the spoon in the dream had been the one given by his mother) and to the foreskin fetish. Here we see behind the idealizations and denial the true picture of the depressed deprived child's feelings of despair (cf. Spitz and Wolf, 1949).

This dream, which is from the middle of his fourth year of analysis, led to the discussion of his attitude of *negativity*. He now described himself as an *un-person*, someone who has never existed, never really experienced anything. All his life, he had merely precipitated events and had remained aloof and dissociated from them – an onlooker, neither nourishing nor nourished. Another theme parallel to this attitude of negativity was his secret sense of being special, that inside he had a very precious something which he could never share, hence could not experience himself either. One cannot exaggerate the life-saving value of this illusion for this patient. It enabled him to survive his adolescence and the regressive depressive apathy in analysis. He had often felt quite objectively that there was no point in his going on living, but he could not kill himself. He was external to this ideal inner self and he had no right to destroy it.

This led to his anxieties about :

(i) over-stimulation through identification with the mother, the castrated sexual mother ;

(ii) fear of being emptied out, left totally vacant like a shell, and abandoned, i.e. being robbed of primary self and breast-mother ;

(iii) dread of his own wish to surrender to the sadistic mother and an acute anxiety about passive annihilation ;

(iv) dread of males and an archaic form of castration anxiety.

The fetishistic practices had reversed these fears. It gradually became quite clear to the patient that his passionate love of his mother in his childhood had been very shallow. Basically he had sealed himself off and lived a pseudo-existence through identification with her moods. This in turn had made masculine-phallic development impossible. He had not really participated. Very early on he had split off into two persons : the clinging phobic anxious child intimately tied to the mother and the negativistic withdrawn boy fixated on his fetishistic internal objects. His attitude to everyone had been one of phobia and paranoid suspicion. He had later added to this a cunning use of language which cancelled all relationships through verbal badinage.

This patient as a child had reacted to the ugly discord between his parents with a regression to a very private and encapsulated state of fantasy. His schematic memories witnessed this and his fetishistic practices enacted it. What characterized these fantasy states was an unintegrated mixture of the most archaic feelings, part-object relations, and excessive erotization. Payne (1939) and Gillespie (1940) have emphasized the importance of sadism and introjection-projection mechanisms. Gillespie (1940) has further stressed the admixture of incorporative tendencies with phallic strivings. In the contents of my patient's fetishistic fantasies all these elements were grossly and flagrantly present. In fact, I consider that one of the primary functions of his creation of fetishistic fantasies regarding the foreskin was to encapsulate and control these very primitive and sadistic impulses. What constitutes the specific threat to the fetishist's ego is the regressive fusion of phallic stage strivings with oral and anal impulses and part-object relationships. In my patient's childhood the mother's overt hostility towards, and de-valuation of, the father, and the sudden and violent break-up of the home led to the child's:

(i) identification with the mother, both as a source of security and a denial of castration threat from the father;

(ii) feminine identification with mother as a way of maintaining internal possession of father (penis);

(iii) regression to part-object aspects of the parents (father as penis, mother as vagina-foreskin) and the attempt to concoct a parental couple through an amalgam of these two part-objects in one foreskin-penis;

(iv) collusion with mother's passionate emotionality, the over-stimulation from this leading to excessive sexualization of these fetishistic reverie states.

The anxiety states which this patient had experienced in childhood were diffuse and acute, verging on panic all the time and yet without much psychic content to them. He could all too easily feel depersonalized and terror-stricken, to which he reacted with either apathetic depression or acting out, or hypochondria. He felt a threat of disintegration and annihilation was forever nagging at him inwardly. It was this type of anxiety state which had exag-gerated castration anxiety. In the fetishist, as Greenacre (1953a), Payne (1939), and Gillespie (1952) have emphasized, it is the more archaic anxiety states that over-load castration anxiety at the phallic phase. This patient's ego had reacted to it by dissociations. These dissociations in the ego were maintained through denial, omnipotent idealization of mother, regressive use of incorporative mechanisms and their sexualization and the total suppression of sadistic-aggressive behaviour.

Payne (1939) has singled out the specific importance of sadism and the failure to integrate it to sexuality and ego-process in the fetishist. She stated that the sexual aim in the fetishist is to kill the love-object. I have shown earlier how in the fetishistic practice the

162

ejaculation of the partner and consequent detumescence were experienced unconsciously by the patient as 'sexual murder' of the penis. The awareness of this murderous wish then led to attempts at undoing through tender nursing and care. In this the fetishist's ego is very like the obsessional's: it continuously oscillates between an archaic wish for sexual fusion and a murderous attack on the object. Both processes intensify the ego's need for self-protection. It is this that leads to exploitation of phobic attitudes and deadening of affectivity in the fetishist. The fetishist's relation to his object is a more sexualized ego-interest than an instinctual investment and love. Gillespie (1939) has pertinently remarked that in the fetishist 'the theme of satisfaction is dependent on frustration, or rather a sort of partial frustration', and that one of the safeguards needed by the fetishist is 'just that he should be frustrated'. In my patient there was never once an experience of full sexual satisfaction. Satisfaction meant extinction and annihilation. It entailed either the ego's surrender to a masochistic archaic wish for total incorporation or a sadistic annihilation of the object in the excited state. Sexuality was exploited only for erotization of defences and archaic frightening part-object relationships. What Anna Freud (1952) has described as negativism and dread of emotional surrender in the pervert is a further aspect of this threat of annihilation.

In this patient the separation from the father and the involvement with mother's emotionality sabotaged the phallic strivings and development and over the course of his childhood and adolescence led to fixations on fetishistic reveries and diffusion of his identity both as a male and as a person.

CONCLUSIONS

I have discussed material from the treatment and life-history of a male homosexual patient who had suffered acute ego-distortion from a pathogenic involvement with his mother's mood and personality from the age of three onwards. The questions I want to ask are:

(i) why the patient as a child did not develop a severe psychotic illness?

(ii) what enabled him to create so early a fetishistic inner reverie state that protected him against total surrender to the mother's pathological intrusions upon his personality?

I think it is feasible to answer that the ego's capacity to dissociate and create a fetishistic reverie protected it from total submergence in mother's pathology. The libidinization from the mother also facilitated the stabilization of the fetish. The fetishistic reveries protected the ego against psychotic breakdown. What had compelled the patient to seek treatment was the unconscious knowledge of the threat to his ego through acting out of the fetishistic fantasies. The question as to what enables a child to create a fetish is not so easy to answer. In my patient there was certainly a good early feeding relation to the (breast) mother and to a stable healthy nanny. It was around the beginnings of the phallic phase that the traumata began to happen. The emergent oedipal (negative and positive) relations were disrupted by these traumata and a collusive pre-oedipal regressive relation to the mother materialized instead. The maturational processes and growth enabled the ego, however, to fight a defensive self-protective battle through dissociation and regression. I have tried to show how the fetishistic object and the foreskin fetish comprised the early infantile self and the primary object (mother). The fetish is built like a *collage*: it envelops complex and archaic affects, psychic processes, and internal part-object relations and manages to sustain them in an unintegrated state. I am inclined to say that in the capacity to create a fetish we see the inherent strength of the infant-child ego and its capacity to save itself from total collapse and disintegration. The capacity to create a fetish presupposes that maturationally the ego has access to its synthetic functions. The basic mechanisms involved are: splitting, denial, isolation, idealization, somatization, objectivation, and sexualization. The primary anxiety affects relate to dread of surrender to excitement and the exciting object, sadism, and threat of body-dissolution, and annihilation and being abandoned. The fetish is both a phobic and a counter-phobic phenomenon. This duality of the fetishistic phenomena relates them closely to obsessional states. Through the fetish the ego tries to find a way out of its negativity and paranoid withdrawal and through the process of sexualization tries to bind the aggressive, sadistic, and uncontrollable rage impulses. The fetish enables ego-functioning and object-relationships, the extreme obverse of which is autistic withdrawal.

The interplay of two distinct types of psychic processes are prominent in this patient: one related to his ego-functions and the other to sexual excitement. The ego-functioning had been crippled by a severely apathetic, phobic attitude throughout the childhood, adolescence, and youth of this patient. During this period he had maintained a highly organized excitement and emotionality in which masturbatory fantasies about the foreskin-penis were the dominant integrating factor. The case-history shows how the patient as a child had reached a rudimentary phallic phase of psychosexual development. These intense phallic-genital excitements had been both sponsored and encouraged by the contemporary care-taking environment and object-relations. The breakdown of the parental environment had led to a chaotic regression to pregenital modes of oral-anal incorporative fantasies, but the penis-imago had been retained throughout these vicissitudes, though in a pathologically dissociated precarious state. Henceforth the most striking feature of this patient's internal reality was the intense and amorphous excitement that this foreskin-imago could mobilize in him. I have also suggested that these phallic excited sexual states operated as a manic defence (Winnicott, 1935) and were exploited as a defence against acknowledgement of the disruptive upheavals of his childhood and the consequent threat of ego-disintegration, despair and dissolution of personality. He had later found a way out to reality and object-relationships through acting out this encapsulated phallic-cum-pregenital amalgam of internal excitement and sexual frenzy. This had enabled him to achieve a pathological ego-mastery over his impulses and the object as well as to force his ego out of its phobic-paranoid attitude of apathetic mistrust. But if this acting out had served the function of a rescue operation, it had also threatened him with a total loss of self through surrender to sexual impulses and the object. He had sought treatment because of his amorphous state of lack of identity and purpose in life. I am proposing here that this type of internal anxiety-situation constitutes the basic predicament for the fetishist. Fetishism is a state of omnipotently, but precariously, controlled mania. Hence it is at once intensely pleasurable and frightfully vulnerable. What the patient had sought from his treatment was the assimilation of this manic sexual fetishistic excitement and affectivity into an ego-capacity that could be related to the self, the object, and the environment. This he has certainly achieved through his analysis. During the past ten years since his analysis, the patient has lived an active and creative professional, social, and intellectual life as a member of his own culture, doing good work in an atmosphere of social belongingness.

Freud from the very beginning had stressed the crucial role of castration anxiety in the genesis of fetishism. Researches since then, particularly those of Glover, Payne, Gillespie, and Greenacre, have emphasized the role of early internalized anxiety-situations, object-relations, and vicissitudes of body-ego development which characterize the peculiar intensity of the fetishist's castration anxiety. In my case material all these factors are vividly present. This case-history tries to show how these early anxiety states and excitatory experiences reinforce the castration threat in the fetishist. Furthermore, it is possible to point out from where the as-if adult quality of the fetishist's sexual exploits and behaviour derives its ego-syntonicity. It is the phallic-genital excitement that holds the dynamic clue (cf. Katan, 1964). At the point of childhood traumata both the ego and psychosexual development have achieved phallic status though they are not stabilized as yet. The regressive process brings with it an influx of pregenital impulses and archaic psychic functioning. This regressive process is collusively reinforced by the mother's behaviour in many subtle ways (cf. Greenacre, 1960a). Hence the bizarre, hopeful, and absurd nature of all fetishistic phenomena. The mutative factor, however, remains the intensity of phallic affective excitement and the regressive intrusion of pre-genital part-object relationships in the fetishist. The omnipotent control of the object to discharge this manic phallic excitement is a most characteristic feature of the fetishist personality. Through it the archaic part-object relationships are held in control. This does not reduce the threat to ego-stability in any way. In fact, it exaggerates it. The very media by which the fetishist is compelled by his internal anxieties and impulses to seek reassurance, through collusion with external objects and reality, expose the ego to severe and persistent danger situations. Hence the acuteness of the threat of castration (annihilation) and ego-collapse in the fetishist. The ego is never in full mastery of the internal crises or external objects. The exploitation of primitive mechanisms, like splitting, projection, incorporation, and idealization by the ego, in order to create the illusion of omnipotent control interferes with its normal functioning. The fetishist achieves his sense of security, self-esteem and well-being entirely through his manipulation of the agitated excitability of the penis-imago and the complex archaic pregenital impulses and object-relations inherent in it. This exploitation increases the threat of over-stimulation to the ego and faces it with the predicament of either total exhaustion and annihilation or masochistic surrender to the object. The failure to neutralize sadistic impulses and their fusion with libidinal strivings without modification of murderous intent exaggerates further the threat to the object and the retaliatory threat to the self (Payne, 1939).

It is in this internal constellation of pregenital sexual impulses, primitive object-relations, and affectivity that we can fully decipher the necessity of the maternal imago as a phallic object for the fetishist. Freud (1927e) had explicitly stated that the psychic content of fetishistic practices is the fixation on the phallic mother-imago: 'the fetish is a substitute for a woman's (the mother's) penis that the little boy once believed in and – for reasons familiar to us – does not want to give up'. My case material suggests that the phallic mother imago upon which the fetishist is fixated is composed from sensations derived from the self-phallus in the excited states and the maternal object towards whom these are directed. Also involved are passive longings for the father's penis. Through a *tour de force* of psychic functioning the fetishist in his childhood creates a unitary imago from experiences and characteristics that belong to two different persons: the self and the object. I have shown how the foreskin fetish in my patient had attributes both of the self and the mother as well as of the father. Once these features have been coalesced they are dissociated from reality-testing *vis-à-vis* the external object. It is at this stage that denial plays such an important role in the psychodynamics of fetishism. It is this that relates fetishistic phenomena specifically to transitional object type of psychic functioning (cf. Winnicott, 1953). The instinctual regression is reinforced by ego-regression to more archaic and magical forms of psychic functioning. The fetish is created out of the sensations of self-body and object-perceptions. The threat to the body-ego from anxiety of annihilation (castration) is averted by projecting the penis-imago to the mother, who is then incorporated as a phallic omnipotent object. This has the added advantage that not only is the threatened penis-imago rendered safe but the archaic bond of security with the mother is also re-established. Similarly, the father's penis is internalized as a magical food-object. The maintenance of this complex affectivity and psychic functioning entails severe curtailment of the ego's growth and development. Hence the fetishist is a person deluded by the certainty that he has access to, and omnipotent possession and control of, a magical object.

The fixation on the internal magical object interferes with the neutralization of aggressive and sexual impulses in the fetishist.

ALIENATION IN PERVERSIONS

The specific ego-pathology in the fetishist thus relates to the failure to establish 'secondary autonomy'. Hartmann (1964) has defined his concept of 'secondary autonomy' as:

> . . . many, though not all, ego activities can be traced genetic-ally to determinants in the id or to conflicts between ego and id. In the course of development, however, they normally acquire a certain amount of autonomy from these genetic factors. The ego's achievements may under some circumstances be revers-ible, but it is important to know that in normal conditions many of them are not. The degree to which its activities have become functionally independent from their origins is essential for the undisturbed functioning of the ego, and so is the degree to which they are protected against regression and instinctualiza-tion. We speak of the degrees of this independence of the ego as the degrees of secondary autonomy. (Hartmann, 1964, p. xi.)

In Hartmann's idiom we could postulate that fetishism is a patho-logical substitute for 'secondary autonomy'. It is this specific type of ego-pathology that accounts for the complexity and bizarre qualities of the fetishistic phenomena.

PART II

The patient returned after an absence of six years and sought further treatment. I shall recount the clinical narrative as it evolved. The patient had kept in touch with me for the first four years by occasional correspondence giving news of how he was getting on. There had been a total absence of fetishistic sexual practices and a distinct abatement of fetishistic reveries in him. He had been able to settle down to a new area of research and was beginning to reach a point where he could start publishing his work. Then for two years I had heard nothing from him. One day, the patient rang me and said he was in town and would like to see me. The man I saw now impressed me by a completely different quality to his body presence. Of course, he was ten years older than the person whom I had first seen, but it was not his age that impressed one, but a certain burnt-out quietude in him. He sat down and told me what had happened to him in the last two years.

One night two years ago, he had been out walking and it was a sultry night. He saw a youth prowling around, and the youth evidently was trying to be picked up. The patient started to talk to him and took him home to his flat. There he performed fellatio on him. The experience had been without any real excitement for the patient. He paid the youth a small amount of money and sent him off. Some two hours later, there was a knock at his door and it was the police. The patient absolutely panicked, and immediately made the first wrong move. He asked to see a solicitor before giving any statement. The moment he had done it he realized he had admitted his guilt. This patient by his education was a lawyer, though he had never practised law. The police agreed to it, and the case started. The boy had accused him of seducing him to the police, and of performing obscene acts on him. The police had actually come to enquire from him whether the boy was telling lies. They had no intention of accusing him to start with. Then the patient got a lawyer to defend him, and here he made a second mistake.

The lawyer advised him to fight the case on a technical point, and as the process of law evolved the patient became more and more certain that he had not a chance of acquittal, because his plea had been made on the wrong count. But he did absolutely nothing. He was sentenced to two years' imprisonment in his country, which was not England. He accepted this with a singular quiet and resignation. In fact, it was quite obvious to me, as he was telling the story and I was listening to it, that he had devoutly wished for it. At this point in the narrative he paused and reminded me how very early on in his treatment some ten years ago, I had once remarked to him that he was looking for an asylum where he could be totally safe and protected from the compulsion to enact his fetishistic reveries on the one hand, and an ungraspable state of anxiety and agitation which he experienced on the other. He went to rather a tough prison, where most of the other prisoners were real criminals. He was given a single room, on request, and he spent fifteen months in it. Then he was allowed to come out because of his good conduct. According to the patient's account, this has been the quietest period in his whole life. He was also allowed to continue working on his research, and it was, from his point of view, a strange irony that while he was in prison some of his work began to be published and draw international recognition.

On coming out of prison, which was some five months before he returned to his analysis, he had arranged to come to England with the intention of having more analysis. As I sat and listened to this patient, he could see that I was deeply grieved by his news. He had suffered a great deal, but, according to him, it had really helped him to be a person, and for the first time he could tolerate himself as a human being and not be continuously seeking somebody else to experience himself through.

These are the events before the treatment started. He wanted to come only once a week because his intention was solely to assimilate all that had happened, and I agreed with that. The patient now lived in one room in a boarding house, and continued with his particular research from there.

Watching him for the first three months of his renewed treatment, what struck me was the extreme absence of any sort of object-relationships or human contact in his life. This very intense person had lost all his fire. Just as he used to be obsessed with his foreskin fetishism before, now he was totally engrossed and preoccupied with his research. It amazed me to see how much isolation and bereftness a human being can tolerate. He was not depressed or apathetic or sick in any manner. He is just an alienated isolate in human society and lives from that stance.

There were three important items which he wanted to understand:

(i) How it had come about that he, who had had such a vast experience in seducing boys, should have so mishandled the situation that the boy should go to the police and tell on him;

(ii) Why was there this compulsion in him, with all his legal knowledge, to ensure that he was convicted.

(iii) How did the period of imprisonment and its solitary isolation personalize him into acceptance of himself as a human entity.

When we examined the episode of picking up that boy in greater detail, what distinguished it from all his other earlier experiences was his lack of interest in the whole activity. He was functioning, as it were, from a conditioned response to this boy's solicitation. The reason why the boy had reported him to the police was because the patient had insulted him. After the fellatio, he had remarked to the boy: 'Your semen tasted rancid.' This remark had been quoted against him at the trial. When I asked him to tell me more about why he had made that remark, he said that now that he looks back on it, what he really wanted to say was: how absurd and meaningless the whole ritual of his seduction was. But he felt that would mean nothing to the boy, so he had made quite a fatuous remark. At this point I began to enquire from him why he had not let me know that he was in trouble. He said he had thought of it many times, but there were two reasons. First, he did not want to hurt me and make me anxious, because he was quite sure he would get convicted.

Secondly, he had somewhere a lurking suspicion that I might manage to intervene or advise his lawyer and create a medical defence for him, by which he might be acquitted. In fact, he never mentioned either to his lawyer or in the cross-questioning that he had ever had any sort of psychiatric or analytic treatment. In fact, he had made absolutely no defence whatsoever.

From here, of course, we started to explore his need for an asylum. The imprisonment had its precedents in his life. After finishing his education at university as a young man, when everybody had thought that he would have a brilliant career ahead of him, because he was a very gifted and successful student academically, he had opted out completely and gone and worked as a labourer in the mines, quite anonymously and away from home. This had been interrupted by his being called up for war service, where he had served a very harrowing two years in a Japanese prisoner-of-war camp, and was one of the few people from his particular camp who survived. Both these experiences are the precursors to this imprisonment. It was when he had come out of the prisoner-of-war camp and re-started his life after the war, and had started treatment with his first analyst, that his sexual practices had begun, as reported earlier in Part I. But what was significant for us now was not the commencement of his sexual practices, but his life as a labourer in the mines, and his two years as a prisoner-of-war. He had lived during this time in what he described as an opaque state of mental inertia. He did everything he was told to do most obediently, and would then just come to a standstill and stay like that. In his own words, it was really very much like a catatonic state. He had no fantasies in that state that he could recall. It was this particular capacity not to register his environment that had saved his life during his prisoner-of-war years. The Japanese were very cruel, sadistic, and exploited every excuse to inflict physical injury on the prisoners. The casualties in that particular camp had been excessive, but he had got by without a single act of assault by a soldier, and, according to his description, he was the only prisoner who escaped being hurt or physically molested.

But this had in some way frightened him also, and this is why he had gone to his first analysis. He had felt threatened that he would lose all contact with reality without finding any relatedness to himself. According to his logic and narrative, the great difference of his recent imprisonment was that he had the relationship to me very alive in him. So I enquired what his five years of relationship to me had meant to him, because in fact I had always been very impressed by a certain aloof, reticent and distant quality in his transference, and I had always respected it and never interfered with it by interpreting it either as resistance or as defence. His own statement about his relationship to me was that I was the first person he had met who actually cared about him and was totally unintrusive. And then he made a most insightful comment about what he called the one inevitable failing of the analytic relationship. He said he had felt safe only for fifty minutes a day, five times a week, but he was still exposed to this extraordinary panic in him, which I had often interpreted to him but which at that time he had no cognizance of in his own experience because what he used to experience was the frenzy of the fetishistic reveries and practices. In the prison cell he had a guaranteed, regulated, protective environment. To him, it had been a very healing experience indeed, and for the first time he was alive in his psyche and self, without being harrowed either by this ungraspable anxiety in him or hounded by his fetishistic fantasies. Also, time had become something tangible and real for him.

From here, he began to talk about his mother. She was very ill when he arrived in England, and she was also very old, but he had not told her he had come to England, and as far as the family were concerned, they still believed him to be abroad. What he recalled now as most significant from his relationship to his mother was what he described as her frantic terror of life. Throughout his childhood, in spite of the fact that both her husbands were well-off and had provided her with a good environment, she had lived in a frenzied dread of destitution and poverty. She had imprinted upon him all her febrile, anxious moods, and his only way of self-protection had been to dissociate his own true self.

Later on, he could be in touch with this self only through his opaque, mindless, affectless states. We could see that the fetishistic reveries and practices were his attempt to reach out towards life and build up some experience, because the regressive pull to hide away completely in this extremely private state was tantamount to annihilation of the ego. In this context, one could now see the whole of his fetishistic experience as a highly organized manic defence. I am using the concept of manic defence as postulated by Winnicott

(1935). Winnicott's concept of manic defence has three basic components. In his own words: 'It is a part of one's own manic defence to be unable to give full significance to inner reality.' Furthermore, Winnicott argues that: 'Omnipotent fantasies are not so much the inner reality itself as a defence against the acceptance of it', and adds: 'In manic defence a relationship with the external object is used in the attempt to decrease the tension in inner reality . . . for making good is only real when the destruction is acknowledged.' I have earlier referred to the salient features of manic defence as epitomised by Winnicott (p. 27, above). It was possible for me now to use this concept of Winnicott's in an extensive way to help this patient to see that in his case *there was no inner reality*, because his mother's intrusive impingements had made it impossible for him to build up an inner world of his own. All he had by way of a personal self was a state of opaque absence from mind and soma. For him to opt for this constituted a maximal threat to his own existence, and this was the real paradox of his personality. Before he had come to treatment with me, during his first analysis, he had provided his own self-cure through fetishistic practices. I had managed to wean him from that practice of self-cure and enable him to sustain some sort of personal ongoing, but he still felt extremely threatened by the very presence of the human environment around him.

In the prison cell, in that guaranteed routine of life and private leisure, he could draw upon his internalized relationship to me, which was neither stimulating to him nor demanding in any way, to build up his own self-experience as a person. What he had returned to analysis for was to assimilate more fully in the interpersonal relationship to me the full scope and significance of all these experiences.

While we were engaged in this work, the patient received the news that his mother had died. By the time the news had reached him the mother had been dead and buried a fortnight. It had been his latent fear since his arrival that his family might find out he was in England and thus he might have to attend the funeral. He knew his mother was gravely ill. The night he heard the news of his mother's death he had the following dream:

'I am travelling with my mother in a cargo boat to a foreign country. Suddenly my mother feels very ill. The boat stops at a deserted port. I carry my mother in my arms to the shore and lay her down. I take off my coat and put it under her head. When I look at her I realize she has died. I cover her over with my raincoat. It was raining heavily now.'

His voice trembled with emotion while telling the dream: a phenomenon I had never encountered in him before. He recovered himself quickly, however, and remarked: 'You would say the rain is my tears.' And of course it was. I wish I could have quoted Paul Ricoeur (1965) to him:

> D'une troisième façon la Symbolique du Mal fait appel à une science de l'interprétation, à une herméneutique: les symboles du mal, tant au niveau sémantique qu'au niveau mythique, sont toujours l'envers d'un symbolisme plus vaste, d'un symbolisme du Salut. Cela est déjà vrai au niveau sémantique: à l'impur correspond le pur, à l'errance du péché le pardon dans son symbole du retour, au poids du péché la délivrance et, plus généralement, à la symbolique de l'esclavage celle de la libération; plus clairement encore, au plan des mythes, les images de la fin donnent leur sens véritable aux images du commencement . . .

But I did not need to, anyway. He continued to explicate it himself. He felt the dream epitomized his whole relation to his mother. She had engendered in him the illusion that he and she were one unit and the rest of the world was a separate hostile entity. Hence in the cargo boat there is no captain and no crew, I added: he agreed. This had escaped him. But the tenderness of his behaviour to his mother had impressed him profoundly, since he had reacted to her physical nearness with vomitive distaste from puberty onwards. He emphasized how on waking from the dream he had a very lucid and distinct awareness that his mother was *really* dead now, and he reminded me that in his 'first analysis' (as he calls it), I had once remarked that he would not feel really free to live his own life until his mother died. I had no memory of that remark myself.

He had had to wait for three days after the dream for his next session, and in this period he reported that he had lived exactly in the same mood as in the Japanese prison camp – namely, one of opaque, mindless, non-somatic existing. But he had not panicked from it. On the contrary, he had observed it with a certain curiosity. He had not been able to do any work or even go out for a meal. He had stayed put in his room and lived off eating what food he had. It was a totally placid and peaceful existence, where nothing happened. And now he himself postulated that he believed that this state was what he had been escaping from since early childhood. He thought that all his memories from childhood and all his fetishistic fantasies and practices were a flight from this state. He asked me what I thought of it. Before I could speak, he added one further comment: 'It is as near to a catatonic state as you can imagine.' I remarked that he was describing more an autistic state than a catatonic one. That what had impressed me about his dream was that it was all so perfectly mimed: there was little affect or relating in it. Even his grief had been wept for him by the clouds. I pointed out that we had reached the end of the session, that I would think about all that he had said and reported, and would say more next time. But meantime I wanted him to know how sad I was I had failed to enable him to relate to his mother during her lifetime, since she was so obviously the only person he had loved in all his life.

In the weeks that followed this, the patient explored much more sensitively the phenomenology of his opaque, mindless, non-somatic state of existing. As he reflected over his whole life afresh, and in a way for the first time, he could see how from very early childhood there was in him a proclivity to sink towards this state, and this constituted his true self, and he experienced it as a real threat to him. My own attempt to make sense of it to him and myself was on the following lines: that in his early relation to his mother, and right through his childhood, there had been so much intrusive impingement on him by his mother that his only area of privacy and personal existence was to be in a state of self where none of the ego-apparatuses operated. Alongside there had been a precocious seduction of all his ego capacities into a concern for the mother, but this concern, if it dislocated him from himself, had one advantage: it also gave him the experiential cum executive scope to enlarge and differentiate his ego-id capacities and functions. So that from the very beginning of his life a marked split has operated in him. In the area where he feels true to himself he is non-existent. All his ego-functions, including his id-tensions, had been from the start usurped by his mother. Later on, the whole manic machinery of his fetishistic reveries, and penultimately the fetishistic sexual practices, created a satellite existence for him, in which he has lived ever since. In this sense, the fetishistic experiences had a dual defensive function: they kept him protected from affective surrender to his mother from concern, and they also alienated him from that state of autistic, blank, private self which was tantamount to non-existence.

The work in this period certainly made us both re-examine some of the hypotheses that I have offered in the first part of this chapter about the nature, role and function of the fetish in his life. None of what we are saying now contradicts that, but it does underline very heavily the fact that in certain infant-mother relationships there can be such gross intrusion on the infant, mixed with seduction of his ego-id capacities into precocious hyper-function, that the true self of the person can be a very opaque state of nothingness. This self is what the perversion-formation protects the person of the patient from, and yet the very success of this mechanism keeps him alienated from his self.

It is still too early to say anything as to how this patient will personalize *vis-à-vis* the human environment. There are certain signs that he is beginning to feel the need of the human environment as a nutrient necessity for him also, but the facts are that the patient now lives a life which, by ordinary standards, is extremely lacking in human contact, and there is no doubt that with the disappearance of the manic defence a certain instinctual fervour and dynamism has gone out of his existence. This, perhaps, is the great hazard of the analytic cure of a pervert's self-cure. But today, he is a person real in himself, creative in his intellectual pursuits, unharrowed by that ungraspable anxiety in himself, and beginning to live a life which to him is meaningful, sentient and true, and has a purpose as well as a direction in terms of its future.

7

Cannibalistic Tenderness
in Nongenital Sensuality

Les philosophes ordinaires ont soumis l'homme à la
nature pour s'accommoder aux idées recues: prenant un
vol plus rapide, je te prouverai, quand tu voudras, qu'il
n'en depend nullement.—DE SADE

FREUD, in his *Three Essays on Sexuality* (1905*d*), had given the
whole concept of cannibalism a new dimension. He had dis-
criminated cannibalistic features in infantile sexuality. Freud
considered the cannibalistic desires of infantile sexuality intimately
related to sadism and the aggressive factor in the libido. To the
cannibalistic pregenital sexual organization Freud further attributed
the aims of incorporation of the object and obtaining mastery over it.

Pursuing the route indicated by Freud, I shall offer a different
significance of the cannibalistic features in adult human sexuality,
be it in the foreplay preceding genital intercourse or in perversions
proper, where it usurps unto itself an exclusive role and purpose.
Following Freud, almost all analytic thinkers have placed too much
emphasis on the sadistic and coercive nature of the cannibalistic
impulses. I shall try to show that it has tender features as well, and
serves functions other than those of incorporating and mastering
the not-self object. Of course Freud was using the adjective
'cannibalistic' to signify a special property and intent of a component of infantile sexuality, and was fully aware that it was in
aim and character different from that human conation the noun
'cannibalism' signifies.

CLINICAL MATERIAL

As I mentally scan my clinical material, four cases strike me as
having an element in their sexual experiences that I have not
cognized and evaluated so far. One such case is that described in
the previous chapter. My homosexual male patient, who had the

compulsion to suck off anonymous young lads whom he picked up at random from the streets, brought a fervent tenderness to the mouthing of their excited genitals and devouring their seminal substance. He experienced the lads genitally in his mouth with an idolizing affectivity, which for the duration of the act made them almost sacred objects to him. It was equally characteristic of him that his appetite and fervour faded in direct ratio to his growing familiarity with them as persons whenever that eventualized, which was not often.

When I examine other samples of such clinical data it strikes me that familiarity with the object does not so much breed contempt as it engenders inhibitions. As if the capacity to sustain a certain impersonal distance both from the object and the self is a pre-requisite to certain types of sexual intimacy and pleasure, be it in perversions, or the foreplay, i.e. the facilitating ambience for satis-factory heterosexual genital intercourse. In ordinary so-called normal genital sexuality, many disturbances accrue from the incapacity to relate to the object in this dual fashion: distantly and impersonally as a body-thing-person, and affectively as a cherished being.

I shall now give two case-histories which I hope will throw some light on this issue of cannibalistic tenderness in sensual intimacies.

The first is that of a young woman in her late twenties who had been referred for analytic treatment because of acute phobia about seeing people vomit or encountering a vomit in subways and buses. The phobia had reached the point where she had to force herself to get out of the house to go to her work; sometimes she failed to overcome her fears and stayed home. She was a goodlooking, attractive, and curvaceous woman. She was illiterate and came from a working-class background.

Her father had died when she was a child, and she had grown up with a promiscuous mother, fending for herself from a very early age. Her sexual life had started early and passionlessly in a de-sultory way at fifteen. She had an illegitimate child at seventeen, whom, at her mother's instigation, she had abandoned in a subway when seven weeks old; she had little guilt or remorse about it. Some years later she had met a soldier and married him simply to have a man around the house. He turned out to be a lay-about, and she had to support him most of the time. According to her, he was over-sexed (her phrase), and she submitted to him but received no pleasure or joy from it. She had a fondness and natural talent for ballroom dancing and gradually acquired enough proficiency to be able to find employment in one of the many dancing schools that started just after the war.

Though I am talking about a case I treated some twenty-three years ago, certain features of her analysis have stayed vivid in my memory. She was my first training case, hence I took and kept extensive notes. She was not a difficult or recalcitrant patient, but a very secretive and frightened one. The whole ritual of the analytic process – lying down, free associating, etc., filled her with an admixture of confusion and bemusement.

I, on the other hand, brought to the task the militant rigour of a novice. It did not fare well. She was often silent and rarely attended five sessions consecutively. But somehow, she stayed the required training period of two years, and then suddenly she disappeared. I have always felt a gratitude for her patience with my methods of working at the time.

I heard nothing for more than a year. Then, one day, she rang and asked to see me. Of course, she had not corresponded because she could not write. During this year she had left her husband and started to live with a young man who had a regular job and cared for her. She came some half-dozen times and sat and talked. I was very impressed with the way she had mended her life. She was no longer teaching youngsters to dance but had taken a regular job as an usherette in a cinema, and was happy with it.

Now she was able to tell me something which she said had made it impossible to have treatment and continue with it. She had felt too guilty and embarrassed about it. The gist of the situation was that every now and then she would be very attracted to a young lad of fifteen to twenty while teaching him to tango and would then 'rub him up' (her phrase) into a state of acute sexual excitement, take him to a lavatory, and then tenderly suck him off. She gave a rather witty and graphic account of how sweet and pathetic the lads looked standing there, trousers around the ankles, bashfully looking away while she mouthed and caressed them to ejaculation. She said she felt so happy when they 'eased up' and looked sheepishly triumphant after the event. She did not think then she did anything immoral but felt I would have been censorious or given, what she called, some of my 'fancy stuff', which she had never understood. She was able to contrast the tenderness and joyously timid playfulness and pleasure of these sensual intimacies with the 'horror' of being 'poked into' by her husband. It was only when she had met this young man, who had a preference for fellatio, that she was able

179

to find relating and sexual pleasure with him. Occasionally they made love, but largely they enjoyed mouthing each other. She made the remark: 'One gets to know them better with the mouth than in the cunt.'

I never saw her again, and to this day I cannot figure out why she had come back for those few sessions. My hunch is that it was to say 'thank you' and also to comfort me for having tried to fool me for two years, which I had been aware of at the time.

The second case I want to report is that of a man whom I saw for some three months. In all he had some thirty sessions. He was an American in his early forties and had sought help while in London on business because his fifth marriage was breaking up and he was, for the first time, feeling depressed and dismayed about it. A rich, highly educated man, he had had various types of psychotherapy since adolescence. He started by telling me that he had not consummated any one of his marriages. The pattern was roughly as follows.

He picked up sexually inexperienced and innocent young models (which his particular trade made readily available to him) and initiated them sensually to masturbatory practices, fellatio, and cunnilingus. It was an imperative of his regime of passion that the girl be a *virgin* in the total sense of the word, meaning even sexually unaware and naively muted. He very patiently 'seduced' them in this way: he licked, sucked, and bit them, but never penetrated them. He married them because, he said, 'without possession it is perverse and promiscuous'.

Of course, the girls gradually awakened to their womanhood and he was quite sympathetic to that. He would let them have proper 'lovers' so long as he felt their true sensual cherishing and pleasure lay in their nongenital sensual intimacies with him. Invariably the girls ran into someone with whom they fell in love, blackmailed him for cruelty, and sought divorce. He had actually given away a large part of his wealth in alimonies.

One phrase of his had impressed me. He had remarked while talking of refusing intercourse 'my penis is still unabused like a lad of seventeen's'. As I look through my meagre notes, I find that like the woman about whom I have reported, he too had emphasized the cognitive richness of experiencing his own and another's body through mouthing, as opposed to intercourse. He had, in fact, compared intercourse to two blind persons knocking into each other trying to identify each other. This remark had evidently impressed me because I made a note of it later. I find one further remark of his significant. He had stressed again and again how refusal of intercourse was necessary for him because it sustained a certain 'lack of cosiness' between him and his girl. He dreaded, he said, the taking-for-granted quality which he noticed in all his married friends who had genital intercourse with their wives. He felt they lost awareness of each other and were taken over by their genitals, while disregarding each other as persons. He prided himself on his extremely sensitive and differentiated awareness of the body responses of his wives and how he cultivated, extended, and actualized these qualities in them with tenderness and patient cognizant care.

He felt he alone had actualized the full potential of their sensuality; the others merely exploited it afterwards. I need hardly say that therapeutically I effected little change in his habits. What I did manage to convince him of was that perhaps possession through marriage was not as necessary to his sensual habits as he thought. That somewhere he did feel guilty about 'frustrating' his girls genitally and compensated by giving them alimonies. This meagre and obvious comment seemed to amaze him and he felt that henceforth perhaps he could manage it without marrying. I did not hear from him once he returned to America so do not know how he fared.

The fourth case is that of an intelligent professional woman in her late forties who had consulted me only a dozen times. She had sought therapeutic help because things had begun to go wrong in her relation to her husband, after some thirty years of a happy marriage. She had given her husband three lovely children, who were now grown up and at university. According to her account, her husband had always been an aggressively virile man and all she had to do was to 'submit to his erections' (her phrase), which she had always managed both without resentment and without participant pleasure. In recent years, her husband had become more demanding in terms of foreplay and this, she found, made her both resentful and negatavistic toward him, even in their nonsexual relation. She was afraid that if she did not overcome her prudishness about fellatio, which her husband desired, in time he would seek other women and their marriage would be ruined. She had specifically emphasized how well she knew her husband as a person and that they were very good friends all their married life. At this point I had interposed: 'But you do not seem to have included his body as part of him as a person.' This startled her, and the notion that the human body was something that could *know* and be *known* in its own right intrigued her imagination. She had always considered sexuality as a sort of localized genital assault to which a woman submitted with un-grudging obedience. When I saw her next, after an interval of some four weeks, she looked curiously happy in a bashful way. She reported how she had coaxed and compelled herself to touch and suck her husband's genitals and let him do the same to her – that after she had got over her distaste about it her whole experience of her own body and that of her husband's had 'dramatically changed'. I asked her what she meant by 'dramatically changed', and she explained that they no longer talked and related to each other with words only, but with touch and taste as well. And how much more tenderness she had discovered both in herself and in her husband since she could initiate and participate in this type of fore-play.

DISCUSSION

I am well aware that there is little that is metapsychologically deep or profound about the clinical material reported here. I have advisedly restricted my account to certain sensual details of the sexual experiences of these patients. To encrust this material with other data from these cases would add little to the understanding of the cannibalistic features and only confuse the issue with ponderous and extraneous erudition.

In psycho-analytic literature, beginning with Freud and Abraham, and later Melanie Klein, a vast amount has been written about the role of cannibalistic oral-sadistic fantasies in the causation of various syndromes, from impotence and frigidity to melancholia and suicide. I am not discussing *fantasy* but practical sensual states and acts that involve the mouth and sexual organs, as well as the whole body, for their true sensual gratification for the person concerned.

The role of the mouth as a *cognitive* organ has been discussed very insightfully by Rene Spitz (1955). Spitz argues that 'the level of coenesthetic perception belongs to what I would call the experi-mental world of the primal cavity,' and he concludes 'the mouth as the primal cavity is the bridge between inner-reception and outer-perception; it is the cradle of all external perception and its basic model: it is the place of transmission from the development of intentional activity, for the emergence of volition from passivity'.

It is my belief that in analytic writings far too much emphasis has been placed on the destructive and aggressive elements of the fantasy systems relating to oral activity and the mouth. Spitz offers us a large new area of research regarding the cognitive and integrative role of orality and the mouth through its experimental activities.

I believe that in certain types of foreplay and some perversions we can find the data for exploring the true creative function of mouth in adult sexuality as well as ego-functioning. In the four cases referred to there is an unmistakable dread of losing 'sight' of the self or the object through genital intercourse. Mouth activity integrates manual, tactile, and visual elements to the intimacy with the object and thus retains a differentiated separateness of the body-ego and self-state, as well as the identity of the object. In this 'transitional area' (to use Winnicott's concept) mutuality is established while retaining distance and separateness. The cannibalistic impulses render themselves to a richer utilization in adult sensuality than we have recognized so far. Also, they can engender a tenderness which is without threat of fusion and, hence, loss of separate body-self existence.

In this context it is relevant to consider Willi Hoffer's ideas (1949). Hoffer's argument is:

> The differentiation of the ego from the id shows itself on the infant's body-surface when, in the service of the oral partial instinct and for the sake of autoerotic pleasure, two sensations, an oral one and a tactile one, are aroused simultaneously by finger-sucking. Such a situation does not usually arise before the 12th week when, quite intentionally and no longer reflexively, the hand is put into the mouth in order to relieve oral tension.
>
> In general psychology the function of the hand has mainly been studied as that of an organ which grasps. I am not suggesting that before this grasping function manifests itself, the hand is merely an attachment to the mouth, but that from intra-uterine life onward it becomes closely allied to the mouth for the sake of relieving tension and within this alliance leads to the first achievement of the primitive ego. From now on the hand cannot relinquish the function of relieving tension and in this way it becomes the most useful and versatile servant of the ego.

Hoffer further elaborates his hypothesis:

ALIENATION IN PERVERSIONS

I am inclined to believe that the hands, after being libidinized during the intensive sucking period, now function more independently of the oral zone and are more under the influence of the eyes, playing the part of an intermediary between eyes and mouth. They have developed from instruments serving as a means for discharging tension into tools which control the outer world. They have at this stage become a most active extension of the growing ego.

The argument I am offering for consideration is that the mouth and the hand play a cognitive role in the transitional area of sensual foreplay, which is the facilitating ambience for true genital sexuality, and, in perversions, the whole of its experiential terrain. To differentiate and define the creative role of cannibalistic tenderness in nongenital sexuality is not to give it a new autonomous status in its own right but merely to attribute to it that which can be its positive and incremental asset. I am well aware that in the contemporary cultural climate there is a fatuous idealization and exploitation of pregenital sexuality as an end in itself. Knowing of the self and the other entails the psychic, the affective, the relational, and the physical. The last of these constituents has not received our attention in an impartial way. In spite of Freud's heroic attempt to free sexuality from social preconceptions and antipathies, one gets the impression that the bias of the analytic writers to treat 'pregenital sexuality' as at root and in essence regressive and primitive has sustained the cultural prejudices in an oblique form.

We should consider a new concept, namely that of 'metonymic cannibalism', where a part of the whole body is eaten either symbolically or concretely. My clinical material indicates that in 'metonymic cannibalism' a specific transformation of the aggressive and sensual intents, i.e., those of incorporation and mastery, into that of tenderness can actualize.

To do justice to our avowed task of understanding the complexity of human sexual experience as one that is essential and germane to true psycho-social health we should be able to comprehend what in Walt Whitman's verse are

> arms and hands of love, lips of
> love, phallic thumb of love, breasts
> of love, bellies press'd and glued
> together with love.

184

8

Ego-Orgasm
in Bisexual Love

Work of sight is achieved,
now for some heart-work
on all those images, prisoned within you;
for you overcame them, but do not know
them as yet.
Behold, O man within, the maiden within
you!—creature wrung from a thousand
natures, creature only outwrung, but
never as yet, belov'd.—R. M. RILKE, *Turning*

THERE has been little discussion of bisexual love in psycho-
analytic literature because it has been confused mostly with
latent homosexual love. Freud, in an early paper 'Hysterical
phantasies and their relation to bisexuality' (1908a), did broach
this subject. The argument offered here is that for certain persons
bisexual love is an authentic and necessary human experience,
which can become distorted through repressions and reaction-
formations as much as heterosexual love. What characterizes
bisexual love is that it is almost exclusively an ego-experience, that
is, the ego's way of relating to and cherishing an object of the same
gender identity. In such relationships the id-energy is neutralized
and turned to use in the ego's passionate *interest* in the object. The
climax of such cathexis of the object is ego-orgasm. The pathological distortions here can lead to ego-perversities in object-
relating, just as in the area of id-experience they lead to perversions
proper.

CLINICAL MATERIAL

I shall present material from a phase of the treatment of two
patients. My emphasis will be on the phenomenology of the processes concerned and not their aetiology. It is my experience that
sometimes our bias to evaluate new experiences in a patient in

terms of our habitual aetiological concepts robs us of the opportunity of learning from our clinical material.

The first patient I want to report from is a young woman of
thirty. She has been in analysis for some two years because of her
dissatisfaction with the *quality* of her experience of herself and others.
Of a rather schizoid-depressive temperament, she felt her relationships were meagre in their intensity and range, compared to what
she felt was her potential. She is a sensitive person with artistic
leanings but has not done much with them. She had been married
at the age of twenty. When she started analysis she had just separated
from her husband, because she felt they were merely wasting each
other with a cosy non-relating that, in social terms, was perfectly
respectable and adequate. She had a keen feeling that if she did not
do something she would waste her whole life. After separation she
had become very depressed and felt utterly unable to harness her
resources to a positive way of life. She went through a prolonged
phase of promiscuous experimenting with men and got little
sensual satisfaction from it. Some eight months before the episode I
shall focus on she had met a man some ten years older than herself,
and started to live with him. In this relationship she was able to
find true pleasurable genital satisfaction and she could begin to
surrender to her female sensuality and enjoy his maleness. She
complained of a lack of corresponding emotional richness in the
relationship and felt she had become too attached to and dependent
on him, which was again keeping her indolently suspended. It was
in this climate of relating in her life that she decided to give her
artistic leanings a chance and joined an art school to learn to
draw and paint. Such actualized initiative was quite a step forward
for her.

Some two months after starting at this art school, one day in the
drawing class she encountered a young girl, who had modelled for
them in the nude. The patient had been strangely fascinated by this
girl's body and presence. She tried hard to capture her exact figure
in a most realistic drawing. During the interval for tea she was
surprised to find that she had gone to the model and started to talk
with her. The model was a foreign girl who was not a professional
and was doing modelling to earn a little extra money during her
stay in London. She herself was a student in her own country. The
patient had been surprised by her venturesomeness in approaching
the girl at all. By temperament and character she was a reticent and
bashful person, who rarely spoke with anyone unless spoken to first.

When the model returned for the rest of the session, the patient found herself 'all excited inside' and curious. She could not draw at all because 'I was all in my eyes and not in my hands'. After a few attempts she had given up drawing in that session, sat back and looked intensely at the model. After the class she surprised herself further by going to the girl and inviting her to dinner, which the girl accepted all too readily.

This is as far as the things had progressed when the patient had come for her analytic session that day. She was in a rather strange state of excited puzzlement. She is not a person who speaks a lot in the sessions. In this session, however, her silences were vibrant and seething. She had given me a brief account of the encounter so far and then had gone on to talk about what she would cook and how she would dress. These details interested me because I had not known her to bother much about such matters before. She was a woman who dressed elegantly anyway. I had made no comment all through this session but carefully noted a certain alerted quality of awareness of the other girl in her.

When the patient came for her next session there was élan about her I had not registered before. She was more than happy in her mood; she was positively gay, and talked with a verve and vehemence new for her. She recounted the evening in minute detail, as if she was relishing reliving it in the session. The model had arrived dressed in a long evening dress and had looked very beautiful. The patient had decided to wear a trouser suit for the occasion. She had cooked a delicious meal and had served champagne. It was indeed a celebration. Her boy-friend had unfortunately not taken to this festive occasion with equal fervour and had accused the patient of making too much fuss over the girl. But what struck me was that even her boy-friend's malaise had not dispirited the patient. He had retired to bed early and she had stayed up late talking with the girl. She gave me all this material in a rather eruptive and exuberant manner. I had a distinct feeling that she was not going to let me have a say in the matter either.

The model had posed for them again, and again she had merely doodled and had been more engrossed with the body-presence of the girl. She gave me a very vivid picture of what the girl looked like and detailed her physique with relish. Towards the end of the session she astounded me by simply telling me that at lunch the model girl had mentioned she had to get out of the youth hostel and find a place to stay, and the patient had straight away invited her to stay with her, which the girl had accepted. It never occurred to her to consult her boy-friend. A most unusual piece of behaviour for her.

This went on the whole of the week. She was a changed person. All her lassitude had vanished. She was deeply interested in the girl's life and curious about what she did and studied. They shopped together; went to cinema and theatres together. She was utterly engrossed with the girl and there was a definite ecstatic quality about her experience of the girl. She had in a certain measure taken her over and was companioning her with an ego-interest and vigour I had not seen in any of her relationships before. The boy-friend had rather peevishly stepped aside and in her sessions she gave me little scope to interpret. She was full of the plenitude of her well-being in her relation with the girl. The model girl was evidently a very intelligent responsive person and met the patient's zeal with a matching generosity of affection.

The girl had signed on as a model for one week only. On the last day of that week the patient really applied herself to drawing the girl in the class and produced a truly successful drawing – which earned her praise from her teacher. When I saw the drawing I too was impressed. The model was a very beautiful curvaceous girl, with a gentle joyous face, and the patient had drawn her with meticulous attention and appetite. I was very tempted to draw attention to the obvious homosexual interest in the model, but abstained. The girl stayed one more week with the patient and they developed a deep friendship for each other. One could detect a certain manic element in the patient's exuberant relating to the girl but to bias the description with the use of the word 'manic' is to smudge the flavour of her true experience.

When her friend left, and they had been two weeks together, she was sad and felt the lack of her companionship but she did not react to it with depression. This detail was crucial for my evaluation of her total experience. As we settled back into the rhythm of her analysis it was possible for me to say to her that up till now in her relation to her boy-friend I had heard her talk of her sensual surrender and sexual orgasms, but what she had made me witness, especially during the second week of her relationship with the model girl, was her experience of a sustained ego-orgasm. She was deeply relieved that I had not interpreted it all in terms of a lesbian affair, which in certain cantankerous moods her boy-friend had in-sinuated to her. She felt liberated in herself. Her boy-friend tried to make her feel guilty that there had been no sex life between them during those two weeks. She was explicitly aware of her lack of sexual desires during this period and said all the energy had gone into her relation with the girl. She insisted that she had never once even felt any desire to touch or cuddle the girl. That visual absorption of the girl's physicality was enough for her. As she gradually spelt out the finer and more latent details of her experience, she began to be aware how 'potent' and competent she had felt during those two weeks. It had given her quite a different experience of her ego-capacities and ego-interests. She felt sufficient and authoritative in herself. It was in this context that I was able to interpret to her that she had projected her female element (her gender identity) onto the girl and had been able to operate non-conflictually from her male element and personalize it as an asset in herself, without any competitiveness or castrative intent *vis-à-vis* the men. I disregarded deliberately her boy-friend's begrudging and nagging behaviour towards her. He had felt left out and disregarded. But it was not the patient's intent to do so. What she had achieved for herself was actualization of her male element through what one could describe as a bisexual love affair. I think it is very important clinically to be able to distinguish such bisexual in-loveness with its accompanying ego-orgasm from homosexuality proper. A further gain to this patient from this relationship has been a true experience of emotional surrender to another person, without intimacy or sexual exploitation. This has given her a new confidence in her own emotions and her ability to contain and share them.

It is, however, imperative that one should remember that the success of this affair was largely due to transference coverage by me. The fact that it was a limited experience, in time and range, was almost guaranteed by the transference relationship to me. It is my belief that similar experiences when initiated and lived out in ordinary life can set up a pattern of ego perversity, in contrast to sexual perversion, which can be very damaging to the affective richness of heterosexual object-relating, because they are sustained then by a split between the sexual and affective experiences.

The second case I wish to report is that of a man of forty-one. Some three years ago he had sought therapeutic help for two reasons: largely because his wife, who had been in analysis for some years, nagged him that he should have some analysis too because his emotional involvement with her and the children was rather flat and insipid, and partially because he had an uneasy feeling that, despite his enormous professional success and prosperity, as a person he was not thriving. I had agreed to see him once a week and have done so for three years. He has made a positive and creative use of his encounters with me.

By any diagnostic criteria he is a normal individual in the context of his cultural values. He was born in an affluent middle-class home and grew up a happy child, given all the conditioning of a puritanical Christian family life. He did well at university and started his own business in which he has done very well. He married when twenty-three and has lived a fairly pleasant and happy family life with his wife and three children. There was never a deep passionate relationship between him and his wife, but that is nothing unusual in his class and culture. By temperament he is an industrious, just and honourable person. Little in his life has moved him deeply and he enjoys most things in a routine ordinary way. He had throughout a satisfactory genital relation with his wife and was very fond of his family and devoted to them. He was often puzzled by his wife's occasional incriminations that he was lacking in passion. He could never quite make out what it meant.

His relations with his colleagues were amicable, mutual and extremely friendly. In fact, he got real pleasure from their company. He is a cultured and educated man and had remarked himself: 'If you come out of the English public schools one thing you are good at is sublimated homosexual friendships with men.' Yes, he had quite a few choice and dear friends, with whom he went shooting, etc. And, of course, within the ethos of his culture it was quite simple to pick up floosies here and there and lay them, without in any way seriously jeopardizing the marriage or feeling too guilty about it.

It is well known how difficult it is clinically to handle persons who have neither symptoms nor any explicit area of stress in their life. Since he was willing to work with me, I was equally intrigued to work with him.

If one sees a patient once a week the patterns of his life emerge slowly. In time it was possible to discern that this man's life was divided into three distinct parts: his life with his wife and children, congenial and affectionate; his life at work, industrious and just; and his life with his men friends, carefree and joyous. And yet one sensed a certain caution and restraint everywhere. He was not a man who let anything happen to him. He was aware of it too. Everything, including his sexual pleasures, was well organized. One thing bothered him from time to time: his wife's acute jealousy of his friendships with men. He did not know what to do about it, nor could he understand her reasons for it.

One was impressed by his massive and successful egotization of all affects and his capacity to discharge instinctual tensions crudely and simply through genital intercourse, with his wife and others. He is a handsome man, who takes good care of his body and physique. I must stress one fact. Though this man spoke easily and there was little in his narrative to capture one's clinical imagination, I have never been bored by the ordinariness of his material. I had a vague sense that he was searching for something and in time it would actualize, if one could provide him unintrusive therapeutic ego-coverage.

As the clinical process, very slowly, gathered its innate momentum the patient began to question his 'lack of intensity of emotional response' (his phrase) in all spheres and relationships of his life. He could begin to see that other people behaved differently and had a richer involvement with each other, and that his life was lacking in this increment to experience; that he was more interested in persons than involved with them. It was in this climate of self-questioning that the episode, that I shall report now, occurred.

The patient had gone abroad on one of his usual shooting trips for a week. I received a cable from him after a week that he had decided to extend his vacations by a fortnight and would return then. When he returned he recounted the following story.

The group at the shoot was an international one: folk from various countries, doing more or less the same things. On the second day the patient found himself attracted to a man, who he thought was a little younger than him. He sought him out and became almost infatuated with his presence. They spent a lot of time talking together. The younger man was also married and had children. He was a refined and educated artistocrat from another country, with a very stark and chiselled handsome face. The patient described the physique and particularly the face of the man in great detail. He was a little self-conscious while talking about it and had remarked: 'I sound like a girl talking about her first crush!' But I had noted the intensity of his visual experience of the object. This reminded me of the girl's account of her encounter with the model.

During the week the patient had developed a close friendship with the man and a fantasy began to compulsively preoccupy him. He wanted to invite the man to join him on a fortnight's vacation in the Bahamas, where there would be sunshine and they could relax together. He was acutely uncomfortable in himself about it, but eventually managed to broach the subject with his friend. His friend suggested the patient should accompany him to Morocco for two weeks where he was going to join his wife and children and they had a house there. The patient agreed to it and went there.

According to the patient's report, he had returned after two idyllic weeks in Morocco with his friend. He had got on splendidly with his wife and children and spent a lot of time with his friend. Nothing like this had ever happened to him before. He felt he had absolutely adored the man and had been totally engrossed with him during this time. They had done a lot of things together and enjoyed them. And he was happy to leave at the end of two weeks because he had felt the experience had saturated itself to completion.

He did not feel sad at leaving his friend, nor had he any nostalgic yearnings about him. He felt that for the first time he had abandoned himself to a relationship and let things happen without arranging them. There was certainly an element of ecstasy in his experience of his friend. On return to London he had thought a lot about it and now he could understand what his wife had meant by her accusations of lack of passion and involvement in him. And since his return his sexual relations with his wife had a different and deeper quality.

In my comments I picked on his phrase about 'talking like a girl about her first crush'. I tentatively suggested that one could talk of the intensity and saturation of his emotional interest in his friend as an ego-orgasm. This made immediate sense to him and he added that now he could see the *lack* in his sexual experiences. I further pointed out that so far all he had experienced was sensual surrender in local genital intercourse without the increment of corresponding affective surrender to the object.

The patient was himself aware of the therapeutic gain to him from this letting-go of his controls and thus allowing himself to feel the surrender to his affective involvement with his friend and the intensity of his ego-interest in him. He felt that his relations so far with his male colleagues and friends could be said to have an element of perversity in them, in so far as they left him dissociated, but his 'affair', as he jocularly called it, with his friend had true value as a further step in his self-realization.

What I am trying to draw attention to is a specific type of dissociation that often not only goes unnoticed in analyses but can even be exaggerated through the analytic process. The dissociation is between the male and female elements in the personality of a given person. If this dissociation is not resolved the person can learn to function fairly adequately in terms of local genital sensual surrender to the object of the other sex without affective surrender. The dissociated affectivity is then acted out in what I would like to call ego-promiscuous fleeting attachments with objects of the same sex. These impulsive friendships seriously curtail and impoverish the affective surrender in and belonging to heterosexual relationships.

Anna Freud (1952) has discussed this in the context of capacity or incapacity for object-relationship in terms of negativism and dread of emotional surrender. Drawing upon the analyses of homosexuals and impotent persons, who even when they regained physical potency through analysis retained 'emotional impotence', Anna Freud concludes:

> Further analysis then reveals that this fear of passivity is capable of a deeper, non-sexual explanation. The passive surrender to the love object may signify a return from object love proper to its forerunner in the emotional development of the infant, i.e. primary identification with the love object. This is a regressive step which implies a threat to the intactness of the ego, i.e. a loss of personal characteristics which are merged with the characteristics of the love object. The individual fears this regression in terms of dissolution of the personality, loss of sanity, and defends himself against it by a complete rejection of all objects (negativism).

In the two cases presented here there was a definite blocking of affect and a negativistic caution about affective involvement until the experience of in-loveness with their friends. Anna Freud (1954a) in another paper draws a significant distinction between object tie and ego-interest. Discussing the transference of a female patient she states: 'She seemed to replace at least some of her passion for the artistic atmosphere by a similar passion for the analytic one. But this devotion did not extend to my person; it avoided it; what should have been an object tie had been turned into an ego interest.'

For me this is a most significant and fateful distortion of the ego's quality of relationship and affective involvement with an object. All too often one sees patients in consultation who have had so-called successful analyses, where their genital functioning has been restored but where this subtle distortion in their ego-functioning has gone unnoticed. Hence they shift from object to object in a desultory way, while maintaining a sort of genital-constancy with a heterosexual object. To see their predicament in terms of inhibition of homosexual interest is misleading.

It is in this context that I find Winnicott's (1965a) hypothesis of 'The split-off male and female elements to be found in men and women' most instructive. After presenting material from a case Winnicott states: 'I had never before fully accepted the complete dissociation between the man (or woman) and the aspect of the personality that has the opposite sex.' Winnicott's argument is too rich and complex to be detailed here. But it is this hypothesis that has enabled me to do the sort of work I have reported above. We have to tolerate the slow emergence of the bisexual patterns and not confuse them with that deployment of pregenital sexuality which we meet with in homosexuality.

The concept of ego-orgasm I also borrow from Winnicott. He discusses it in his paper 'The capacity to be alone' (1958a). Since this concept of Winnicott's is little known and he himself dwelt upon it only once, I would like to give it at length in his own words:

I would now like to go a little further in speculating in regard to the ego-relatedness and the possibilities of experience within this relationship, and to consider the concept of an ego orgasm. I am of course aware that if there is such a thing as an ego orgasm, those who are inhibited in instinctual experience will tend to specialize in such orgasms, so that there would be a pathology of the tendency to ego orgasm. At the moment I wish to leave out consideration of the pathological, not forgetting identification of the whole body with a part-object (phallus), and to ask only whether there can be a value in thinking of ecstasy as an ego orgasm. In the normal person a highly satisfactory experience such as may be obtained at a concert or at the theatre or in a friendship may deserve a term such as ego orgasm, which draws attention to the climax and the importance of the climax. It may be thought unwise that the word orgasm should be used in this context; I think that even so there is room for a discussion of the climax that may occur in satisfactory ego-relatedness. One may ask: when a child is playing, is the whole of the game a sublimation of id-impulse? Could there not be some value in thinking that there is a difference of quality as well as of quantity of id when one compares the game that is satisfactory with the instinct that crudely underlies the game? The concept of sublimation is fully accepted and has great value, but it is a pity to omit reference to the vast difference that exists between the happy playing of children and the play of children who get compulsively excited and who can be seen to be very near to an instinctual experience. It is true that even in the happy playing of the child everything can be interpreted in terms of id-impulse; this is possible because we talk in terms of symbols, and we are undoubtedly on safe ground in our use of symbolism and our understanding of all play in terms of id-relationships. Nevertheless, we leave out something vital if we do not remember that the play of a child is not happy when complicated by bodily excitements with their physical climaxes.

The so-called normal child is able to play, to get excited while playing, and to feel satisfied with the game, without feeling threatened by a physical orgasm of local excitement. By contrast, a deprived child with antisocial tendency, or any child with marked manic-defence restlessness, is unable to enjoy play because the body becomes physically involved. A physical climax is needed, and most parents know the moment when nothing brings an exciting game to an end except a smack – which provides a false climax, but a very useful one. In my opinion, if we compare the happy play of a child or the experience of an adult at a concert with a sexual experience, the difference is so great that we should do no harm in allowing a different term for the description of the two experiences. Whatever the unconscious symbolism, the quantity of actual physical excitement is minimal in the one type of experience and maximal in the other. We may pay tribute to the importance of ego-relatedness per se without giving up the ideas that underlie the concept of sublimation.

Bisexual love is essentially *playing*. In both the cases reported one can identify the quality of ego-interest as playing with an object. Furthermore it is limited in the scale of time. The argument I am offering is that if we fail to evaluate such experiences in terms discussed above then we engender a quite false sense of guilt in terms of homosexual implications, which in turn leads to a reactive exaggeration of local genital sensual surrender with corresponding depleted casual but compulsive attachments to friends of the same sex. I do not believe it is possible for persons who need an experience of such intensity of ego-orgasm in bisexual love to arrive at their personalized wholeness, to achieve it outside coverage by the analyst in the transference as auxiliary ego. This is largely due to what Anna Freud rightly describes as dread of disintegration of their intactness as person and ego from the regressive potential in the experience.

Lastly, I want to return to Freud's (1905*d*) statement about perversions: 'It is impossible to deny that in their case a piece of mental work has been performed which, in spite of its horrifying result, is the equivalent of an idealization of the instinct.' I wish to offer a corollary to that and say that in bisexual love a neutralized instinctual element is added to the ego interest in the object which leads to the *idolization* of the object. Both cases reported bear this out explicitly.

9
The Role of Will and Power
in Perversions

Whoever invades people's
privacy corrupts them.—MOHAMMED

THERE are those that fuck from *desire*; and those that fuck from *intent*. The latter are the perverts. Because intent, by definition, implies the exercise of will and power to achieve its ends, whereas desire entails mutuality and reciprocity for its gratification. This distinction was brought home to me by the simple and lucid account given by a young female patient of a phase in her life.

CLINICAL MATERIAL

The patient, a young married woman, was recounting certain happenings in her life when she was some twenty-three years of age. At that time she had just started her career as a fashion model and was living with a man, to whom she had committed herself seriously. Because of her youth, intelligence and winsome fragile beauty she was often invited to dinners in high society. At one such dinner she found herself seated next to an elderly, rather shapeless and plain man. He overheard her telling the person on her other side that she was leaving for Rome next morning to model there. She was excited about this new opportunity in her career. This man casually enquired from her when she was leaving and by what flight. She was utterly astounded to find him at the airport waiting for her. With ceremonious casualness and unintrusive ease he told her he had decided to go to Rome for a day since he loved that city. He offered that she should travel first class with him, knowing full well she was travelling economy class. She was so confused by the sudden turn of events that she accepted his offer. On arrival in Rome he escorted her to her hotel; left her to get on with her work and invited her to join him for lunch. They lunched together and at the end of it he let it be known to her that he had not booked himself in any hotel because he was returning to London that evening.

They had eaten and wined well and she felt obliged to invite him back to her hotel. He had made no passes at her and she felt very intrigued by his conversation and interest in her. When they reached her hotel-room she felt herself curiously sexually roused and desired to fuck him desperately. She took it for granted that he must have wished to 'screw' her (to use the patient's phrase), otherwise why would he have gone to all the trouble. She let her desire be known to him and was taken aback by his polite and gentle refusal with the discreet explanation that he had met her by accident and it was all too much of a good thing; he had no intention of exploiting her naive generosity; that he would not seduce her *but* if they met again in London and she agreed to spending a weekend in Rome with him he would not fail her.

When she had returned to London, she had waited to hear from him for a few weeks. Nothing happened and gradually she got absorbed with her usual life: professionally and with the man she was living with. Then some six months or so later just as she got another job in Rome, he had rung her saying he was going to be in Rome that week and he had heard she was going to be there too, so could they lunch together. Since he had rung her at her home and her steady boy-friend was in the room at the time she thought it expedient to say yes to his assignation. He quietly and firmly told her at which restaurant he would be waiting for her on the agreed day.

In spite of her grave misgivings and an acute sense of guilt she turned up for lunch as agreed. After lunch he persuaded her out of returning to her work and took her for a tour of the town. They had dinner and returned to his hotel And then he fucked her all night as she had never been fucked before. This, in spite of the fact that on meeting him again she had been horrified by how ugly a man he was and repulsed by it. Yet, there was an authority to his ways, she said, which coerced her to comply. And there were no lies on his side. He had candidly told her that he was a *happily* married man, and had discovered that no marriage could survive if there wasn't the *third* to increment it. They had a sexual orgy of calculated pleasure for a week and she had neglected her professional work dismally. He had left her neither energy nor time for it.

On return to London her lover changed his tactics. He kept her tantalized and on edge: ringing her out of the blue for lunch, fucking her and then vanishing completely. She found his wilful intrusions on her life irresistible. Gradually he managed to break up her relationship with her steady boy-friend, who was a rather quiet and sad youth. Then he set her up in a small flat but his availability was never predictable. He insisted on the one hand that she sustain her professional work and yet on the other hand he mocked and denigrated her efforts to work. Thus he achieved his aim: he succeeded in demoralizing her *vis-à-vis* her professional ability and made her utterly dependent on him.

Gradually he introduced her to some of his friends. Being his mistress was not a role she cherished; yet she accepted it with the same passivity as other roles he capered her through. He forced her to live a life totally alien to her. Passion alone ruled their ways.

One thing, however, had struck her forcibly all along. His *need* that she should *resist* him a little. Hence his insistence she should work, though he left her with neither the time nor the energy for it. He could love her only if he sensed some resistance in her which his power could then smash. Even though she felt herself to be little more than a walking corpse, she had to maintain a pretence of independence, and paradoxically a certain willingness on her part. Humiliating her yielded him a diabolic increment to sensual enjoyment. She had bouts of intense rage and it gave him great satisfaction to be able to conquer her rages with his will and passion. This bizarre existence persisted for a year or so. She became more and more depersonalized and at the same time sort of addicted to her stance of the victim. Gradually a boredom began to seep into their orgiastic intimacies. Then her lover compelled her to participate in three-somes. He managed to pick up the most unpalatable partners to fuck her. It was this that made her wake up suddenly from her trance of abject fascination with and awesome surrender to his will. One day she suddenly left him.

I have abstracted from the material which the patient had taken a week to recount. It had a wholeness and a certain quality to it quite different from the rest of her experiences. She was herself mystified that she could have let all that happen to her and with such intensity as well as conniving passivity. I had at one point casually remarked that her story reminded me of Pauline Reage's novel *Histoire D'O*. She had laughed and told me that she herself had been reminded of that story while living with her lover and had in fact given him that book to read, and he had taken its 'methods' seriously. She had wryly added the comment: 'only the pornographic literature is truly instructive and idealistic!'

Two facts need to be reported from the patient's adolescence and childhood because they throw significant light on the *necessity* of this perverted episode in her life. The first fact is, that though during her puberty and school years the patient had been a very compliant and brilliantly studious girl, she had collapsed into a long bout of depression waiting to go to the university. This had lasted some eight months. Once in the university her whole style of living had changed. She had neglected her studies and had got carried away by the social life available. She was aware of the forced and rather manic quality of her sexual exploits during the university years. She had barely managed to pass her examinations and afterwards a strange apathy had engulfed her. She was no longer interested in anything intellectual and had taken to modelling merely to keep herself mobile. She had, with a certain wisdom, established her first serious and stable relationship with the sad youth. But they were both equally crippled and there was little zest or sap in their relationship. They were each other's keeper, and when she had met her lover she had been acutely apprehensive lest she break down completely into acute depression and give up all hope as well as initiative towards life. The *break out* into perversion was the obverse of a *breakdown* into acute incapacitated depression. The second fact was that of the war, which had completely disrupted the familial milieu of the patient's childhood. The father had gone away on military service and the patient had lived a harassed peripatetic existence with her mother and siblings, moving from place to place and never knowing how long any situation would last. When she had gone to school as a boarder, she had escaped into her intellect, read voraciously and books became her almost total reality. How the traumatic unpredictability of her childhood existence repeated itself, in a sexualized and transformed manner, during her perverted episode with her lover we shall discuss later.

THEORETICAL DISCUSSION

In psycho-analytic literature perversions have been largely discussed in terms of the strength of pregenital impulses, weakness of the ego with the resultant intolerance of anxiety and the pressure of a severe and archaic super-ego. In this paper I shall not concern myself with these matters. Instead I shall focus on the role of *passive* will and *active* will in perversion-formations. Unfortunately a serious handicap restricts our researches here. All perversions accrue from a symbiotic complicity between two persons, which is both unconscious and empathetic. We see the total dynamics from the point of view of one party only and that biases our theories. The *active* will of her lover would have been quite ineffective if the *passive* will of my patient had not met it with equal appetite. Just as the *passive* will of my patient, on its own, would have suppurated merely apathy and depression.

Jean Paulhan in his preface to *Histoire D'O* titled 'Du Bonheur dans L'Esclavage' states:

> . . . there is a grandeur and there is a joy as well in abandoning oneself to the will of others (lovers and mystics are familiar with this sense of grandeur, this taste of joy) and in finding oneself, at last! rid of the weight of one's own pleasures, interests and personal complexes.

In clinical psycho-analysis our concern with the pathology in perversions has somewhat hidden from us a certain climate of psychic functioning and sensual pleasure which has specific qualities of its own: both for good and evil. Listening to my patient's account I had been very struck by a certain impersonality in her towards what her own body had experienced. The patient herself had had to overcome a definite ego-resistance in her during that phase to be able to let her 'passive' will have its way and surrender to the 'active' will of her lover. Only thus a desire that 'is strange, alien, all but unbearable' (to use Paulhan's words) had fructified into experience, and there unmistakably 'existed a certain mysterious equilibrium of violence' (another one of Paulhan's diagnostic phrases about *Histoire D'O*). The argument of this article is that it is the confluence of 'active' will and 'passive' will in two persons, autonomously separate yet symbiotically empathic, that enables all these factors to actualize into experience.

I have no intention of offering a cogent conceptual structure. My aim is to state the problem in a way that I feel could help us to examine the psychodynamics of perversions afresh. I want to focus on a certain quality and distance in a person's way of *using* the object and the own body. The role of the will, active or passive, is to sustain a committed impersonality towards desire and object (own body or the other's).

For my purposes two simple definitions of will are sufficient:

Strength of mind and moral fibre (*The Penguin English Dictionary*)
Puissance intérieure par laquelle l'homme et aussi les animaux
se déterminent à faire ou à ne pas faire (*Littre*)

Hence I consider will a special function and capacity of the
individual. The question now arises whether we can find some clues
to the formation of the active or passive will in the pervert. One such
clue became available from the treatment of my patient.

After narrating the episode with her lover my patient had drifted
away from it and in analysis had become engrossed with discussing
her present life. Some three weeks later she reported a dream from
a weekend. This had been a particularly harassing weekend for her.
Her children had been fractious and demanding. They had a lot
of house-guests over the weekend and her husband had irritated and
provoked her into a terrible temper by teasing her about her not
being able to enjoy the company of their guests. On Sunday she had
retired to bed rather early trying to avoid an explosion into rage
with her husband. During that night she dreamt: 'I was with my
lover and he was ferociously fucking me.' The dream was physically
acutely sentient and on waking she had a vivid recall of it. It had
made her feel both guilty and frightened. She had also felt extremely
hesitant about telling me the dream. After telling the dream she had
quickly shifted to talking about her very early childhood, just after
her father had left for the war. First I had felt she was trying to
escape from the dream into a rather innocent period of her past, but
as she recounted her memories one feature was predominant in
them: rage. She had a clear recall of how she would flare up into a
temper tantrum at the slightest frustration and her mother would
shut her up in her room until she said 'sorry'. And if she had a
temper tantrum with her siblings she always came out worse, since
she was the youngest and they could easily overpower her physically.
This had lasted till she was five or six and then suddenly she had
become a compliant and docile child, who became almost addicted
to reading books.

In this context and from these associations it was possible to show
the patient how her dream was a way of coping with a rage, that
had threatened to spill over into her familial reality and damage her
relation to her husband. The patient had been herself surprised by
the explicit physicality of her dream. The lack of symbolic elaboration had impressed me too, and I pointed it out. From here the
patient started to recall and discuss the years of 'frantic masturba-

tion', from the age of fourteen to seventeen. When angry or depressed she would withdraw to her room and masturbate, many times a day. There was little fantasy or sensual pleasure attached to the masturbatory activities. They were mechanical and perfunctory, executed in a depersonalized state.

As her trust in the analytic process and me increased, she began to put together a vague but compulsive theme which had accompanied her masturbatory mood and practices. In her own words, it was 'a boring, unromantic and repetitive theme of being coerced into sexual intercourse by a physically unattractive person'. Sometimes there were other persons also watching her being 'humiliated in this way' (her words) and a few times they would all fuck her in turn. But she would often shy away from the last turn of events and focus only on being fucked in this unmutual and degrading manner. The patient had a firm conviction that during her first acute depression before going to university she had become unable to masturbate and all these fantasies had faded away. She could not mobilize any sensual aliveness in her during that bout of depression.

From here onwards, in the analysis of this patient, it became possible to work with her towards a deeper understanding of the *necessity* (and I use that noun advisedly!) of the perverted complicity with her lover during a certain phase in her development. As her first account had clearly indicated she was in a depressed listless mood when she had encountered her lover. Now, she was able to spell out her experience of her depression in greater detail. She was more than depressed at the time she said. She was immobilized in a listless apathetic boredom. It took all her determination to go to work and often she did it in a noticeably perfunctory manner. Her emotional and sexual life with her steady boy-friend had no colour or zest to it. She had often felt inclined to distract herself with masturbation but could not be bothered. In fact she felt rather suicidal at times and was frightened by fleeting dark ruminations about death. When the affair with her lover had first started she had been surprised by the passion and sensual fervour he could tantalize out of her. Their orgies were abundant and his inventiveness in sexual techniques surprised her innocence. Compared to his sensual expertise her masturbatory fantasies had been so monotonously bleak and uninspired, she said. She had met his demands with avid and exuberant empathy as well as response. Yet all along she had a certain feeling that all he could ever get her to do sexually was already 'known' to her in a vague and mysterious way. Sometimes she had even wondered whether he was not merely enacting with her and for her, what she had always wished for but been unable to cognize or print into awareness and desire. They were mutually interdependent for what they actualized as sexual *happenings* between them; but the role that each played was different. Only her passive will actualized his intents into shared sensual experiences. As the whole picture of their relationship gradually began to cohere into focus I was very impressed by the fact that though at first it had looked that she had been the 'victim' of her lover's crazy sexual fantasies and demands, in fact his fantasies and active will did little more than print and execute the unspoken demands of her mute and transparent passive will. Even the acute anguish her lover had caused her from his brutal indifference at times, from his unpredictability and tyrannical behaviour seemed to be in response to the mysterious demands of her passive will. She desired first but invisibly, what he intended and executed wilfully and explicitly afterwards.

As my clinical experience grows I see more and more clearly what a crucial role a certain intensity of psychic pain and rage play in all perversions. In the finished products of perversions these are often all too successfully hidden behind the bizarre sexualization of the events entailed. In order to understand the role of these factors in the reported episode in this patient's life I have to go back to the beginning of her analysis with me.

The patient had been referred to me because she was in a state of acute agitated depression. Attempts to alleviate her depression by medication had not succeeded and the patient feared she was heading towards a breakdown, like before going to university, only this time she felt she had no routes of escape left open to her. She was well aware that she was facing another crucial developmental crisis and now she felt only psychotherapeutic help could see her through it. She had been happily married for some ten years and reared her children with a joyous mutuality with her husband. Now they were growing up and she had to harness her resources towards creating a new autonomous life of her own. Of course she had grave misgivings about launching on a long analytic treatment and it was not easy for her to submit to such explicit dependence on another human being. She was a wilful and determined woman. In the first consultation she had been too depressed and incapacitated to give a detailed account of her life and I had not pushed her for one. As I looked at and listened to her I could sense an intact vitality in her and a resolute purposefulness towards life which as yet had not found its true shape and direction in her person. She had also impressed me as someone to whom life had really happened. She did not strike me as one of those neurotics who live their lives in that inert terrain where inhibitions and fantasying exclusively arbitrate existence. I had accepted her for analytic treatment on this premise. One thing, however, had puzzled me a great deal: why had this intelligent woman waited for so long and suffered so much before seeking therapeutic help? The answer to this began to emerge when it became possible to explore the relation between her depressive states and the perverted episode in her life.

According to the patient's account, until her experiences with her lover her depressions reduced her to a state of total inertia. She could neither relate to anyone nor accept any type of relating. She would withdraw into a global apathy in which she experienced only a dead sort of pain and burnt out rage. All this had changed during the time spent with her lover. The dead pain had changed into actual suffering and anguish related to a real person. And her rages became sentient and articulate. She felt murderous towards him and acted with considerable violence in mood and language. He helped her to exteriorize her pain and her rage. Furthermore he made them bearable with the increment of the sensual element. In this constellation of experiences it was easy to establish the *necessity* of this perverted affair for her. Had she broken down into a severe depression instead of breaking out into this perverted alliance, one wonders if any therapist would have been able to meet the demands of her resourceless regression and its devouring apathy. Her relationship to her lover initiated experiences for her; it gave her an anchorage in life. It did not merely engender insights leaving her to find the initiative in herself and for herself. It seems to me that we as therapists are rather poorly equipped to mobilize the 'passive will' in a person. The pervert here has the advantage over us, in so far as he can initiate experiences and execute them through his 'active will'. This certainly is true in the life-experience of this patient. Of course the pervert as therapist is direly handicapped when it comes to weaning himself from his own neediness and vulnerability in the complicity he engenders.

Here I would like to briefly discuss one detail from this patient's experience that had intrigued me greatly, namely that the relationship started to break up when her lover began to compel her into sexual experiences with other men, which she had explicitly fantasied about while masturbating in adolescence. The enactment of what she had fantasied by her lover yielded neither pain nor pleasure to her, only arid disgust and embarrassed shame that she could not come to terms with. This had made him feel very *powerless* with her, and all his ruses to intimidate her by withdrawal of attention or by scathing criticisms of her prudishness had little effect on her. She would not panic and this made him more powerless and infuriated. Suddenly she began to see him as a rather pathetic person who had no resources, when powerless, to sustain himself. It seems to me that the active will of the pervert operates only in an area of illusion where his victim through her passive will demands and endorses his active will. Powerlessness creates the same panic and rage in the pervert as helplessness does in other syndromes.

As the analytic work gained in complexity it began to be clear how a need to search for power in the other in order to integrate and actualize herself had played a crucial role in the three significant contractual relationships that this patient had entered into during her life so far. The first was with her lover (the perverted contract); the second was with her husband (the conjugal contract) and the third, and the most recent, was with me (the analytic contract).

The patient had given a vivid account of the pervert-contract, as detailed above. About her conjugal contract she was less clear. She had married a man of considerable authority, sagacity and status. She loved him deeply and with a fearful sensitivity. She was somewhat inordinately apprehensive about her cultural and social inadequacies *vis-à-vis* him. Her husband was a kind and generous man with a distinctive style of life. She felt that at last she belonged to a person and a home, and yet felt awesomely insecure because of her own incapacities to share and relate in a playful confident manner. The conjugal contract had engendered in her a basic trust that belonging was possible for her. She felt homed and loved. Her anxieties were about her meagre use of what was available to her. She would be too reactively adaptive and conciliatory and then on some silly and minor issue boil to silent rages in herself. Attempts to contain and screen these rages left her depressed and devitalized. It was in this crisis that she had sought the third contract: the therapeutic transference contract.

Here I shall focus on only one aspect of her transference, namely her need to find the exercise of will and power in her analyst. It is customary in most of the analytic literature to present the role of the analyst as a neutral passive one, reflecting what is being projected onto him by the patient. This is only partially true. In fact the analytic situation is a highly sophisticated and artificial construction, where the analyst plays a very fateful role, using both will and power. The analytic situation is initiated by the analyst making specific demands that a patient has to be able to meet, at least minimally, if the therapeutic contract is to actualize at all. The demand on the patient to lie down looking away from us, to talk without being talked with, to verbalize whatever thought or memory comes into his mind without asking what comes into ours – all these are functions of the analyst's will and power. The fact that the clinical process needs these demands should not blind us to the character and nature of our demand. Naturally to our demands the patient confronts counter-demands, which we generally treat as resistances in the patient to the analytic contract. This is another exercise of our will: the analytic situation provokes resistance in the patient which we then help the patient to resolve.

In this patient, from the beginning, I was impressed by her need to ask questions. In almost every session she would ask me for guidance on some issue pertaining to her daily life. At first I treated her questions with the customary evasive silence or condescending grunt. This, however, always left her dejected and frightened. I tried to interpret her need for reassurance, particularly in relation to her latent negative feelings. But all this had little effect and I myself began to feel I was behaving hypocritically. She usually asked me quite sensible ordinary questions, which it was not difficult to answer. What characterized her questions was that they all sought to find out how she should act or behave in some social or familial situation. Once I decided to answer her questions, what followed was very revealing. She would instantly accept and agree to what I said. But then she would *play around* with what I had said: question and correct it, until she would find the right solution for herself. I was very struck by her capacity to play with different possibilities of conduct, once I had suggested a course. If I abstained she would invariably go inert and become resourceless. This use of the analyst's will and power with which she could identify and internalize, proved extremely helpful to her.

During this phase of analysis the patient became acutely aware of how different was the play of her children from what she recalled from her own childhood. Theirs was imaginative, spontaneous and sharing. Her childhood had been spent in long monotonous fantasies, with little actual play. One could best express it in Winnicott's phrase and say she had been 'locked in the fixity of fantasying' (Winnicott, 1971, p. 31). This further convinced me that in asking the questions this patient was trying to find an area of playing in the analytic situation. I was reminded of Winnicott's (1971) statement: 'Psychotherapy takes place in the overlap of two areas of playing, that of the patient and that of the therapist. Psychotherapy has to do with two people playing together' (p. 38). This led me to ask myself how was playing in the 'analytic contract' different for this patient from participation in 'games' that her lover had made her an accomplice to during her 'perverted contract'. There was no doubt that her lover had sensed her latent sexual fantasies and desires with a singular empathy. In this context he had actualized her unconscious for her. How was this actualization different from making the unconscious conscious, which is the task of the analytic contract? The crucial difference seemed to lay in the different *use* of the patient as a person, by her lover and by her analyst. Once a basic rapport had been established between their sexual fantasies, her lover compelled her into the role of his 'subjective object'. He had to devalue and disrupt all functions in her that gave her a separate identity and existence. She was merely a puppet that actualized through his will and command, his intents and fantasies. Until the end of their relationship she had not been aware of her own sexual fantasies playing an equally important role in their relationship. What she had experienced was merely an intensely excited and passive surrender to his will. This mechanism of splitting plays a decisive role in sustaining that sense of innocence that characterizes the 'victim' in the pervert-contract. It is this splitting that makes the victim impersonal to her fate in the pervert-contract and leads to the idolization of active pervert's will and power. Hence there is little mutuality and reciprocity in the 'victim's' role in the pervert-contract. The abject resourceless unsharing mood of Sade's heroines are a vivid proof of this. In the analytic contract, per contrast, she sought help to be enabled to find her own will and power in her life situations. The empathy she required was in the service of the actualization of her own capacities and functions towards personal autonomy.

This brings me to the last point I wish to discuss here. Just as the neurotic lives through his fantasies (conscious and unconscious), the pervert lives through his actions. This internal necessity *to act* makes the use of will and power imperative for the pervert. The psychic energy that is utilized in becoming aware of oneself, in the pervert becomes available to his will in the mastery of his object. The pervert knows himself only through his victim's actualization of his intentions. It is this which constitutes the essential poverty of the pervert's experience. What is essential for him in fact happens to and is experienced only by the other. The pervert stays an onlooker to what he perpetrates as actions through the other.

10

From Masochism
to Psychic Pain

Mon art est une impasse.—MALLARME

FIRST I shall give three statements by three patients on the same Monday. A young man in his mid-twenties started his session by saying: 'I am feeling very anxious because I am meeting the parents of my girl-friend for the first time tonight.' The second patient, a business man in his late forties, started by saying: 'The deal went through successfully last Friday and we have been celebrating it all weekend, yet I feel depressed today.' The third patient, a woman in her late thirties, arrived, lay down, and was silent for some twenty minutes. I sensed she had started to cry quietly. Eventually she said: 'I am in pain and I do not know why. My children came from school last Friday and they have done so well the last term that we all went out and enjoyed ourselves. I arrived here eager to tell you that and now I am crying and in pain for no reason.' No one would have had difficulty in making sense to the young man why he was anxious. He had been living sexually with the girl for some months, and the associations soon led to oedipal feelings and one could explain it in terms of conflict between the ego and the id. The business man's depression was not difficult to explain either. He is a self-made man, and every financial success causes him guilt. One can utilize the concepts of conflict between ego and super-ego in that context. The pain of the female patient I found hard to make sense of. I was surprised to hear myself telling her that only a good familial experience had enabled her to come to a session and *be* in her pain, a pain she could not print psychically but to which she could now take the risk of *the other* bearing witness, without intrusive explanations or precipitate need to assuage it for her.

It is my inference from what I know of the history of religions, especially the three monotheistic ones, that it is precisely this need in the human individual for his or her psychic pain to be witnessed silently and unobtrusively by *the other*, that led to the creation of the omnipresence of God in human lives. Over the past two centuries

210

and more, with the increasing disappearance of God as the witness-
ing *other* from man's privacy with himself, the experience of psychic
pain has changed from tolerated and accepted suffering to its
pathological substitutes, and the need has rapidly increased for
psychotherapeutic interventions to alleviate these pathological
masochistic states. All symptom-formations are masochistic in an
essential measure, as Freud (1895*d*) was the first to discover and
state at the end of *Studies on Hysteria*:

> When I have promised my patients help or improvement by
> means of a cathartic treatment I have often been faced by this
> objection: 'Why, you tell me yourself that my illness is prob-
> ably connected with my circumstances and the events of my
> life. You cannot alter these in any way. How do you propose
> to help me, then?' And I have been able to make this reply:
> 'No doubt fate would find it easier than I do to relieve you of
> your illness. But you will be able to convince yourself that much
> will be gained if we succeed in transforming your hysterical
> misery into common unhappiness. With a mental life that has
> been restored to health you will be better armed against that
> unhappiness' (p. 305).

As the knowledge and the clinical expertise of psycho-analysis has
increased and become more effective during the past seventy years,
it seems from reading the literature, that we have become too
ambitious in curing miseries, and even trying to obviate the necessity
of psychic pain in human self-relating. T. S. Eliot in his book,
After Strange Gods, had anticipated this:

> At this point I shall venture to generalise, and suggest that
> with the disappearance of the idea of Original Sin, with the
> disappearance of the idea of intense moral struggle, the human
> beings presented to us both in poetry and prose fiction today,
> and more patently among the serious writers than in the
> underworld of letters, tend to become less and less real. It is in
> fact in moments of moral and spiritual struggle depending
> upon spiritual sanctions, rather than in those 'bewildering
> minutes' in which we are all very much alike, that men and
> women come nearest to being real.

Some forty-two years later, in a recent essay, Louis Dupré (1976)
regrets: 'Unfortunately, the therapeutic success of depth psychology
has become one of the main obstacles preventing a full theoretical
exploration of the unconscious self' (p. 103).

All this may sound rather wild and irrelevant metapsychologic-ally to you regarding the topic I have chosen to discuss. But the problem of psychic pain cannot be adequately enquired into, either in terms of the topographic model or the structural one. But once we get to postulating about the self, we hover dangerously near the reaches of mysticism and literature proper, because as Dupré rightly states: '. . . the self far surpasses the boundaries of individual personhood' (p. 123). Please do not mistake me for idealizing religion and God's role in human lives. Man has a unique genius to use perversely his own best inventions and creations. And God, as well as religion, have not escaped such abusage.

To return to our metapsychology. If Freud struggled all his life to define and explicate the psychodynamics of the pathogenic transformations of psychic pain, as mourning and melancholia (1917e), anxiety (1926d) and masochism (1924c), he did not quite succeed in postulating the role and nature of psychic pain. One reason for this, I believe, is, that after having established the intra-psychic structures id, ego and the super-ego (ego-ideal), Freud (1923b) did not wish to confuse the issues by including the concept of the self.

And this is where I come stuck. For even a tentative definition of psychic pain demands some clear definition of self. I believe, from clinical experience and my reading of literatures, that just as the various painful affects are experienced by the ego, psychic pain is experienced by the self. If you can accept my inability to offer adequate or any definitions of self or psychic pain, I wish to propose a hypothesis for discussion. It is: *masochism is a special variant of manic defence that the ego uses for holding together the self from a psychic pain that threatens to annihilate it, and hence the ego.* I further want to say, in parenthesis, that I am using the concept of masochism, not only as a sexual perversion, but as an affect that the ego creates with characters, real or imaginary, in *the space of fantasy*, to use Paul Ricoeur's (1976) excellent concept, to create and sustain an atmosphere of pain, that stays under its control and can be libidinized. In these cases the task of analysis is to enable the ego to relax its omnipotent control-systems so that the person's self can experience psychic pain, without threat of annihilation.

In all masochistic experiences, intrapsychic or interpersonal, there are always three persons: the subject, the desired *other* who will cause him pain, and the *witness*, a part of the subject's ego, that registers and experiences the painful affect this contract (to use

Smirnoff's concept (1969)) actualizes. In commenting on my female patient's state of 'being in pain', I said she needed a witness and an *other* for her to experience her 'being in pain'. So we see that the basic ingredients of the experience of psychic pain and masochistic pain are the same. What needs investigation is how in some persons the ego can shift the register of experience from one psychic plane to another, and thus bring it under its manipulative control.

I believe that, today, once again, we have to start, as Freud did in 1895, by giving a true phenomenological account of our clinical encounter with our patients, without paralysing the ambiguities of the therapeutic exchange by coercing them into the strait-jacket of our metapsychological preconceptions. Therefore, I hope, you will bear with a certain naïveté in my account of the case material from my female patient who said 'I am in pain', in my attempt to explicate my hypothesis.

She had been referred to me, by a physician, after she had taken an overdose of barbiturates. In her first consultation she gave briefly and candidly the account of her life-history. Over the past five years she had been getting more and more depressed, and the medications of her physician had not helped much. She had taken the overdose after her two sons had returned to school, because she had been utterly apathetic and unable to do anything for them or her husband. She felt she was beginning to harm them now.

As to her past she stated it with an impersonal veracity and exactitude. She spoke slowly but lucidly. She had lost her parents at the age of three and been taken into care by her parents' very close friends. She spoke of them with reverence and gratitude. She emphasized that she had rarely felt overtly unhappy, but had not made any emotional relationships with her 'aunt' and 'uncle' (as she called her adopting pair) or with anyone else. She was good at sports and grew rather precociously to be a tall tom-boyish girl. But she could not study or read sufficiently. The fact that she was very good at track-sports, somehow enabled her to stay at the various schools she went to, in spite of her dismal academic record. She had been a compliant and affable girl, both at home and school.

She had been brought up in the countryside, and at the age of seventeen she asked her 'aunt' and 'uncle' whether she could leave school and come to London and try her own way into life. They had been so despairing about her, having taken her abroad on holidays, where she had been equally apathetic, that they agreed to it.

For some two years in London she did various jobs, such as part-time waitress, au-pair girl, shop assistant, etc. Then at the age of nineteen she met a man, some twelve years older than her, and within a few weeks she married him. She stressed the fact that she had married a virgin. In the next three years they had two sons and she reared them herself, though her husband was rich and has ample staff. It was only when the sons had to go to public school, because where they lived there were no good schools around, that she began to relapse into apathy again.

She told me that her physician had cautioned her that I might not accept her for psychotherapy if she could not come five times a week. But, she said, she lived a very long way away, and could come only twice a week. I agreed to take her into twice weekly psychotherapy.

When I thought about the consultation, after she had left, I was struck by certain features that were quite new to my way of handling such a first consultation. This woman had motored 150 miles to come and see me, yet she had stayed only some twenty minutes; and I had made no attempt to prolong the consultation and enquire further into her history: e.g. what her parents had died of; what had suddenly released in her the motivation to come to London at seventeen and discover living for herself. I had been very impressed by her manner of telling her life-story: as if she had talked about someone else. Furthermore I did not get the impression she was depressed; rather, I felt, she had made me a witness to a person absent from their own being. Paula Heimann (1950) was the first to state that the counter-transference is more than an affective subjective response, but that it is also an instrument for perception. I would add, especially, for the perception of those psychic and affective states that a person cannot verbalize. It is also my experience that counter-transference works best, as a perceptual tool, if it works silently, and unobtrusively, as Balint (1968) would have said. Precipitate counter-transference interpretations can initiate a reactive as-if dialogue between the analyst and the patient, from which the person of a patient can stay absent for ever (cf. Castoriadis-Aulangier, 1975). I, also, had not known throughout the consultation, *whom* to address my questions to.

In the four months that followed this first consultation, the banality of the patient's material was matched only by her affability of manner and a reticent but compliant trust in me. Gradually I became convinced that she was making me experience

214

a total psychic inertia and incapacitation. This, I felt, must have been her life-stance until the age of seventeen. I heard about her current life only: the troubles with her staff, the drought and the garden perishing from lack of rain, etc. etc. But I could never persuade myself to render her debris of narrative into interpretative intrusion. I suffered my incapacity, but I also noted that each time she reported a little more participation in the running of her household.

Then one day she arrived looking more in her being and body. I also knew she was expecting her sons for the long summer vacations that weekend, and I did not wish a repeat of their last visit. So I decided to ask her what had suddenly coaxed her to seek living, as against just existing, at seventeen. She was silent, and I could almost touch her bashfulness whilst she was silent, and then she said it was such a ridiculous accident that I would laugh at her if she told it to me. I told her I was not easily amused. I had deliberately chosen to say something personal about myself, because I felt that alone would perhaps encourage her to share something personal about herself. It worked!

There is a verse in Shakespeare that reads:

> so full of shapes is fancy
> That it alone is high fantastical.
> (*Twelfth Night*, I,1,15.)

What I heard was little less than the 'high fantastical'. At about the age of seventeen a girl at her school had succeeded in getting matey with her. One Sunday they had gone to the local cinema to see a romantic film, as advertised. But unfortunately, she said, it turned out to be a cowboy film. One scene in it caught her attention. A rough and rugged gunman walks into a saloon, grabs a can-can girl, pulls her over his knees and spanks her. The local bravados take him on and he shoots them all dead. She could not recall what happened afterwards.

Going to bed that night she started to tell herself 'a story' (as she called it). It had myriad tiny variations, but the central theme was as follows:

'She is sitting in a bar. It is around lunch-time. A man comes in and sits besides her. They start to talk. He tells her his hobby is collecting rare and ancient pistols. He asks her whether she would like to see them. She winks at him and agrees. They arrive, sometimes at his flat, at others, at his office. Of course he has no pistol collection. They pet and somehow she induces him to spank her for her prankishness. He pulls her across his lap, pulls up her skirt and is about to spank her when he finds some excuse to stop. She must leave (his wife or maid or secretary will return shortly). She feels deeply affronted and decides to leave. As she is leaving he pretends to slap her bottom and does not. She then leaves humiliated, enraged and vengeful.'

She could see her 'story' as if on a screen. It was this 'story' that had awakened her and made her come alive. She wanted to discover the world. Her 'aunt' and 'uncle' had been amazed at her change of mood from blank compliant listlessness, to an energetic lively girl. She had lived in this 'space of fantasy' for some two months, when she had talked her girlfriend into venturing forth and coming to London with her.

Once in London she had done various jobs, but lived with her 'story' and made no dates with youths. One day she met her husband and was married within weeks. To her dismay, once her sex-life started, the fantasy faded away. No matter how hard she tried she could not make it work. She did not enjoy her sex-life, but she added: 'since my husband did, I went along with it'. Telling the 'story' had taken up the whole of the session, and it was on a Thursday, so she left without my being able to say anything; which was just as well.

It was in the next session that she had cried silently and been 'in pain'. After she left I noted that she had made no reference to her 'story' in this session. Which convinced me that the pleasure-pain of 'the story' and the *blank* pain of her crying were two sides of the same coin.

When she returned for her next session, she asked if she could sit and talk with me. I agreed, of course. There was a sombre vitality of presence in her that struck me instantly. She recounted that when she was driving home, after the last session, suddenly a thought crossed her mind: 'my parents died in some accident'. Once this idea entered her consciousness, it became as obsessive as 'the story', she said. The past forty-eight hours she had done nothing but to find out how her parents had died, and she did: by going through the back-numbers of the local weekly journal of the town where she was born. She came of high gentry, and so she had felt sure that there would have been notice of her parents' death in the local paper.

According to her the statement in the weekly was brief. It merely stated that on such and such a Christmas day, Mr and Mrs X were killed on their way home after Christmas lunch. Their car had skidded on an icy road and rammed into a tree. When the police arrived, they found the parents dead and a child alive in her dead mother's lap. She did not say any more in that session, but told me, that since she had been so upset, her husband had driven her, and could she leave early as he was waiting for her.

Now I shall briefly summarize the clinical work of the following six months. At first the patient was in cold but lucid rage with her 'aunt' and 'uncle' for not telling her *how* her parents had died. She realized they had done so to spare her pain, but one day she remarked: 'They petrified my mental life by sparing me suffering. Now I realize I grew only physically; otherwise I was totally absent.' She could not have stated it more succinctly. As she worked through the complex maze of her recollections, she herself was astonished at the paucity of her living experience psychically.

Gradually we were able to piece together the causes that had made her young life 'an arid terrain', to use her phrase. The traumatic death of her parents had been so sudden that her emergent ego-functions could not cope with it. Instead of mourning, what had happened was a global paralysis of psychic functioning. She existed through her body, since physiology can defy all psychic trauma and continue its ordained course.

When we came to deciphering as to how she had been awakened into living, and to seek a life of her own by a meagre cowboy film, her narrative changed in many ways. Only two things in the film and her 'story' now seemed significant to her: the alive lap, and the killing by the gunman, which in the 'story' is sublimated into the person collecting rare pistols. We could now see that in her memory she had retained, somewhere and somehow, the difference between the lap of the living mother and the dead mother. She had all her life unconsciously sought that lap to come alive again so that she could live. To explain it in terms of guilt would be glib; for her it was a necessity for coming alive. It also explicated why in the 'story' the wish does not achieve its end. That would have obviated the unconscious historical past and put it in the instinctual urgencies of the adult femalehood. This taught me that in all masochistic fantasy or practice there is always a kernel of psychic pain, that has been lived and lost, and instead, proliferations of screen-fantasies take its place.

Towards the end of the sixth month, after the session when she had cried and said 'I am in pain', she arrived one day and said she had been in the same pain the last night and her husband had got very anxious and she had told him that '*such* pain does not kill one, and asked him to please just stay by me, and it will pass'. I told her that she was telling me that she could now do without my care and holding. She sat up surprised and said: 'I could never have found the courage to say it to you!' As a parting gesture, since we both realized it was her last session, I quoted her a verse of Rainer Maria Rilke:

> Love consists in this
> that two Solitudes protect and
> touch and greet each other.

Pornography and the
Politics of Rage and Subversion

PORNOGRAPHY: obscene writings or pictures intended to
provoke sexual excitement.
(The Penguin English Dictionary)

I ACCEPT the above as an adequate definition: and shall try to
explore the nature of 'provocation' and the quality of 'sexual
excitement' which is engendered by pornographic literature and
imagery. In order to make my point I offer two examples of pornographic writing, taken at random:

> '*Yes, Lovely* –' Her voice came to him, somewhere near a
> scream, it seemed, as a hot, white spinning haze began en-
> veloping him, 'Yes, YES, LOVELY –' she said – His arm was
> gliding, penetrating, he was almost up to his elbow, he was
> drenching wet, nearly out of his head, he began to stroke, he
> stroked and stroked, she was writhing under it, it was a pump-
> ing stroke, he stroked more rapidly, feeling the very depths of
> her meeting his loving fist, each time it thrust home in her, he
> stroked and stroked, she began to scream, he was in a wild
> dream, the sweat poured off him, she couldn't have been
> drenched more, he plunged and stroked, up to his elbow.
> (F. Polim, *Pretty maids all in a row.*)

A man we had never seen previously, said that amiable
whore, came to the house and proposed a rather unusual
ceremony: he wished to be tied to one side of a stepladder: we
secured his thighs and waist to the third rung and, raising his
arms above his head, tied his wrists to the uppermost step. He
was naked. Once firmly bound, he had to be exposed to the
most ferocious beating, clubbed with the cat's handle when the
knots at the tips of the cords were worn out. He was naked, I
repeat, there was no need to lay a finger upon him, nor did he
even touch himself, but after having received a savage pound-
ing his monstrous instrument rose like a rocket, it was seen to

219

sway and bounce between the ladder's rungs, hovering like a pendulum and soon after, impetuously launch its fuck into the middle of the room. He was unbound, he paid, and that was all. (Sade, *The 120 Days of Sodom.*)

Even a cursory examination of the somatic events described leaves one in no doubt of their physical impossibility for a woman and a man. To push a whole fist and arm up the genitals would entail rupture, violence and enormous damage to the organ involved. But the author disregards all that. Instead, the sensation reported is one of pleasurable ecstasy. Similarly, Sade's character, after the thrashing he receives, is in no way enfeebled or injured; he just walks robustly away after the event. And the example I have quoted is, by Sade's standards, a rather mild one. For persons to be severely injured, girls to be maimed in sexual orgies, their toes cut off, etc., is routine in the adventures undertaken in the Sadeian *écriture*. No matter what is done to the human body, it never gets really damaged or incapacitated. Every character remains the same after the event as before. Pain hinders nothing, and pain teaches nothing. Sade's Justine stays whole and innocent and ignorant from the beginning to the end of that narrative.

If the somatic events described in a pornographic *écriture* – I prefer to use the French concept of *écriture* to the English word 'writing', because it implies a specific intent in the use of words – are utterly unfeasible in terms of the actual human body and its capacities, then the question arises: from where do these 'somatic events' derive their authenticity and potential to stimulate the reader sexually? The answer lies in the specialized use of words in pornography. Here they do not describe human experience, but instead simulate or concoct a completely non-human somatic event. The very absurdity and unfeasibility of this event lends it a new power: it has transcended the innate physical limits of the human body to experience pain and excitement.

This specialized use of words has another quality: the mentalization of instinct. What are described are not spontaneous, shared, humanly sexual experiences, but highly elaborate and synthetic events which are the concoction of the mind through words. Though, overtly, the experiences are meant to be physical, and concrete, in fact these events can happen only in the mind, and in that conjuring void which is the terrain of pornography. It is this characteristic which puts pornography beyond the scope of ethics and morality.

It can be evaluated only aesthetically and psychologically, not judicially or ethically.

Since pornography is exclusively a perverted mind-game that has little to do with ordinary sexual experiences, it is necessary to examine it more closely, aesthetically and psychologically. The aesthetics of pornography are a conglomerate of lacks. Rarely does it achieve the quality of literature proper. With due apologies to Apollinaire, Jean Paulhan, Geoffrey Gorer, Georges Bataille and Roland Barthes, no one can really claim any virtues for the style of Sade. One has to admit that Sade's *écriture* is boring, oppressively repetitive and without invention – the same somatic events are concocted in a claustrophobic space with an obsessive and indefatigable insistence. There is also little imagination or invention or characterization in pornography; and Sade again is the prime example. And there is never any emotion, object-relation or self-experience. But I anticipate: that belongs to the psychological examination.

It is when one considers pornography aesthetically that one discovers that it is as false in its pretensions to be literature as it is lacking in its claim to be the vehicle of heightened instinctual experiences. Here pornographic writers have struck lucky, with the hysterical outcries of outraged Europeans, reared in their puritanical traditions. The whole issue has been sidetracked. The real issue is not that pornography is immoral but that it is pathetically bad literature. An ironic and absurd situation has arisen *vis-à-vis* pornography in contemporary European cultures. While pornographic writers will engage in endless debate with the cultural moralists – those anachronistic and eunuched custodians of culture's failing vitality – they are dogmatically intolerant of any suggestion that pornography retails poor literature and sick psychology to those resourceless individuals who have not the means to evaluate it and can only become its hapless accomplices.

This is the first cultural area where pornography is most subversive. Since it neither draws upon nor extends the reader's imagination and sensibility, it offers him/her a limited world of omnipotent verbiage, insinuated and fabricated as somatic events, with their built-in faked climaxes and orgasms, at which the accomplice can feel both complacent and excited. The genius, if one may use that word, of pornography rests in its confidence-trick. It aligns itself with the incapacity of a given individual and a culture to actualize experiences from personal initiative – both as real life and as literature. It is the incapacitated writer's revenge on the tradition of true literature in a culture. If it takes a culture centuries to actualize, through one of its members, the *Confessions* of a Rousseau or the *Four Quartets* of an Eliot, it entails merely a desperate addiction to personal affliction to bring about a Sade or a William Burroughs.

The chief sin of pornography – and one must use that concept since pornography has become sacred today – is that it is not literature proper. No, much worse, that its intention and achievement are to dislocate literature from its vital role in the life of the individual and the culture. Pornography negates imagination, style and the tradition of man's struggle to use language to know and enhance himself.

Now let me turn to the psychological aspects of pornography. What I am offering is a personal point of view or, to borrow a felicitous phrase of Nietzsche's, 'regulative fictions'. My psycho-analytic training and practice have naturally biased me in a certain direction and lend a specific conceptual slant to my 'regulative fictions'. I believe that pornography alienates its accomplices – one cannot talk of them as its readers – both from their self and the *other*. What masquerades as mutual and ecstatic intimacy through somatic events is in fact a sterile and alienated mental concoction. It is this characteristic which made me once remark that pornography is the stealer of dreams. In it there is neither scope for reverie nor for object-relations. Everything is imprisoned through words in a violent and tyrannical game with the own body-self and the *other*. Its time is the perpetual and static present. Hence the nostalgic atmosphere of pornography.

Anna Freud (1952) has diagnosed the essential predicament in perversion-formations as the dread of emotional surrender. One could argue that the crucial predicament in pornography resides in the incapacity for sensual surrender. Here lies the fascinating paradox at the root of pornography. Overtly it is militantly devoted to describing states of ecstatic sensuality and abandonment to a mutual orgastic pleasure. But all that it actualizes is an orgiastic expertise in the physical manipulation of the own body-self and the *other*'s bodily organs. Hence a certain manic quality, which infests the narrative. If one reads the two specimens that I have quoted, one cannot fail to sense a certain quality in it, very much like that of an apoplectic fit.

So the next question is: what is the nature of affect that these somatic events are trying to actualize, externalize and distribute (one cannot call it share). My answer to that is: *rage*. The only true achievement of pornography is that it transmutes rage into erotic somatic events. I advisedly use the word 'transmutes' and not 'sublimates'. Because of the peculiar use of words in this *écriture* there is none of that assimilation or working-through of the affect of rage, which sublimation would entail. It abreacts and encapsulates the transmuted rage into pleasurable somatic events, but with the violence of rage still wholly there. Now, as Barrington Cooper once remarked to me, violence is not a quarrelsome emotion; it entails an absolute demand for submission. What in health can be experienced as sensual surrender, in pornography becomes abject submission through violent events. But as my example from Sade shows, it is both female and male degradation. Genet too has given us this bizarre spectacle of degradation, mutilation and violent submission in vivid, hieratic and hallucinatory terms.

The capacity of pornography to transmute latent rage into violent, erotic events encapsulated in language lends it three potent functions: subversion, therapeutics and instruction. It is subversive in so far as it negates the *person* through its somatic expertise. The accomplice/reader can reach and participate in this type of *écriture* only in very specific states of depersonalization and dissociation. It is therapeutic in so far as it transmutes the threat of total violence and destruction from latent rage in the individual and the culture into manageably distributed, dosed and eroticized language. In a macabre way the therapeutics of pornography achieve Freud's demand for analytic treatment: 'where Id was there shall the Ego be'. In pornography it is all ego and only the ego; no id, no body, no person. The id, the person and the body are merely exploited to establish and actualize the machinery of somatic events. Its instruction lies in that it has to *teach* the tricks to its accomplice/reader for its peculiar reality to be participated in. And here again the Divine Marquis set the pace, when he all too awarely wrote his *Philosophy in the Bedroom*. In Madame de Saint-Ange's postulate to Eugénie: 'May atrocities, horrors, may the most odious crimes astonish you the most forbidden, 'tis that which best rouses the intellect ... 'tis no more, my Eugénie; what is of the filthiest, the most infamous, that which always causes us most deliciously to discharge.' Sade most insightfully exposed the omnipotent role of intellect in these somatic events, and the absence of instinct.

This specific hyper-functioning of intellect, through the creation of somatic events imprisoned in words, not only alienates but also isolates the reader/accomplice just as much as it does the characters in pornography. Geoffrey Gorer (1962b) in an article on 'The pornography of death' accounts for this phenomenon in an interesting way:

> Pornography on the other hand, the description of tabooed activities to produce hallucination or delusion, seems to be a very much rare phenomenon. It probably can only arise in the literate societies, and we certainly have no records of it for non-literate ones; for whereas the enjoyment of obscenity is predominantly social, *the enjoyment of pornography is predominantly private.*

My contention here is that this privacy, or what I call isolation, is a further subversive function of pornography. The banal fact is that pornography is largely, if not exclusively, used for masturbation.

Sartre in his mammoth study *Saint Genet – Actor and Martyr*, discussing the whole function of masturbation in Genet's books, has this to say:

> Seeking excitement and pleasure, Genet starts by enveloping himself in his images as the polecat envelops itself in its odour. These images call forth by themselves words that reinforce them; often they even remain incomplete; words are needed to finish the job; these words require that they be uttered and, finally, written down; writing calls forth and creates its audience; the *onanistic narcissism ends by being stanched in words.* Genet writes in a state of dream and, in order to consolidate his dreams, dreams that he writes, then writes that he dreams, and the act of writing awakens him. *The consciousness of the word is a local awakening within the fantasy; he awakes without ceasing to dream.*

I am not so convinced as Sartre is that the phenomenon of dream is involved in Genet's writings; it strikes me that it is the other way round. All of Genet's compulsive onanistic fantasizing compensates both for his incapacity to dream and his incapacity to relate to the other. And pornography, in this sense, is an objectivization of these incapacities in its authors. One can go to the extreme and say that pornography is little more than masturbation writ large. Or, in Sartre's postulate, 'the onanist wants to take hold of the word *as an object*'.

If, aesthetically, pornography is lacking in imagination and, psychologically, in both emotion and object-relation – and if, physically, it symptomizes a lack of spontaneous instinctual impetus and desire – then one can define it as exclusively preoccupied with the mental pursuit of sensations to the exclusion of both emotions and object-relations. It aims to conjure up somatic events through words, and these are its only reality. If an accomplice/reader becomes too addicted to the given reality of pornography, then there is definitely a disruption of his own inner capacities to grow and personalize as a human adult. The trouble with pornography is not that it is against God's law but against nature's law in so far as it subverts the growth of the human adult into selfhood.

I have so far used the concept 'somatic events', and have given two sorts of example of them. But one needs to examine the character of these events in more detail. Though they purport to be sexual in nature, in fact sexuality is merely exploited, to express violence and rage, either against the self-body or the other-body. The champions of pornography and pornographic writers themselves often make out that what they are trying to remedy are the inhibitions of instinctual experience in the individual through prudish cultural prejudices. Their claim is that they are trying to free the individual, to be more vitally and sentiently his instinctual, sexual self. And yet what pornography achieves in fact is the opposite of what it claims to set out to do. As Sade and Sartre have pointed out, the mind and the word usurp in fact the natural function of instinct in human experience and misappropriate the instinctual drive to a hyper-mental concoction of often brutal imagery, in order to establish somatic events which disregard the person and being of the characters.

So one sees that there is a specific type of split involved in the concoction of these events. First, the instinctual sexual drive is dissociated from natural bodily expression, sharing and gratification through object-relation. Second, this mutilation of the sexual drive is then used to create a very specific type of violence through language, a violence that is further eroticized to make it palatable. But the facts remain the same: negation of the self and object. It is in this particular redistribution of the instinctual drives of sex and aggression that the true pathology of pornography rests. It has replaced sexual freedom and sharing by a mental act of coercion on the body-self and object into extreme stances of submission and humiliation. In this context one can say that the politics of pornography are inherently fascistic.

So far, by and large, I have looked at the negative aspect of pornography. It cannot, however, be denied that a cultural revolution has been realized through pornography, from the Divine Marquis to Saint Genet. To my knowledge nobody has so far tried seriously to account for it; and one cannot write it off as a fatuous phenomenon. Pornography is both a symptom of specific processes of the devitalization of instinct in a culture as well as in the individual, and an attempt at a cure of the symptom. Hence, my emphasis on the therapeutics involved in pornography. It is necessary now to understand more about the nature of the symptom and its functioning, on the one hand, and the character of the revolution that pornography has created in European cultures on the other. It is no use saying that both the symptom and the revolution can be done away with by legislation. As my quote from Geoffrey Gorer indicates, the advent of pornography is very much linked with literacy, and in recent decades advertising media have added a vast and new vocabulary of visual imagery to pornography.

All serious thinkers – be they poets or psychologists or philosophers – in this century have been concerned about a distinct dehumanization of man's relation to himself. It is my contention that with the Industrial Revolution and the advent of scientific technology in European cultures man began to consider himself neither in the image of God nor of man, but in that of a machine which was his own invention; and pornographic *écriture* and imagery try to make of the human body an ideal machine, which can be manipulated to yield maximum sensation. These sensations are derivative of instinct but essentially aggressive in intent. What David Holbrook has called 'the cult of death circuit' in certain types of modern literature is only one side of the coin, the other being the pornographic circuit. Both of them are essentially nihilistic towards the realization of the individual's psychic potential, both within himself and in his relation to others.

CHRONOLOGICAL BIBLIOGRAPHY

The material in this book was written over a period of years, and it may be of interest to readers to know the exact chronology:

1962 'The role of polymorph-perverse body-experiences in ego-integration'. *Brit. J. Med. Psychol.*, 35.

1963 'The role of infantile sexuality and early object-relations in female homosexuality'. In *The Pathology and Treatment of Sexual Deviation*, ed. I. Rosen (London: Oxford U.P.).

1964 'Intimacy, complicity and mutuality in perversions'. Originally published as 'The function of intimacy and acting out in perversions'. In *Sexual Behaviour and the Law*, ed. R. Slovenko (Springfield: Thomas).

1965,
1979 'Fetish as negation of the self: clinical notes on foreskin fetishism in a male homosexual'. Part I (1965) published as 'Foreskin fetishism and its relation to ego-pathology in a male homosexual'. *Int. J. Psycho-Anal.*, 46, Part I. Part II (1979).

1968 'Reparation to the self as an idolized internal object: a contribution to the theory of perversion-formation'. *Dynamische Psychiatrie*, 1.

1969 'Role of the "collated internal object" in perversion-formation'. *Int. J. Psycho-Anal.*, 50.

1972 'Pornography and the politics of rage and subversion'. *Times Literary Supplement*, 4 February.

1973 'Cannibalistic tenderness in nongenital sensuality'. *Contemporary Psychoanalysis*, Vol. 9, No. 3.

1973 'The role of will and power in perversions'. Published in French as 'L'alliance perverse' in *Nouvelle Revue de Psychanalyse*, No. VIII.

1974 'Ego-orgasm in bisexual love'. *Int. Rev. Psycho-Anal.*, 1.

1976 'From masochism to psychic pain'. Published in French as 'Ne pas se souvenir de soi-meme' in *Nouvelle Revue de Psychanalyse*, No. XV.

I would like to take this opportunity of thanking the editors and publishers concerned for doing me the honour of publishing my work in the first place. Without their help my book could not have taken its present form.

BIBLIOGRAPHY

Abraham, K. (1920). 'Manifestations of the female castration complex'. In *Selected Papers on Psycho-Analysis* (London: Hogarth).

Alpert, A. (1959). 'Reversibility of pathological fixations associated with maternal deprivation in infancy'. *Psychoanal. Study Child*, 14.

Arlow, J. A. (1954). 'Report: Panel on Perversion: theoretical and therapeutic aspects'. *J. Amer. Psychoanal. Assoc.*, 2.

Bacon, C. L. (1956). 'A developmental theory of female homosexuality'. In *Perversions*, ed. S. Lorand and M. Balint (New York: Random House).

Bak, R. C. (1953). 'Fetishism'. *J. Amer. Psychoanal. Assoc.*, 1.

——(1968). 'The phallic woman: the ubiquitous fantasy in perversions'. *Psychoanal. Study Child*, 23.

Balint, M. (1950). 'Changing therapeutic aims and techniques in psycho-analysis'. *Int. J. Psycho-Anal.*, 31.

——(1952). 'New beginnings in the paranoid and depressive syndromes'. In *Primary Love and Psycho-Analytic Technique* (London, Tavistock, revised edition, 1965).

——(1968). *The Basic Fault* (London: Tavistock Publications).

de Beauvoir, S. (1954). 'Must we burn Sade?'. In *The Marquis de Sade* (New York: Grove Press, 1966; London: Calder, 1966).

Bellak, L. (1963). 'Acting out: some conceptual and therapeutic considerations'. *Amer. J. Psychotherapy*, 17.

Benedek, T. (1952). *Psychosomatic Functions in Women* (New York: Ronald Press).

Bergler, E. (1951). 'Lesbianism'. In *Counterfeit Sex* (New York: Grune & Stratton).

Bird, B. (1957). 'A specific peculiarity of acting out'. *J. Amer. Psychoanal. Assoc.*, 5.

——(1958). 'A study of the bisexual meaning of the foreskin'. *J. Amer. Psychoanal. Assoc.*, 6.

Bonaparte, M. (1953). *Female Sexuality* (London: Imago; New York: Int. Univ. Press).

Bouvet, M. (1958). 'Technical variations and the concept of distance'. *Int. J. Psycho-Anal.*, 39.

Brierley, M. (1932). 'Some problems of integration in women'. *Int. J. Psycho-Anal.*, 13.

——(1936). 'Specific determinants in feminine development'. *Int. J. Psycho-Anal.*, 17.

229

BIBLIOGRAPHY

Brody, M. W. (1943). 'An analysis of the psychosexual development of a female with specific reference to homosexuality'. *Psychoanal. Rev.*, 33.

Brunswick, R. M. (1929). 'The analysis of a case of paranoia'. *Ment. Dis.*, 70.

——(1940). 'The pre-oedipal phase of libido development'. *Psychoanal. Quart.*, 9.

Buxbaum, E. (1960). 'Hair pulling and fetishism'. *Psychoanal. Study Child*, 15.

Bychowski, G. (1945). 'The ego of homosexuals'. *Int. J. Psycho-Anal.*, 26.

——(1954). 'The structure of homosexual acting out'. *Psychoanal. Quart.*, 23.

——(1956). 'The ego and the introjects'. *Psychoanal. Quart.*, 25.

Caprio, F. S. (1957). *Female Homosexuality* (London: Peter Owen).

Castoriadis-Aulangier, P. (1975). *La Violence de l'Interprétation* (Paris: Presses Universitaires de France).

Coleman, R. W., Kris, E. and Provence, S. (1953). 'The study of variations of early parental attitudes'. *Psychoanal. Study Child*, 8.

Delay, J. (1963). *The Youth of André Gide* (Chicago: Chicago Univ. Press).

Deutsch, H. (1930). 'The significance of masochism in the mental life of women'. *Int. J. Psycho-Anal.*, 11.

——(1932). 'On female homosexuality'. *Psychoanal. Quart.*, 1.

——(1942). 'Some forms of emotional disturbance and their relationship to schizophrenia'. In *Neuroses and Character Types* (1965).

——(1944). *The Psychology of Women*, Vol. I.

——(1945). *The Psychology of Women*, Vol. II (New York: Grune & Stratton).

——(1965). *Neuroses and Character Types* (New York: Int. Univ. Press; London: Hogarth).

Dupré, L. (1976). 'The mystical experience of the self and its philosophical significance'. In *Psychiatry and the Humanities*, Vol. I, ed. J. H. Smith (New Haven: Yale Univ. Press).

Eissler, K. R. (1939). 'On certain problems of female sexual development'. *Psychoanal. Quart.*, 8.

——(1953). 'Notes upon the personality of a schizophrenic patient and its relation to problems of technique'. *Psychoanal. Study Child*, 8.

Ekstein, R., and Friedman, S. W. (1957). 'Acting out, play action and play acting'. *J. Amer. Psychoanal. Assoc.*, 5.

Eliot, T. S. (1934). *After Strange Gods* (London: Faber).

Fain, M. and Marty, P. (1960). 'The synthetic function of homosexual cathexis in the treatment of adults'. *Int. J. Psycho-Anal.*, 41.

Fenichel, O. (1929). 'Analysis of a dream'. In *Collected Papers of Otto Fenichel*, 1st series (New York: Norton; London: Routledge, 1955).

——(1945). *The Psycho-Analytic Theory of Neurosis* (New York: Norton; London: Routledge, 1946).

Ferenczi, S. (1914). 'The nosology of male homosexuality'. In *Contributions to Psycho-Analysis* (London: Hogarth, 1950).

——(1923). 'Stages in the development of the erotic sense of reality'. In *Thalassa* (New York: Psychoanal. Quart., 1938).

——(1925). 'The psycho-analysis of sexual habits'. In *Further Contributions to the Theory and Technique of Psycho-Analysis* (London: Hogarth, 1926).

Fraser, A. W. (1963). 'A relationship between transitional objects and preconscious mental processes'. In *Modern Perspectives in Child Development*, ed. A. J. Solnit and S. A. Provence (New York: Int. Univ. Press).

Freud, A. (1949). 'Certain types and stages of social maladjustment'. In *Indications* (1968).

——(1952). 'A connection between the states of negativism and of emotional surrender'. In *ibid* (1968).

——(1953). 'Some remarks on infant observation'. In *ibid* (1968).

——(1954*a*). 'The widening scope of indications for psycho-analysis'. In *ibid* (1968).

——(1954*b*). 'Problems of infantile neurosis—a discussion'. *Psychoanal. Study Child*, 9.

——(1959). 'The nature of the therapeutic process'. *Bull. Philadelphia Assoc. Psychoanal.*, 9.

——(1968). *Indications for Child Analysis and Other Papers* (New York: Int. Univ. Press; London: Hogarth, 1969).

Freud, S. (1895*d*). *Studies on Hysteria. Standard Ed.*,* 2.

——(1905*d*). *Three Essays on the Theory of Sexuality. Standard Ed.*, 7.

——(1905*e*). 'Fragment of an analysis of a case of hysteria'. *Standard Ed.*, 7.

——(1908*a*). 'Hysterical phantasies and their relation to bisexuality'. *Standard Ed.*, 9.

——(1914*c*). 'On narcissism'. *Standard Ed.*, 14.

——(1914*g*). 'Remembering, repeating and working-through'. *Standard Ed.*, 12.

——(1915*f*). 'A case of paranoia running counter to the psycho-analytic theory of the disease'. *Standard Ed.*, 14.

——(1916–17). *Introductory Lectures on Psycho-Analysis. Standard Ed.*, 15–16.

——(1917*e*). 'Mourning and melancolia'. *Standard Ed.*, 14.

——(1919*e*). ' "A child is being beaten" '. *Standard Ed.*, 17.

——(1920*a*). 'The psychogenesis of a case of female homosexuality'. *Standard Ed.*, 18.

——(1922*b*). 'Some neurotic mechanisms in jealousy, paranoia and homosexuality'. *Standard Ed.*, 18.

——(1923*b*). *The Ego and the Id. Standard Ed.*, 19.

——(1924*c*). 'The economic problem of masochism'. *Standard Ed.*, 19.

——(1924*d*). 'The dissolution of the Oedipus complex'. *Standard Ed.*, 19.

——(1925*j*). 'Some psychical consequences of the anatomical distinction between the sexes'. *Standard Ed.*, 19.

——(1926*d*). *Inhibitions, Symptoms and Anxiety. Standard Ed.*, 20.

——(1927*e*). 'Fetishism'. *Standard Ed.*, 21.

——(1931*b*). 'Female sexuality'. *Standard Ed.*, 21.

——(1933*a*). *New Introductory Lectures* ('Femininity') *Standard Ed.*, 22.

——(1940*e*). Splitting of the ego in the process of defence'. *Standard Ed.*, 23.

——(1950*a*). *The Origins of Psycho-Analysis* (London: Hogarth, 1954; New York: Basic Books).

*The Standard Edition of The Complete Psychological Works of Sigmund Freud, published in 24 volumes (London: Hogarth; New York: Norton).

BIBLIOGRAPHY

Fries, M. E. (1946). 'The child's ego development and the training of adults in his environment'. *Psychoanal. Study Child,* 2.

Gillespie, W. H. (1940). 'A contribution to the study of fetishism'. *Int. J. Psycho-Anal.,* 21.

——(1952). 'Notes on the analysis of sexual perversions'. *Int. J. Psycho-Anal.,* 33.

——(1956). 'The general theory of sexual perversions'. *Int. J. Psycho-Anal.,* 37.

——(1964). 'The psycho-analytic theory of sexual deviation with reference to fetishism'. In *The Pathology and Treatment of Sexual Deviation,* ed. I. Rosen (London: Oxford U.P.).

Gitelson, M. (1958). 'On ego distortion'. *Int. J. Psycho-Anal.,* 39.

Glauber, P. (1949). 'Observations on a primary form of anhedonia'. *Psychoanal. Quart.,* 18.

Glover, E. (1932a). 'The relation of perversion-formation to the development of reality sense'. In *On the Early Development of Mind* (1956).

——(1932b). 'On the aetiology of drug-addiction'. *Int. J. Psycho-Anal.,* 13.

——(1938). 'A note on idealization'. In *On the Early Development of Mind* (1956).

——(1940, 1959). 'The problem of male homosexuality'. In *Roots of Crime* (London: Allen & Unwin, 1960; New York: Int. Univ. Press).

——(1943). 'The concept of dissociation'. In *On the Early Development of Mind* (1956).

——(1949). *Psycho-Analysis* (London: Staples).

——(1955). *The Technique of Psycho-Analysis* (London: Baillière, Tindall & Cox; New York: Int. Univ. Press).

——(1956). *On the Early Development of Mind* (London: Imago; New York: Int. Univ. Press).

Gorer, G. (1962). *The Life and Ideas of the Marquis de Sade* (London: P. Owen).

——(1962a). 'The Marquis de Sade'. *Encounter,* 18.

——(1962b). 'The pornography of death'. In *Death, Grief and Mourning in Contemporary Britain* (London: Cresset Press, 1965).

Greenacre, P. (1948). 'Anatomical structure and superego development'. In *Trauma, Growth and Personality* (1952).

——(1950a). 'General problems of acting out'. In *ibid* (1952).

——(1950b). 'Special problems of early female sexual development'. In *ibid* (1952).

——(1952). *Trauma, Growth and Personality* (London: Hogarth; New York: Norton).

——(1953a). 'Certain relationships between fetishism and the faulty development of the body image'. *Psychoanal. Study Child,* 8.

——(1953b). 'Penis awe and its relation to penis envy'. In *Drives, Affects and Behaviour,* ed. R. M. Loewenstein (New York: Int. Univ. Press).

——(1954). 'Problems of infantile neurosis'. *Psychoanal. Study Child,* 9.

——(1955). 'Further considerations regarding fetishism'. *Psychoanal. Study Child,* 10.

——(1956). 'Re-evaluation of the process of working through'. *Int. J. Psycho-Anal.,* 37.

BIBLIOGRAPHY

——(1959). 'On focal symbiosis'. In *Dynamic Psychopathology in Childhood*, ed. L. Jessner and E. Ravenstedt (New York: Grune & Stratton).

——(1960a). 'Further notes on fetishism'. *Psychoanal. Study Child*, 15.

——(1960b). 'Regression and fixation'. *J. Amer. Psychoanal. Assoc.*, 8.

——(1960c). 'Considerations regarding the parent-infant relationship'. *Int. J. Psycho-Anal.*, 41.

——(1963). 'Problems of acting out in the transference relationship'. *J. Amer. Acad. Child Psychiat.*, 2.

——(1968). 'Perversions: general considerations regarding their genetic and dynamic background'. *Psychoanal. Study Child*, 23.

Greenson, R. R. (1960). 'Empathy and its vicissitudes'. *Int. J. Psycho-Anal.*, 41.

——(1964). 'On homosexuality and gender identity'. *Int. J. Psycho-Anal.*, 45.

Hartmann, H. (1952). 'The mutual influences in the development of the ego and the id'. In *Essays* (1964).

——(1956). 'Notes on the reality principle'. In *ibid* (1964).

——(1964). *Essays on Ego Psychology* (New York: Int. Univ. Press; London: Hogarth).

Heimann, P. (1950). 'On counter-transference'. *Int. J. Psycho-Anal.*, 31.

——(1952). 'Certain functions of introjection and projection in early infancy'. In *Developments in Psycho-Analysis*, ed. J. Riviere (London: Hogarth).

Hoffer, W. (1949). 'Mouth, hand and ego-integration'. *Psychoanal. Study Child*, 3–4.

——(1950). 'Development of the body ego'. *Psychoanal. Study Child*, 5.

——(1952). 'The mutual influences in the development of ego and id: earliest stages'. *Psychoanal. Study Child*, 7.

Holbrook, D. (1972). *Sylvia Plath and the Problem of Existence* (London: Athlone Press).

Horney, K. (1926). 'The flight from womanhood'. In *Feminine Psychology* (1967).

——(1933). 'The denial of the vagina'. In *ibid* (1967).

——(1939). *New Ways in Psycho-Analysis* (New York: Norton; London: Kegan Paul).

——(1967). *Feminine Psychology*, ed. H. Kelman (New York: Norton; London: Routledge).

Hunter, D. (1954). 'Object-relation changes in the analysis of a fetishist'. *Int. J. Psycho-Anal.*, 35.

James, H. M. (1960). 'Premature ego development'. *Int. J. Psycho-Anal.*, 41.

——(1962). 'Infantile narcissistic trauma'. *Int. J. Psycho-Anal.*, 43.

Jones, E. (1927). 'The early development of female sexuality'. *Int. J. Psycho-Anal.*, 8.

——(1933). 'The phallic phase'. *Int. J. Psycho-Anal.*, 14.

——(1935). 'Early female sexuality'. *Int. J. Psycho-Anal.*, 16.

Kanzer, M. (1957a). 'Acting out, sublimation and reality testing'. *J. Amer. Psycho-Anal. Assoc.*, 5.

BIBLIOGRAPHY

——(1957b). 'Panel report: acting out and its relation to impulse disorders'. *J. Amer. Psychoanal. Assoc.*, 5.

——(1958). 'Image formation during free association'. *Psychoanal. Quart.*, 27.

Katan, A. (1960). 'Distortions of the phallic phase'. *Psychoanal. Study Child*, 15.

Katan, M. (1964). 'Fetishism, splitting of the ego, and denial'. *Int. J. Psycho-Anal.*, 45.

Kaufmann, I. C. (1960). 'Some ethological studies of social relationships and conflict situations'. *J. Amer. Psychoanal. Assoc.*, 8.

Keiser, S. (1956). Review of *Female Sexuality* by M. Bonaparte. *J. Amer. Psychoanal. Assoc.*, 4.

——(1958). 'Disturbances in abstract thinking and body-image formation'. *J. Amer. Psychoanal. Assoc.*, 6.

Keiser, S. and Schaffer, D. (1949). 'Environmental factors in homosexuality in adolescent girls'. *Psychoanal Rev.*, 36.

Kestenberg, J. (1956a). 'Vicissitudes of female sexuality'. *J. Amer. Psychoanal. Assoc.*, 4.

——(1956b). 'On the development of maternal feelings in early childhood'. *Psychoanal. Study Child*, 11.

Khan, M. M. R. (1960a). 'Clinical aspects of the schizoid personality: affects and technique'. In *The Privacy of the Self* (1974).

——(1960b). 'Regression and integration in the analytic setting'. In *ibid* (1974).

——(1962). 'Dream psychology and the evolution of the psycho-analytic situation'. In *ibid* (1974).

——(1963a). 'The concept of cumulative trauma'. In *ibid* (1974).

——(1963b). 'Ego-ideal, excitement and the threat of annihilation'. In *ibid* (1974).

——(1964). 'Ego-distortion, cumulative trauma and the role of reconstruction in the analytic situation'. In *ibid* (1974).

——(1969). 'Homosexuality as sexual nursing of self and object'. Published in Dutch in *Inval.*, Inhould 1.

——(1974). *The Privacy of the Self* (London: Hogarth; New York: Int. Univ. Press).

Kinsey, A. C., Pomeroy, W. B., Martin, C. E. and Gebhard, P. H. (1953). *Sexual Behaviour in the Human Female* (London: Saunders).

Klein, M. (1928). 'Early stages of the Oedipus conflict'. In *Love, Guilt and Reparation and Other Works, 1921–1945* (London: Hogarth, 1975; New York: Delacorte).

——(1932). 'The effects of early anxiety-situations on the sexual development of the girl'. In *The Psycho-Analysis of Children* (London: Hogarth, 1975; New York: Delacorte).

Kris, E. (1951). 'Some comments and observations on early autoerotic activities'. *Psychoanal. Study Child*, 6.

——(1955). 'Neutralization and sublimation'. *Psychoanal. Study Child*, 10.

Kronengold, E. and Sterba, R. (1936). 'Two cases of fetishism'. *Psychoanal. Quart.*, 5.

234

Lacan, J. and Granoff, V. (1956). 'Fetishism: the symbolic, the imaginary and the real'. In *Perversions*, ed. S. Lorand and M. Balint (New York: Random House).

Lampl de Groot, J. L. (1928). 'The evolution of the Oedipus complex in women'. *Int. J. Psycho-Anal.*, 9.

——(1933). 'Problems of femininity'. *Psychoanal. Quart.*, 2.

Van der Leeuw, P. J. (1958). 'The preoedipal phase of the male'. *Psychoanal. Study Child*, 13.

Lewin, B. D. (1950). *The Psycho-Analysis of Elation* (London: Hogarth; New York: Norton).

Lichtenstein, H. (1961). 'Identity and sexuality'. *J. Amer. Psychoanal. Assoc.*, 9.

Loewenstein, R. M. (1950). 'Conflict and autonomous ego development during the phallic phase'. *Psychoanal. Study Child*, 5.

Lorand, S. (1930). 'Fetishism in statu nascendi'. *Int. J. Psycho Anal.*, 11.

Lorand, S., and Balint, M., eds. (1956). *Perversions, Psychodynamics and Therapy* (New York: Random House).

Mahler, M. S. (1969). *On Human Symbiosis and the Vicissitudes of Individuation*, Vol. 1 (New York: Int. Univ. Press; London: Hogarth).

Mead, M. (1962). *Male and Female* (New York: Morrow; London: Penguin).

Milner, M. (1952). 'Aspects of symbolism in comprehension of the not-self'. *Int. J. Psycho-Anal.*, 33.

Mittelmann, B. (1955). 'Motor patterns and genital behaviour: fetishism'. *Psychoanal. Study Child*, 10.

Muller, J. (1932). 'A contribution to the problem of libidinal development of the genital phase in girls'. *Int. J. Psycho-Anal.*, 13.

Nacht, S., Diatkine, R., and Favreau, J. (1956). 'The ego in perverse relationships'. *Int. J. Psycho-Anal.*, 37.

Nunberg, H. (1938). 'Homosexuality, magic and aggression'. *Int. J. Psycho-Anal.*, 19.

——(1947). 'Circumcision and problems of bisexuality'. *Int. J. Psycho-Anal.*, 28.

Orr, D. W. (1954). 'Transference and counter-transference'. *J. Amer. Psychoanal. Assoc.*, 2.

Payne, S. M. (1935). 'A conception of femininity'. *Brit. J. Med. Psychol.*, 15.

——(1939). 'Some observations on the ego development of the fetishist'. *Int. J. Psycho-Anal.*, 20.

Rado, S. (1933). 'Fear of castration in women'. *Psychoanal. Quart.*, 2.

Reage, P. (1954). *Story of O* (London: Corgi, 1972; New York: Grove Press).

Reich, A. (1940). 'A contribution to the extreme submissiveness in women'. *Psychoanal. Quart.*, 9.

——(1953). 'Narcissistic object choice in women'. *J. Amer. Psychoanal. Assoc.*, 1.

——(1960). 'Pathogenic forms of self-esteem regulation'. *Psychoanal. Study Child*, 15.

Rickman, J. (1951). 'Number and human sciences'. In *Selected Contributions to Psycho-Analysis* (London: Hogarth; New York: Basic Books).

Ricoeur, P. (1965). *De l'Interprétation: Essai sur Freud* (Paris: Editions du Seuil).

——(1976). 'Psycho-analysis and the work of art'. In *Psychiatry and the Humanities*, ed. J. H. Smith, Vol. I (New Haven: Yale Univ. Press).

Rilke, R. M. (1914). 'Turning'. In *Poems 1906 to 1926* (London: Hogarth, 1957).

Riviere, J. (1929). 'Womanliness as a masquerade'. *Int. J. Psycho-Anal.*, 10.

Robbins, B. S. (1950). 'The problem of femininity'. In *Feminine Psychology* (New York: New York Medical College).

Romm, M. E. (1949). 'Some dynamics of fetishism'. *Psychoanal. Quart.*, 18.

Rosolato, G. (1967). 'Etude des perversions sexuelles à partir du fétichisme'. In *Le Désir et la Perversion*, eds. P. Aulagnier-Spairani *et al.* (Paris: Editions du Seuil).

de Sade, Marquis. 'Philosophy in the bedroom'. In *The Marquis de Sade* (New York: Grove Press, 1965).

——'Juliette ou les prospérités du vice'. In *Oeuvres Complètes* (Paris: Au cercle du livre precieux 1961).

Sandler, J. (1960). 'On the concept of superego'. *Psychoanal. Study Child*, 15.

Sartre, J.-P. (1963). *Saint Genet—Actor and Martyr* (New York: Braziller, 1965).

Schafer, R. (1960). 'The loving and beloved superego in Freud's structural theory'. *Psychoanal. Study Child*, 15.

Schmideberg, M. (1956). 'Delinquent acts as perversions and fetishes'. *Int. J. Psycho-Anal.*, 37.

Schur, M. (1953). 'The ego in anxiety'. In *Drives, Affects and Behaviour*, ed. R. M. Loewenstein (New York: Int. Univ. Press).

Shields, R. S. (1962). *A Cure of Delinquents* (London: Heinemann).

Smirnoff, V. N. (1968). 'Severin von Sacher-Masoch ou l'impossible identification'. *Bull. de l'Assoc. Psychanal. de France*, No. 4.

——(1969). 'The masochistic contract'. *Int. J. Psycho-Anal.*, 50.

Socarides, C. W. (1959). 'Meaning and content of a pedophiliac perversion', *J. Amer. Psychoanal. Assoc.*, 7.

——(1962). 'Report: Panel on Theoretical and clinical aspects of overt female homosexuality'. *J. Amer. Psychoanal. Assoc.*, 10.

Sperling, M. (1959). 'A study of deviant sexual behaviour in children by the method of simultaneous analysis of mother and child'. In *Dynamic Psychopathology in Childhood*, ed. L. Jessner and E. Ravenstedt (New York: Grune & Stratton).

Spitz, R. A. (1955). 'The primal cavity'. *Psychoanal. Study Child*, 10.

——(1962). 'Autoerotism re-examined: the role of early sexual behaviour patterns in personality formation'. *Psychoanal. Study Child*, 17.

Spitz, R. A. and Wolf, K. (1949). 'Autoerotism: some empirical findings and hypotheses on three of its manifestations in the first year of life'. *Psychoanal. Study Child*, 3-4.

BIBLIOGRAPHY

Sterba, R. F. (1957). 'Oral invasion and self-defence'. *Int. J. Psycho-Anal.*, 38.

Stoller, R. J. (1964). 'A contribution to the study of gender identity'. *Int. J. Psycho-Anal.*, 45.

——(1968). *Sex and Gender* (New York: Science House; London: Hogarth).

Stone, L. (1954). 'The widening scope of indications for psycho-analysis'. *J. Amer. Psychoanal. Assoc.*, 2.

——(1961). *The Psychoanalytic Situation* (New York: Int. Univ. Press).

Szasz, T. S. (1957). 'A contribution to the psychology of bodily feelings'. *Psychoanal Quart.*, 26.

Thompson, C. (1943). 'Penis envy in women'. *Psychiatry*, 6.

——(1949). 'Cultural pressures in the psychology of women'. In *A Study of Interpersonal Relationships*, ed. P. Mullahy (New York: Thomas Nelson).

Weigert, E. (1954). 'The importance of flexibility in psychoanalytic technique'. *J. Amer. Psychoanal. Assoc.*, 2.

Weissmann, P. (1957). 'Some aspects of sexual activity in a fetishist'. *Psychoanal. Quart.*, 26.

Wiedeman, G. H. (1962). 'Survey of psychoanalytic literature on overt male homosexuality'. *J. Amer. Psychoanal. Assoc.*, 10.

Winnicott, D. W. (1935). 'The manic defence'. In *Through Paediatrics to Psycho-Analysis* (1975).

——(1945). 'Primitive emotional development'. In *ibid* (1975).

——(1947). 'Hate in the counter-transference'. In *ibid* (1975).

——(1948a). 'Reparation in respect of mother's organized defence against depression'. In *ibid* (1975).

——(1948b). 'Paediatrics and psychiatry'. In *ibid* (1975).

——(1949). 'Mind and its relation to the psyche-soma'. In *ibid* (1975).

——(1951). 'Transitional objects and transitional phenomena'. In *ibid* (1975).

——(1952). 'Anxiety associated with insecurity'. In *ibid* (1975).

——(1954). 'Metapsychological and clinical aspects of regression within the psycho-analytic set-up'. In *ibid* (1975).

——(1955). 'Clinical varieties of transference'. In *ibid* (1975).

——(1956a). 'Primary maternal preoccupation'. In *ibid* (1975).

——(1956b). 'The antisocial tendency'. In *ibid* (1975).

——(1958a). 'The capacity to be alone'. In *The Maturational Processes* (1965).

——(1958b). 'Psycho-analysis and the sense of guilt'. In *ibid* (1965).

——(1960). 'The theory of the parent-child relationship'. In *ibid* (1965).

——(1965). *The Maturational Processes and the Facilitating Environment* (London: Hogarth; New York: Int. Univ. Press).

——(1965a). 'The split-off male and female elements to be found in men and women—theoretical inferences'. In *Playing and Reality* (London: Tavistock; New York: Basic Books).

——(1975). *Through Paediatrics to Psycho-Analysis* (London: Hogarth; New York: Basic Books).

237

BIBLIOGRAPHY

Wittenberg, R. (1956). 'Lesbianism as a transitory solution of the ego'. *Psychoanal. Rev.*, 43.

Wulff, M. (1946). 'Fetishism and object choice in early childhood'. *Psychoanal. Quart.*, 15.

Zilboorg, G. (1944). 'Masculine and feminine'. *Psychiatry*, 7.

INDEX

Abraham, K., 56, 66, 72, 73
acting out, 20, 27–9, 50, 100–4
  as counter-phobic mechanism,
    28
  function in service of tech-
    nique of intimacy in perver-
    sions, 27–9
  role of mechanism, 27–9
activity, fixation on, 20
After Strange Gods (Eliot, T. S.),
    211
aggressive drives in perverts,
    50–1
agoraphobic anxieties, case his-
    tory, 122–33
alienation, 9
Alpert, A., 34
aphanisis, 69
Arlow, J. A., 19, 60, 83, 99

baby, wish for, in male child,
    154–5
Bacon, C. L., 136, 140, 152
Bak, R. C., 136, 140, 152
Balint, M., 19, 89
Beauvoir, S. de, 22
Bellak, L., 27
Benedek, T., 60
Bergler, E., 61
Bird, B., 103, 106
bisexual love, clinical material,
    185–92

discussion, 193–6
ego-orgasm in, 185–96
body-ego development, 92–3
body-experiences, in ego-integra-
    tion, 31–55
body reality-testing, 86
Bonaparte, M., 60
Bouvet, M., 69, 99
Brierley, M., 76, 79, 115, 117
Brody, M. W., 60, 72, 77
Brunswick, R. M., 56, 77
Buxbaum, E., 140
Bychowski, G., 19, 22, 37, 47, 51,
    66, 69, 80, 100, 136

cannibalistic tendencies in non-
    genital sensuality, 177–84
case histories, 177–84
Caprio, F. S., 61, 85
Castoriades-Aulangier, P., 214
castration anxiety, in female
    patient with homosexual
    attachment, 66
Coleman, R. W., 54
collated internal object, case
    history, 122–33
  role in perversion-formations,
    120–38
complicity in perversions, 18–30
confession by pervert, 23–4
counter-phobic mechanism, act-
    ing out as, 28

239